Reuben Kaufman is currently the editor and publisher of the *American Jewish Post*, a weekly newspaper published in Paterson, N. J. He was ordained a rabbi from the Jewish Theological Seminary, and has served in the active rabbinate from 1919 until 1965. The congregations served by him include Temple Beth El in Utica, N. Y., East Midwood Jewish Center, Brooklyn, N. Y., Temple Emanuel, Paterson, N. J., and Temple Beth El, Paterson, N. J. During World War I, Rabbi Kaufman was an Acting Chaplain, AEF, in LeMans, France.

An accredited correspondent to the United Nations, Rabbi Kaufman has written and lectured extensively. His travels have taken him to Poland, Greece, the Soviet Union and Israel, from which he has gleaned first-hand information about Jewish life in these countries. Many of his impressions and attitudes are to be found in his published works which include, *My Trip to Israel*, and *The Philosophy of Judaism*.

Rabbi Kaufman is a member of the New York Board of Rabbis, The Rabbinical Assembly, Mizrachi, B'nai B'rith, The Kiwanis Club, the Rotary Club, as well as other fraternal and religious organizations.

GREAT SECTS AND SCHISMS
IN JUDAISM

GREAT SECTS
AND SCHISMS
IN JUDAISM

REUBEN KAUFMAN

JONATHAN DAVID

Publishers   *New York*

Jewish Sects
Judaism - history

TABLE OF CONTENTS

I

JEWISH PLURALISM AND JEWISH UNITY

Judaism has survived every crisis in its long and checkered history of unparalleled persecution and humiliation. The decimation of one-third of our people in the Nazi holocaust almost sounded the death knell of the Jew. Were it not for the miraculous re-establishment of the State of Israel, the fate of the Jew would have been sealed. When Theodor Herzl declared: "If you will, it is no legend," his words, in a sense, were applied to the legend of the Phoenix. According to our sages, the Phoenix was the only creature in the Garden of Eden that would not eat the forbidden fruit. The Lord blessed the Phoenix and said that it would live forever. Every thousand years, the bird would be consumed in fire; but out of the ashes of the old bird a new one would emerge. By the same token, the new Israel arose out of the ashes of the crematoria in Auschwitz and Buchenwald.

Let us not think, however, that our worries are over, that all problems have been solved, and that the millenium of universal peace has arrived. The issues which vex Israel internally and vis à vis the outside world will be resolved in time, we hope, through the ingenuity of its own statesmen and leaders. But, now that the Galut has, in a measure, run its course, and the Jews of the Diaspora, for the first time in two thousand years, have a place of refuge which will receive them with open arms; now that the Jew is no longer regarded as the pariah of the nations, a fugitive and a vagabond, a man without a country; now that the Jew has shown that he can fight back when under attack

1

—a new challenge faces the Jew, not on the political front where his fate and survival are linked with those of all the other nations of the world, but on the religious front.

It would be a mistake to feel that the establishment of the State of Israel is an end in itself. Many of the sabras in Israel, and those who have become naturalized Israeli citizens, regard their mere living in the Holy Land as the fulfillment of all their obligations to God and to Israel. They refer to the sages who declared that "Whoever lives in the land of Israel is considered to have a God, but whoever lives outside of the land of Israel may be regarded as one who has no God" (Ketubot 110b). It is evident that godlessness and idolatry were the issues which troubled our sages. They felt that while it was possible to serve God anywhere in the world, it was only in the land of Israel that a complete understanding of the nature of God's unity could be acquired, while outside of Israel there was danger of deterioration under pagan influence. Our sages, however, did not mean to imply that living in the land of Israel gives a *hechsher* to be godless or to violate any of the commandments of the Torah.

David Ben-Gurion may be justified in arguing that only he who lives in Israel is a true Zionist, basing his contention on the talmudic dictum. But it must likewise be acknowledged that it is not enough for a Jew to live in Israel, and at the same time repudiate, by his conduct, all the traditions that Israel has preserved throughout the ages, and that have preserved Israel in the Diaspora. The rabbis have stressed the transcendent importance of the revelation on Mount Sinai. The emancipation of the Israelites from their physical bondage in Egypt did not mean that they had attained full freedom. Before they could enter the Promised Land they assembled at the foot of Sinai to receive the Ten Commandments from on High. The purpose of the exodus and the purpose of possessing the Holy Land may be indicated by the transposition of the phrase "With a strong hand hath the Lord brought thee out of Egypt, that the law of the Lord may be in thy mouth." Conse-

2

quently, the challenge for the Jews who live in Israel, as well as for the Jews who are scattered to the four corners of the earth, is to labor in behalf of the complete emancipation of the Jewish spirit. That can be accomplished by accepting the Torah again, as did our ancestors at Sinai when they declared: "All that the Lord hath spoken we will do and obey." The Sinai campaign in 1956 may be just a mere incident in the struggle of Israel for independence. But, perhaps, it may also be regarded as providential. "Remember Sinai" is a divine command which still challenges us today.

One of the distinguishing features of the establishment of the State of Israel is that it has served to unite the Jewish people in the Diaspora, to the extent that, with the exception of the small group of the American Council for Judaism, almost all Jews are proud of Israel and contribute some share toward the development of the ancient land of our fathers. There is a strong feeling of kinship with our brethren in Israel. Culturally, all Jews feel close ties with the Holy Land, because of the common heritage of the Bible and the rich talmudic and rabbinic lore which has been the great reservoir of inspiration from which our scholars in every age and clime have derived their wisdom. But, what of the future? Disintegrating forces exist within our ranks which, if unchecked, will ultimately result in Jewish assimilation and extinction. The cry for Jewish unity has become more articulate in recent days, for unless efforts are made to stop the divisiveness which prevails to an alarming extent, there is more danger now for the segments of Israel to become estranged from each other than ever before in the entire history of the Diaspora. Whatever criticism the ghettos of Europe may have evoked because of their customs and mode of living which were regarded as antiquated and not in keeping with the standards practiced and maintained by the intelligentsia, there is no gainsaying the fact that they provided the dynamic which preserved the Jews from dissolution.

There are prophets of doom who predict that the Jews

in the Diaspora will suffer the same fate as the last of the Mohicans. That is Ben-Gurion's lamentation. Abba Eban, too, has expressed fear of an estrangement between Israelis and Jews living in other countries. They seek a stronger bond of union among Jews everywhere, and particularly between American Jews and Israel, and wish to foster a closer attachment to the culture of Israel.

What is the culture of Israel? It is an all-inclusive term which embraces the entire gamut of literary endeavor, every phase of art, music, drama, folklore, new approaches to philosophy and the sciences, and research in every aspect of the human body, mind and soul. There is a new world, a new civilization unfolding in Israel, which is bound to have repercussions throughout the world. Jews in the Diaspora can unite with their brethren in Israel in this new florescence of culture, in a give-and-take exchange which will be mutually beneficial. The distinguishing feature of this new development is that it is uniquely Israeli; it is "something new under the sun." One aspect of this culture, however, remains an expression of a practical philosophy thousands of years old, a common cultural heritage spelled out in the Torah, the Talmud and the commentaries, and shared by *all* Jews, whether living in Israel or in the Diaspora.

The sages declare: *"V'salmud torah k'neged kulom,* the study of the Torah is equal to all (the other virtues),'' emphasizing that the Jewish religion is equal to *all* the cultural achievements which our Jewish minds have created. Scholastic and cultural triumphs are *parpara'os l'chachma,* appetizers or auxiliaries to wisdom. It is in the field of religion that the Jews in the Galut must cooperate with their co-religionists in Israel in order to create that solidarity which will assure a stable future for our people. It is its religion which gives Jewish culture that uniqueness which distinguishes it from all the cultures of the world. It must not be forgotten that there are four thousand years of an unbroken chain of spiritual and intellectual creativity within Judaism. There has been an admixture of other

4

blends which has served to enrich the main ingredient; in fact, Judaism has embodied all the major cultures of the civilized world. But it has successfully retained the elements which further strengthen the ideals of the Torah, while rejecting all the foreignisms which do not harmonize with the main theme of the One-ness of God and the one-ness of the human race. Now it is imperative that the one-ness of Judaism be maintained, that all the fragmentation in Jewish life today be abolished, and all sectarians join hands in the creation of ONE JUDAISM.

It is gratifying to note an increasing awareness of the need to re-evaluate the meaningful content of the various denominations of Judaism. They are each riding high on a crest of growing membership. But their leaders are beginning to realize that more than membership figures is needed for a vital Judaism.

Amidst the unprecedented growth of temples, synagogues and community centers, there is growing apprehensiveness among our religious leaders that the religious life of our people is very superficial. Congregational worship is one concrete indication of the commitment of the Jew to his ancestral faith. It is regrettable to note that the attendance of the Jews at religious services is the smallest of all religious groups in America. All the talk of being a religious Jew "at heart," without a visible act to substantiate the claim, is idle and vain. One cannot be a Jew at heart any more than a violinist can be a soloist at heart and not be able to play the instrument expertly, or a person be charitable at heart and not make a single contribution to a worthy cause. There is perhaps more truth than is apparent in the commonplace saying, "Hell is paved with good intentions."

The causes of religious apathy are comprised of many factors which require analysis. But the one, outstanding, reason for the corrosive condition which prevails in the observance of Jewish rituals and Jewish traditional practices is the splintering in the ranks of our people which is confusing to the average layman and which alienates

5

him from the essence of the faith, leaving him only with a shell. It would seem that every Jewish leader who is sincere about his Judaism should admit that there is no substitute for the fundamental faith of our fathers. And every attempt that has ever been made to institute improvements, in one form or another, has failed. Even a cursory glance at the history of Jewish sectarianism from the very beginning of our history until today, will indicate that there were circumstances which led to reforms; but when the circumstances ceased to exist the reform sects either sank into oblivion, or only a remnant remained and its significance for the bulk of the Jewish people was practically nil.

Some years ago, the late Rabbi Abba Hillel Silver, courageously declared in essence that "the old time religion is good enough for me." To quote: "Judaism is quite adequate for the spiritual needs of our day. What is needed is not more innovation and reconstruction of Judaism, but the conversion of the Jew to his faith. It is really not a question any longer of less or more Reform, Conservatism or Orthodoxy, but of Godlessness, secularism and materialism which have blighted our people along with other peoples, but which we, because of our unique position in the world, can least of all afford. It is hopeless to try to reach the hearts of our people today by confronting them with the competitive claims of Orthodoxy, Conservatism or Reform. None of these has scored any significant victories in our day, and life is now attacking them all."

This revolutionary declaration put Rabbi Silver in the ranks of those advocating One Judaism, a Judaism loyal to the traditional faith, allowing for disputes within our ranks comparable to the disputations in talmudic times, but deprecating the Iron Curtains which have been set up between one denomination and the other in the Jewish world. Why argue about doctrinal differences and variations in the practice of the rituals? Rituals are important, but they are not issues to fight about, when we have a myriad of problems which concern all Jews, regardless of

6

our individual concepts of the Jewish faith. If we are to combat our common enemies we need all our undivided energies. They should not be dissipated by internecine strife.

The danger of the formation of sects and factions in Judaism was clearly indicated in the plea which Moses made to the Lord shortly before he died. He offered the following prayer: "Let the Lord, the God of the spirits of all flesh, set a man over the congregation, who may go out before them and who may come in before them, and who may lead them out and who may bring them in; that the congregation of the Lord be not as sheep that have no shepherd" (Numbers 27:16, 17). The rabbis note the use of the plural, "spirits," which implies that differences of viewpoints do exist among men, and hence there is a tendency to drift apart into diversified groups. It is for that reason that Moses pleaded with the Lord (in the words of the Midrash): "Lord of the Universe, You know the thoughts of every human being. The thoughts of Thy children are not alike, and when I leave them, I beg of Thee, appoint a leader who will tolerate each one according to his thoughts, as it is written, 'May the Lord of the spirits, etc.'" (Numbers Rabbah, 21.1).

Our sages warned against the formation of sects in their interpretation of the admonition "lo titgodedu," literally translated, "You shall not cut yourselves." The rabbis derived the word titgodedu from the root, "AGD," to bind, implying the formation of separate groups. In Tractate Yebamoth 13b there is a lengthy discussion on the subject of sectarianism. A distinction was made between biblical prohibitions and customs. Different customs are allowed where there is a dispute between authorities that are equally matched. But when there was sharp cleavage among the rabbis in the Talmud who interpreted the same passages in the Bible differently, there was an attempt to create uniformity in practice. "Nimnu v'gomru, they counted (votes) and they decided." Majority ruled, following parliamentary procedure. There were many clashes be-

7

tween the schools of Shammai and Hillel, for example, but in the main, our people have maintained a homogeneity, colored by the individual customs adopted by the Jews living in the Oriental countries and in the ghettos of Central Europe. However, these variations do not touch the basic laws which are embodied in the Shulhan Aruch, and which are the guide for the religious conduct of Jews the world over. There are many divergencies among Jews today, but one must distinguish between the differences of the Hasidim and Mitnagdim on the one hand, for example, and the Orthodox and Reform on the other. The former may vary in minor details, while the latter clash on the fundamentals of the faith.

Today, unfortunately, there is no dialogue between the sectarians. Orthodox, Reform and Conservatives do not come together for the purpose of discussing halachic questions. The recent controversy regarding the "Conservative *Get*" (bill of divorce) which the Rabbinate of Israel refused to accept was not conducted in the spirit of scholarly discussion of the ancient talmudic *tanaim* and *amoraim*. The Conservatives demanded that their form of a *get* should be recognized by the official Israeli *Beth Din* on the basis of freedom of religion. A denial of this demand was stigmatized as an act of discrimination and intolerance. This is a stand which is unparalleled in Jewish history.

The tendency to form cliques, schisms and cults of all kinds has been inherent in the heart of *Homo sapiens* from the beginning of time. God has given man the faculty to think for himself. It is inevitable that men shall look at life from different angles, since the environment and the cultural background of each person varies with the locale in which he was reared, the company he keeps, and the family traditions which continue to influence his character. In every generation, many sects have sprung up among our people. Every precaution that was instituted by our religious leaders, each ritual restriction that was imposed upon the people can be appreciated only in terms of the effort to maintain the integrity and the solidarity of the body politic. When the rabbis ordered: "Make a fence around the Torah" (Pirke Avot, 1:1), their only motivation was to keep the people within bounds and ward off fragmentation. Periodically, the people rebelled against the rigid regimentation, which they regarded as an infringement upon their inalienable liberties. But the long experience of Israel's history has demonstrated the wisdom of our saints and seers of yesteryear. One of our modern poets, Louis Ginsberg, graphically expressed the basic thought in these words:

> *Violin strings, you breathe no sound*
> *When you are loosed, mute you are bound,*
> *Only when fastened and fettered tight*
> *You find the freedom to utter delight.*

II

THE REBELLION OF KORAH

The history of sectarianism in Judaism may have had its beginning with the rebellion of Korah against the leadership of Moses and Aaron as related in the Bible: "Now, Korah, the son of Izhur, the son of Kohath, the son of Levi, with Dathan and Abiram, the sons of Aliab, and On, the son of Peleth, the son of Reuben, took men and they rose up in the face of Moses, with certain of the children of Israel, two hundred and fifty men, they were princes of the congregation, the elect men of the assembly, men of renown, and they assembled themselves together against Moses and against Aaron, and said unto them: Ye take too much upon you, seeing all the congregation are holy, every one of them, and the Lord is among them; wherefore then lift ye up yourselves above the assembly of the Lord" (Numbers 16:1-3). Moses was greatly distressed by the

9

Korah insurrection which was different from the frequent murmurings of the children of Israel who hungered for the flesh pots of Egypt. Here he was dealing with "men of renown" who would have created a serious breach in the organic totality of Jewish peoplehood which he tried desperately to maintain. Moses was disturbed by Korah's demand for recognition of his right to be the prince of the Kohathites, a position which went instead to Elizaphan the son of Kohath's youngest son. Moses squelched the mutiny quickly. Korah's claim was tested in fire. "And the earth swallowed them up, and the earth closed upon them, and they perished from among the assembly."

It would seem that the arguments advanced by Korah and his coterie in questioning the leadership of Moses set the pattern which all future non-conformists followed as they organized dissident groups. "Ye take too much upon you, seeing all the congregation of the Lord are holy." We hear the same argument today. "What right has one Jew to set himself up as a paragon of virtue, above all other Jews?" "I am a good Jew," exclaims the Jew who violates every law in the Code, and who does nothing to show his devotion to Judaism in a tangible form, except perhaps by giving a few dollars to Jewish charity. Now it is true that *yisroel af al pi shechata, yisroel hu*, a Jew who sins is still a Jew. It does not say, however, that he is a "good Jew," any more than a criminal can call himself a good American. But it was not a violation of the law that alarmed Moses. Moses could make allowances for human foibles: "For there is not a righteous man on earth that doeth good and sinneth not" (Ecclesiastes 7:20); "Who can say, I have made my heart clean, I am pure from sin" (Proverbs 20:9). Sin can be confessed and purged by atoning sacrifice. But Korah preached not sin—but sedition.

The further argument that "all the congregation is holy" likewise did not trouble Moses. His willingness to share his divine gifts of prophetic vision with all Jews was evinced in the incident when a young man ran to Moses and said: "Eldad and Medad are prophesying in the camp."

10

Joshua asked Moses to "shut them in." But Moses said to him: "Art thou jealous for my sake? Would that all the Lord's people were prophets, that the Lord would put His spirit upon them" (Numbers 11:27, 29). Moses would not begrudge Korah the honors which he deserved. But the rebelliousness of Korah (as well as the abomination of worshipping the Golden Calf while Moses was on the mountain top to receive the Ten Commandments) went beyond sinfulness, and could not be expiated. Defiance of authority unilaterally, by creating discord and causing ruptures, strikes at the very heart of a people or a country. There is ample evidence for this in many parts of the world where internal strife and civil war have made life intolerable and have resulted in destruction, ruin and ultimate collapse.

This does not mean that differences of opinion must be suppressed. Judaism has always encouraged argumentation and debate. "Come now, let us reason together, saith the Lord, though your sins be as scarlet they shall be as white as snow" (Isaiah 1:18). Our entire Talmud is a record of rabbinic disputes over the diverse interpretations of the Bible and the formulation of the *Halacha* or Jewish law. But it is crucial to take note of the spirit of the dialectics. Our rabbis declare, "Every controversy that is in the name of heaven shall in the end lead to a permanent result; but every controversy that is not in the name of heaven shall not lead to a permanent result. Which controversy was that which was in the name of heaven? Such was the controversy of Hillel and Shammai. And that which was not in the name of heaven? Such was the controversy of Korah and his company" (Pirke Avot 5:20).

The rabbis characterize the fate that befell Korah and his company, as *"srefas neshama v'goof kayam,* the burning of the soul while the body remained intact" (Sanhedrin 52a). The problem with Korah went further than the rebellion against the leadership of Moses and Aaron. It was a revolt against spirit of the Torah of Moses, with the accusation that the Torah was not of Divine origin but that Moses had invented the laws and ordinances of Torah out

11

of his own imagination. As a pretext, Korah questioned Moses with reference to the law of the fringes and affixing the *mezuzah* on the door posts of the homes. It is stated in the Bible immediately before the chapter of Korah: "Speak unto the children of Israel, and bid them that they make throughout their generations fringes in the corners of their garments, and that they put with the fringe of each corner a thread of blue" (Numbers 15:38). Now, Korah argues, if one thread of blue sanctions its use, what happens if the entire garment is made of blue wool? Are fringes still necessary? It is further stated in the Bible: "And thou shalt write them upon the door posts of thy house and upon thy gates" (Deuteronomy 6:4). "Does a house which is full of books need a *mezuzah?*" Korah asked, presumably not for information, but to justify his revolt.

The discussion is reminiscent of the legend concerning a Jew who asked the rabbi, "If one recites the entire Book of Psalms, must he also repeat the *Ashre* (Psalm 145) which is the beginning of the *Mincha* service?" The rabbi gave the answer with a parable: "A man who drives a wagon loaded with barrels containing grease must still grease the wheels of the wagon." The explanation is satisfactory to the pious Jew who appreciates the sanctity of the *mitzvot*. But our brethren who find the laws of the Torah burdensome, and who look for an excuse to circumvent the law, seek logical deductions and sophistical arguments which can prove black, white, and night, day.

"The Ten Spies and assembly of Korah will not have a share in the world to come," declare the rabbis (Sanhedrin 109b). The ten spies who brought an evil report about the Promised Land, as well as the assembly of Korah, will be excluded from the bliss awaiting the righteous in the next world, because of the sins which they committed against God, Moses and the people. They all caused dissension within the camp. The majority discouraging report of ten spies as against the favorable report of the two, Caleb

attack upon our people, in every generation in a different guise, constitutes a study by itself, but we are concerned now with the internecine strife which is equally disturbing and distressing.

III

THE SPLIT KINGDOM

The next serious break within the ranks of Israel came when the Kingdom of Rehoboam split in two, the Kingdom of Israel on the north, with Samaria as the capital, and the Kingdom of Judea on the south, with Jerusalem as the capital.

If Rehoboam had been more conciliatory toward the demand of Jeroboam and all the congregation of Israel that the taxes be lightened, heavy taxes which came as a result of the building operations of his father, King Solomon, he would have saved the day. He rejected the wise counsel of the old men who said unto him: "Speak good words to them, then they will be thy servants forever." Instead, he foolishly followed the impetuous directive of the young men who advised Rehoboam to spurn the demands of the people. "My little finger is thicker than my father's loins. And now whereas my father did burden you with a heavy yoke, I will add to your yoke; my father chastened you with whips, but I will chasten you with scorpions" (I Kings 12:7, 11), exclaimed Rehoboam. We can learn a great deal from the critical period of the division of the kingdom, lessons which can be of profit when dealing with the divisions which are taking place currently on the Jewish religious scene. Shall we, today, follow the sedate admonition of our elders who, while admitting that it is a heavy tax upon the people to carry the "yoke of the mitzvot," realize that it is only by kind words of conciliation that compliance can be attained? Or shall we allow the fragmentation of our ranks not into two kingdoms, as in the case of Rehoboam, but into many segments and many "kingdoms?"

It was in Shechem where Jeroboam broke away from Rehoboam. It had been the intention of the people to make Rehoboam king of the whole of Israel, to take the place of his father, King Solomon. But after the third day, the people proclaimed: "What portion have we in David? Neither have we inheritance in the son of Jesse; to your tents, O Israel; now see to thine own house, David." Rehoboam went back to Jerusalem, and here a group of men threatened to attack the house of Israel and bring the kingdom back; but the man of God, Shemaiah, advised against violent action. Jeroboam then set up two calves of gold, and said unto the people: "Ye have gone up long enough to Jerusalem. Behold thy gods, O Israel, which brought thee up out of the land of Egypt." Thus a new dynasty of kings of Israel was established, which continued until Shalmanesser, King of Assyria, conquered the Northern Kingdom of Israel in the year 722 B.C.E. (II Kings 18:9). He also threatened King Hezekiah of Judah who refused to surrender, by the advice of the prophet Isaiah. The Kingdom of Judah continued to resist the attacks of her enemies until her downfall came in the year 586, when Nebuchadnessar, King of Babylon, besieged Jerusalem and the people were exiled to a strange land.

The chapter relating the division of the Kingdom should be carefully studied, not only by students of history and archeology, but by our statesmen and leaders of today. History has a peculiar habit of repeating itself. Today there are the successors of the "nessers" of biblical times, who are looking with wolves' eyes upon the prey of Israel. Today, we need unity more than ever.

16

IV

THE SAMARITANS

The Samaritan sect was a source of great irritation to their fellow Jews in some of the most critical periods of Jewish history. Sectarianism generally arouses feelings of hostility, which may be manifest by one party or the other. Even an attempt to bring about reconciliation is often frustrated. We find such an inflexible frame of mind prevalent in the time of Zerubbabel, when the Temple in Jerusalem was being rebuilt by decree of Cyrus, King of Persia. The Samaritans offered to join with the tribes of Judah and Benjamin, who had been exiled after the destruction of Jerusalem, in the rebuilding of the Temple. The Bible describes the episode in great detail in the Book of Ezra, Chapter 4.

The Samaritans drew near to Zerubbabel and to the heads of the fathers' houses, and said unto them: "Let us build with you; for we seek your God, as ye do; and we do sacrifice unto Him since the days of Esarhadon king of Assyria, who brought us hither." But Zerubbabel rebuffed them: "Ye have nothing to do with us to build a house unto our God; but we ourselves together will build unto the Lord, the God of Israel, as King Cyrus, the King of Persia, hath commanded us to."

Trouble ensued. The Samaritans did everything they could to frustrate the building of the Temple during the reign of Cyrus and until the reign of Darius. When Artaxerxes ascended the throne, a message was sent to him, slanderous in character: "Be it known unto the king that the Jews that came up from thee are come to us unto Jeru-

17

salem; they are building the rebellious and the bad city and have finished the walls, and are digging out the foundations. Be it known now unto the king, that if the city be builded, and the walls finished, they will not pay tribute, impost or toll, and so thou wilt endanger the revenue of the Kings." An order was issued to stop of the building of Jerusalem. But the building continued, nevertheless, through the encouragement of the prophets, Haggai and Zechariah.

In the second year of the reign of Darius, a letter was sent to him by the Samaritans, asking him to make search in the king's treasury in Babylon whether it be so, that a decree was made by Cyrus the King to build this house of God at Jerusalem. The search was made in the house of the archives, and the decree was found. Tatenai, the governor in Jerusalem, was enjoined from interfering with the building of the Temple, and the king gave the order that the expenses be paid out of the king's treasury, and that all the necessary supplies for the sacrifices be provided to the priests.

There was bitter feeling against the Samaritans for their attempted blocking of the building of the Temple. Ben Sira (1:25) has harsh words against them, as well as against Seir and Philistia. "Against two nations my soul is disturbed, and the foolish nation that liveth in Shechem."

The Samaritan's offer to help build the Temple was rejected on the ground that the population was mixed when the northern kingdom fell to Sargon, King of Assyria, in 722 B.C.E. The Jews living in Samaria were exiled to Babylonia, and Babylonian colonists were sent to Samaria. Not all the Jews were exiled. Many remained. Those who were removed were the priests, the rich, the leaders. The new colonists intermingled with the existing population, and their religious ideas also must have become blended, to some extent.

It is important to note that as a result of the division of the one kingdom under Solomon, two kingdoms were formed, Israel and Judah, and that one after the other fell into the hands of the enemy, with the result that ten tribes

of the Northern Kingdom were lost, and their whereabouts
are not known until this day. There have been many con-
jectures, none of which has been substantiated. The Red
American Indians have been identified with the Lost Ten
Tribes. The British, the Japanese, the Bnai Israel of India,
are also among those that have been mentioned. The one
lesson which must be heeded from the tragic experience of
our people has been expounded in that commonplace saying: "United we stand, divided we fall." That irreparable
loss has never been regained until this day.

The Samaritans again showed their enmity to the body
of Israel when they joined the enemy in the rebellion of
Bar Kochba against the Romans.

The Talmud devotes considerable discussion with reference to the relationship between the Kuthim (Samaritans)
and the Jews. An entire treatise, Tractate Kuthim, deals
with the Samaritans, indicating that their insistence upon
their own interpretation of the Bible was a matter of concern for the rabbis, who felt the need of warning the people to be vigilant in their dealings with the heretics who
did not follow the authorized code of Jewish practice. The
Samaritans' acceptance of Judaism was not regarded as
being inspired by conviction. They were called *gere arayot*,
proselytes of lions, as indicated in the account in II Kings,
chapter 17. When the King of Assyria conquered the Northern Kingdom of Israel, "he brought men from Babylon,
and from Kutha and from Avva and from Hamath and
Sepharvaim, and placed them in the city of Samaria instead
of the children of Israel . . . the nations knew not the manner of the God of the land; therefore he hath sent lions
among them, and behold they slay them, because they knew
not the manner of the God of the land." The Samaritans
adopted the faith of Israel, but in a modified form. In the
discussion whether to regard them as true proselytes or
not, it was decided that in observances which are in keeping with the rabbinic law they were to be trusted, but in
all other matters they were to be regarded as heathens.

There is a dispute among the talmudic sages with re-

gard to the status of the Samaritans. In Tractate Niddah
56b, the Israelites and the Samaritans are put in the same
category respecting the laws of hygiene, because "the Samaritans are true proselytes." But in Tractate Kiddushin
75b, where the sages debate the subject of the marriage
of proselytes, it is stated that R. Eleazar agrees with R.
Ishmael, who maintained that Kuthim are proselytes
(through fear) of lions, and therefore are regarded as
heathens.

Rabbi Akiva, however, was more liberal. He holds that
Kuthim are true proselytes, and the priests who became
mixed up with them are true priests (Kiddushin 75b). But
intermarriage with them was forbidden, because the Samaritans maintained that according to their interpretation of
the verse in Deuteronomy (25:5), with reference to levirate marriage, an *arusa* (an engaged women) is subjected
to *halizah* (levirate release), but not a *n'sua* (a married
women). The interdiction against intermarrying and asso-
ciating with the Samaritans on a religious basis was due
not only to their own interpretation of the Scriptures which
was contrary to that of the rabbis, but to the fact that they
were not thoroughly versed or scrupulous in the details
of the mitzvot. One Tana maintains that it is permitted to
eat the matzoh of a Kuthi, and he fulfills his obligation to
eat unleavened bread as directed in Exodus 12:18. But
R. Eliezar, on the other hand, forbids it, because they are
not fully versed in the principles of the biblical commandments. In respect to marriage, they have no intensive
knowledge of the laws of betrothal and divorce. A woman
may be validly betrothed, yet they thought that she was not
and permitted her to marry another, and that rendered the
children illegitimate.

Maimonides, in his commentary on Mishna Berachot,
end of Chapter 8, summarized the relationship between the
Jews and the Samaritans: "Now I will explain the subject
of the Kuthim, the people whom Sennacherib brought from
Kutha and settled in the cities of Samaria. The Bible states
that they feared God and they served the Lord (II Kings,

17). In course of time they studied the Torah and accepted it literally, and in the commandments which they observed, they were scrupulous, and they were relied upon that they believed in our religion. They did not worship idols until the scholars made search and found that they honored Mt. Gerizim, and they made diligent search and found on that mountain the form of a dove, and they knew that they served idols, and then they regarded them as complete Kuthim (heathens) in every respect. And everywhere in the Mishna where you may infer that the Kuthim are better than the heathens and worse than the Israelites, as it is said: "One may join with a Kuthi in saying grace and the Kuthi may pronounce the blessing," this applied only before they made search. But after they made search they found, as I have indicated, that they are much worse than the heathen. Therefore be apprised concerning this matter, and it will not be necessary to mention this at all wherever the Kuthim are mentioned."

To this day there has been no intermingling with the Samaritans who number only a few hundred in Israel. The sect is fast disappearing, although it is a strange phenomenon that they have lasted throughout the centuries.

V

HELLENISM AND JUDAISM

Translations of the Bible have reached almost every corner of the globe. Written in every language and dialect, even those of the very primitive peoples, they have served to bring the word of God to all segments of the human race. Whether or not this has contributed to the welfare of humanity and furthered the cause of universal peace and brotherhood, is another question. Nevertheless, at least the nations of the world have come to know that there is a divine code which inculcates the principle of "Love thy neighbor as thyself," and the doctrines of the Ten Commandments.

It was the avowed purpose of the Jews who lived in the era following the conquest of Alexander the Great, to bring the teachings of Judaism to the outside world, and the Hellenistic Jews sought to make propaganda for Judaism under a pagan masque.

The translation of the Bible into Greek, the Septuagint, was ordered by King Ptolemy who placed seventy-two elders, each in a separate house, without revealing to them at first the reason for their confinement. He then told them to translate the Torah of Moses. The legend informs us that "the Lord put wisdom into their hearts, and their concepts jibed one with the other and they wrote a single Torah, with thirteen variations." The variations in the translation from the original are enumerated in Tractate Soferim, Chapter 1. Each variation sought to avoid a possible misinterpretation. For example: the opening verse of Genesis, if literally translated, reads: "In the beginning created God," which the philosophers would interpret as an indication that God is not the creator of the world. The translators of the Septuagint uniformly translated the passage to read: "In the beginning God created the world."

With all the precautions, however, the rabbis were convinced that the translation would become a source of assimilation and they declared: "The day that the Bible was translated into Greek was as fateful as the worship of the Golden Calf." The translation was undertaken because the language spoken by the populace was not Hebrew, but Greek. What happened then is the same that has happened in every age of Jewish history. The attempt to popularize the Jewish religion by dressing it in foreign garb did not serve to strengthen Judaism, but in reverse, brought about a demoralization which required the super-human efforts of a small band of loyal zealots to neutralize and combat. It was for that reason that the rabbis looked askance at

22

the whole Hellenistic culture which seemed so glamorous in the eyes of the populace. Philo of Alexandria, who borrowed from the Stoics, admits that the proselytes adopted nothing more than the monotheistic principle. And all his attempts to demonstrate that Jewish law excels Plato's philosophical concept of the ideal republic, proved to no avail. The anti-Semitism of Apion on the one side and the mistrust of the converts on the other, turned Philo's mission to the nations into a mockery. The allegorical method of interpreting the words in the Bible led to eccentric notions and capricious practices, which were embodied in the vast literature of the time, known as the Hagiographa, or Foreign Writings. The rabbis forbade them to be read or studied because they led to heresy, apostacy and paganism. They were not included in the Canon of the Holy Bible. The church, however, has given them recognition, although they did not become part of the New Testament. Paul who formulated the tenets of Christianity came under Hellenic influence. The sect of the Essenes who have recently attained prominence due to the finding of the Dead Sea Scrolls, show a mingling of Greek culture and Jewish traditions. The rabbinic authorities of that period sensed the danger to Judaism, and valiantly fought against the foreign inroads. They condemned the *Minim*, the sectarians and infidels who sought to steer the stream of Judaism into the marshes of paganism, idolatry and superstition.

The rabbis were aware of the disintegrating influence which Hellenism posed for Judaism, and regarded every move, no matter how innocuous on the surface, as fraught with grave danger for the integrity of the faith. The experience of the past must serve as an admonition for the present, because the same influences which prevailed in ancient days are also operative in our day. Hence it is imperative to scrutinize all movements which are seemingly dedicated to the advancement of Judaism but which may prove to be a blessing in reverse.

VI

SADDUCEES AND BOETHUSIANS

The origin of the heretical sects of the Sadducees and Boethusians, mentioned in the Talmud, the Apocryphal literature and the New Testament is obscure. They are reputed to be the descendants of the High Priest, Zadok, who officiated during the reigns of David and Solomon. Zadok's son, Ahimaaz, married a daughter of King Solomon and, became governor of Naphtali. The line of high priests was known as the "sons of Zadok" (Ezekiel 4:15), and took pride in tracing its lineage to the first High Priest, Aaron. However there are scholars who question this theory of the origin of the Sadducean movement.

Another conjecture traces the founding of the sect to the pupils of Antigonus of Socho, a disciple of Simon the Just, who lived in the first half of the third century B.C.E. His two students were Zadok and Boethus. In the first chapter of the Sayings of the Fathers, there is a saying attributed to Antigonus which was misinterpreted by his disciples: "Be not like servants who serve their master for the sake of receiving a reward." Consequently, argued the students, there is no reward in the world to come and there is no resurrection of the dead. This was the beginning of the split between the Sadducean party and the Pharisees.

The Sadducees were connected with the high priests and the dignitaries of the Temple. The constituency of the High Court (*Sanhedrin*) was mostly Sadducean, which gave them strong power. However, the masses of the people, who followed the Pharisees, were not with them, and the conflict between the two parties on questions of ritual and doctrine was bitter.

The Sadducees regarded themselves of a higher order in the social stratum, and for that reason were condemned by the Pharisees as the "haughty" aristocracy. They lived in luxury, and enjoyed life as the goal of man. Having abandoned belief in the hereafter, they believed that man's destiny was in his own hands. They aimed for worldly success, which to them was the *summum bonum*, the only purpose in life, since death marks the end of man, and everything then passes into oblivion.

In the words of the prophet, Isaiah, we may find a characterization of the Sadducean philosophy of life: "And behold joy and gladness, slaying oxen and killing sheep, eating flesh and drinking wine. Let us eat and drink, for tomorrow we shall die" (Isaiah 22:13).

The Sadducees broke away from the law as expounded by the Pharisees, the rabbinic authorities of the time, which meant that they repudiated the *Torah shebe'al peh*, the "Unwritten Torah," which contains the contents of Talmud and the rabbinic lore. The interpretations of the rabbis according to the hermeneutical rules of logic were disputed by the Sadducees, who constantly argued in reverse. The rabbis were warned not to argue or debate with the Sadducees, because they distorted the meaning of the sages to suit their own convictions. Abtalion, the teacher of Hillel and Shammai, said: "Ye sages be heedful of your words, lest ye incur the penalty of exile" (Perek 1:11), which meant, "Do not give them the opportunity of misinterpreting your teachings, lest you be banished in exile." The Talmud relates that R. Joshua ben Parachiah fled to Alexandria because of Sadducean hostility (Sota 47a).

Some rabbis regarded the Sadducees in the same category as heathens, and treated them as such in all legal matters. Others, like Rabbi Gamaliel, placed a Sadducee in the class of heretic Israelites, following the rule, "An Israelite although he has sinned is still an Israelite," the relationship to the body of Israel is not annulled by sin (Kiddushin 36a).

25

Nevertheless, Rabbi Akiva declared that those who read the extra-canonical books, (the Apocrypha which were dominated by Hellenistic influence), the Sadducees and the Samaritans—will have no share in the world to come (Sanhedrin, 90a). They were held in contempt by the Pharisees, because, although they held high positions in the Court and in the administration of communal affairs, they were stigmatized as being ignorant. They interpreted the Bible literally, and were not concerned with the rich storehouse of tradition which the rabbis of the Talmud transmitted from generation to generation. The Sadducees were more concerned with political matters in the struggle with the Romans. Many of them perished in the wars; many were executed by the Romans or sold into slavery. With the destruction of the Second Temple by the Romans, their influence waned, their numbers decreased and they finally disappeared.

VII

THE ESSENES

Judaism was divided into three sects during the talmudic period: the Essenes, the Pharisees and the Sadducees. The basic philosophies of these three aspects of Judaism may be defined simply, as follows: The Essenes believed that everything is determined by destiny; the Pharisees believed in destiny but also in the freedom of the will, as indicated in the Ethics of the Fathers, 3:19, "Everything is foreseen, yet freedom of choice is given"; and the Sadducees believed that there is no destiny at all.

We learn of the colorful life of the Essenes from the writings of Philo and Josephus, who described their daily regimen in detail. According to Philo, the Essenes have no property of their own, neither house nor slave nor farm, nor flocks nor herds, but hold in common everything they have and obtain. They either pursue agriculture or tend to their sheep, cattle or beehives, or practice some handi- craft. Their earnings are in the care of an elected steward who buys the food for their meals and whatever is neces- sary for life. Every day they have their meals together; they are contented with the same food because they love frugality and despise extravagance as a disease of body and soul. They also have their dress in common, a thick cloak in winter and a light mantle in summer, each one being allowed to take whatever he chooses.

Josephus adds a few further details: "Their way of dressing and their general appearance are decorous; they possess neither two cloaks, nor two pair of shoes. At early dawn they rise for devotion and prayer, and speak not a word to one another until they have praised God in hymns. They speak not a word about profane things before the ris- ing of the sun, but they offer up the prayers they have re- ceived from their fathers, facing the sun as if praying for its rising. The purpose of this custom is explained in Bera- chot 9b, to join the *Geulah* (prayer for deliverance from Egyptian bondage), and the *Tefilah* (the *Amida* prayer). It is also in keeping with the verse in Psalms 72:5: 'They shall fear Thee with the sunrise and so long as the moon throughout all generations.' After prayer they go forth each to his work until the fifth hour. Then they put on linen aprons and bathe in cold water before they eat breakfast, none being allowed to enter the house who does not share their views or mode of holiness. For all meals they are dressed in sacred linen garments. Having taken their seats in order amid silence, each takes a sufficient portion of bread and some additional food, but none eats before the bene- diction has been offered by the priest, who also recites the grace after the meal. Both at the beginning and the end they praise God in hymns. After this they lay aside their sacred linen garments used at their meal, put on their work- ing clothes left in the vestibule, and betake themselves to their labors until the evening, when they take supper. There is no loud noise and vociferation heard at their assembly; they speak gently and allow their discourse to flow with grace and dignity, so that the stillness within impresses outsiders with a sense of mystery. They observe sobriety and moderation in eating and drinking. Above all they refrain from all forms of passion and anger as leading to mischief. All pay due attention to the president, and whatever he orders they obey as law."

The initiation into their organization, or closed fraternity (*Chabura*) was very strict. An applicant received his food outside the main hall for a full year after having received a mattock, a linen apron and a white robe, a symbol of *zeniut*, Essene modesty and purity. After having given proof of self-control during this period, he was advanced and his ablutions assumed a higher degree of purity, but he was not allowed to partake of the common meal until, after a trial of two years more, he was proved worthy to be admitted to membership. The oath of a most solemn character was administered to him. He swore to treat with reverence whatever is related to the divinity. He will observe righteousness to all men and injustice to none. He will not hate anyone who has done him an injustice but will pray for his enemies. He swore that he will not communicate the doctrines differently from the manner in which he has received them himself.

The Essenes were very scrupulous in the observance of the Sabbath. They prepared their meal one day previously so as not to touch fire, and during the Sabbath some of them did not rise from their couch. Among the many rigid customs which they observed, they did not handle or look at a coin that had an image upon it, nor enter a city at the gates of which statues were erected.

They claimed to possess by tradition the pronunciation of the magic spell of the Holy Name, and with it to achieve miracles, as the men of old.

VIII

CHRISTIANITY AND JUDAISM

Our study of the many sects which branched out of the Judaism must include Christianity in order to indicate the factors which led either to the extinction of such sects as the Sadducees and Essenes, or to a severing of ties with Judaism as initiation of a new growth, such as Christianity and Islam. The Jewish community in the Holy Land at the beginning of the common era was fragmented into many sects besides the early Christians who were Jews in every respect except their belief in the messianic character of the founder of the new movement. There were the Ebionites, Elkesaites, Ossenians, Nazarites, Nazarenes, Sampsaeans, and many others. The challenge of these splinter organizations was faced by the rabbis of the Talmud, who were more deeply concerned with the fate of Judaism from corrosion within than from the danger of attack from without. Professor Ginsberg, in his *Students, Saints and Scholars* (p. 88), quotes the talmudic dictim: "Israel went into exile only after it became divided into twenty-four sects." We can understand the reason for the insistence upon strict observance of the Torah on the part of the rabbis, who put a fence around the law (*seyag latorah*) as a precautionary measure to prevent any possible break which might lead to the destruction of its fruits.

The period at the beginning of the Common Era was marked by confusion caused by the welter of diverse cultures harboring strange myths, the deification of heathen and pagan demigods, the yearning for an escape or redemption from the thraldom imposed by tyrants—which a savior or messiah could bring. There was a hunger for something new and sensational. In many respects the conditions were not unlike those existing today, with the multiplication of sects and schisms promising salvation and relief from the trials, afflictions and ordeals from which mankind is suffering. The old tradition did not bring satisfaction and comfort, and a new philosophy had to be formulated.

Christianity as it stands today is different from the Christianity of the founder, who had no intention of creating a new religion. The law, the Torah, was regarded as an eternal testament, as indicated in the dictum recorded in Matthew (5:17, 18) : "Think not that I come to destroy the law, or the prophets: I am not come to destroy but to fulfill. For verily, I say unto you, till heaven and earth pass, one jot or tittle shall in no wise pass from the law, till all be fulfilled."

But all this was changed under the influence of Paul, who was responsible for the complete break with Judaism and the establishment of Christianity as an independent and separate religion. Paul was one of the apostles who never saw his Master. He was born in Tarsus, in Asia Minor, and received both a Greek education and a thorough Hebrew education. Becoming a Roman citizen, he came under the spell of Roman culture. He assumed the name Paul, which was a Roman adaptation of his Hebrew name, Saul. He came to Jerusalem to study under the guidance of the Patriarch, Gamaliel I (Acts 22:43), and at first was an observant Jew like all his fellow Jews of his day. In fact he went to Damascus to chastise the Jewish Christians for their heretical views. But he saw a light from heaven and he heard a voice saying: "Saul, Saul, why persecutest thou me?" (Acts, 9:4). Ananias then came to him and said: "Brother Saul, receive thy sight. . . . The God of our fathers has chosen thee, that thou shouldst know His will. Arise and be baptised and wash away thy sins, calling on the name of the Lord." Saul went to Jerusalem and prayed in the Temple. As he prayed he fell in a trance, and he again heard the voice telling him to leave Jerusalem, "for they will not receive thy testimony concerning me."

Paul did not succeed in preaching to the Jews who persecuted him. He therefore decided to preach to the Gentiles, and succeeded in gaining many converts. Realizing, however, that there were many obstacles in the way of the Gentiles accepting the new religion with all the Jewish requirements, such as circumcision, the dietary laws and the Sabbath, Paul assured the new converts that all of these old laws were no longer operative. According to the teachings of Paul, faith freed Christians from the claim and obligation of law. "And they are informed of thee, that thou teachest all the Jews which are among the Gentiles to forsake Moses, saying that they ought not to circumcize their children, neither to walk after the customs."

The conflict between Judaism and Christianity, their similarities and differences, are subjects which have been treated by competent scholars, and are entirely outside the confines of our present treatise. Suffice it to say that we yearn for the coming of the day in our generation when the diverse faiths of the world will inspire their votaries with the humanitarian ideals which we all have in common, utilizing the unique methods and the disciplines which they have accepted through indoctrination and which harmonizes with their philosophy of life. According to the Midrash, Abraham, the Patriarch, proselytized the men, and Sarah converted the women. But through the entire history of Judaism, there had been no attempt to engage in propaganda aimed at converting the heathen, a policy which was adopted by Paul, who declared: "I am the apostle to the Gentiles" (Romans 11:143). Judaism followed the admonition of the prophet Micah (4:5) : "For let all the peoples each one walk in the name of its God. But we will walk in the name of the Lord our God forever and ever."

The Jews have held fast to the Torah and combatted every influence which resorted to suppression and forced disputation in an effort to break down loyalty to the ancestral faith. That loyalty has been maintained at tremendous cost and sacrifice until the present day. Pious Jews propose to continue unswerving devotion to the traditional religion and bravely face the "slings and arrows of outrageous fortune." In our attitude toward Christianity we can follow the declaration of Maimonides: "The teachings of the Nazarene and the Ishmaelite (Mohammed) serve the divine purpose of preparing the way for the Messiah, who is sent to make the whole world perfect by worshipping God with one spirit: for they have spread the words of the Scriptures and the law of truth over the whole world" (Mishne Torah, Melachim 11:4). Jacob Emden likewise pays tribute to the contribution of Christianity to civilization in his words: "The founder of Christianity conferred a double blessing upon the world: on the one hand he strengthened the Torah of Moses, and emphasized its eternal obligation. On the other hand he conferred favor on the heathens in removing idolatry from them, imposing upon them the seven Noahite precepts. Would that all Christians would live in conformity with their precepts. They are not enjoined like the Israelites to observe the laws of Moses, nor do they sin if they associate other beings with God in worshipping a triune God" (*Seder Olam*).

The appeal for Christian unity which was made at the 21st Ecumenical Council, convened by Pope John XXIII, and the effect it has had upon channeling the thoughts of men toward a revaluation of their denominational differences should likewise influence our people to reconsider the cliches which have only served to divide us and split our ranks. The invitation to the "separated brethren" to return to the fold should go even further than the ranks of Christianity. Perhaps it is time to think that all men should go back to the original sources, and hearken to the words of the prophet, Isaiah: "Ye that seek the Lord, look at the rock whence ye were hewn."

The Jew will persist in proclaiming the Ten Commandments and the entire compendium of laws as promulgated in the Torah and in the teachings of the sages in all generations as the only salvation of the human race from the doom of destruction which hangs ominously, like the Damocletian sword, over their heads. The Jew will continue to preach to the world that man will be justified by the law of Moses, and not by faith alone. The belief that faith frees man from the obligations of the moral law is not in keeping with the precepts of Judaism, as enunciated in the declaration of Micah (6:8) : "He hath told thee, O man, what is good and what doth the Lord require of thee, but to do justly, to love mercy, and to walk humbly with thy God."

The Jew will continue to pray and hope for the coming of the Messiah who will fulfill all the prophecies which are contained in holy script. He will not appear until man is deserving of his coming by reason of conduct which must be in conformity with the precepts of the Torah. Mankind is still in the throes of the *chevle hamashiach*, the "birth pains of the Messiah." The Messianic age is fully described in the Book of Isaiah (chapter 11) : "And the wolf shall dwell with the lamb . . . they shall not hurt and destroy in all My holy mountain." Then the Messiah will come.

IX

ISLAM AND JUDAISM

The study of Islam and its relation to Judaism is important for an understanding of the problems caused by sectarianism in Judaism. When Mohammed first began to receive visions of his divine mission to preach the true faith, as he conceived it, he depended upon the Jews for his support. He made an appeal for their conversion to the new faith which proclaimed Allah as the only God, and Mohammed, the "seal of the prophets" (*Khatam al-anbiya*). He was the messenger (*Razul*), appointed by Allah to bring the final revelation of the Creator to mankind. Islam was the last stage of the theophany, the final manifestation of the Lord to man, superceding Judaism and Christianity. The Koran was the perfection and consummating florescence of faith. It is a similar conviction in the mind of every aspiring leader of a new religion or a new reformation, that he is endowed with new, divine vision, that has led to the multiplication of sects in the world. It is for that reason that one of the precepts of faith, as proclaimed by Maimonides, precludes the bifurcation of Judaism into diverse segments. "I believe with a perfect faith that this law will not be changed and there never will be any other law from the Creator blessed be His name." Maimonides aimed this principle of the Thirteen Principles, which are included in our prayer book, at counteracting the claims to superiority of Christianity and Islam. Firmness of faith was the anchor and the ballast which has kept the Jewish ship afloat among the tumultuous waves which have dashed against it during the stormy centuries of history.

Mohammed was provoked by the influential Jews of his day who refused to recognize him as the chief of the prophets, and his love turned to hate. At the beginning, like Christianity, the practices of Islam were similar to Judaism. Many biblical and talmudic laws were adopted by Mohammed. Saturday was the Sabbath. Swine's meat was prohibited and some of the laws of slaughtering were observed, such as requiring the severance of the esophagus (*veshet*) and the windpipe (*kone*). The Moslems practice the rite of circumcision, which is performed on the thirteenth birthday instead of the eighth day after birth. The reason may be found in the biblical account of the circumcision of Ishmael who is traditionally the ancestor of the Arabs. "And Ishmael his son was thirteen years old, when he was circumcised" (Genesis 17:25). The Moslem Yam el-Din corresponded with Rosh Hashanah. Originally a fast day, it was observed on the tenth day of the first month, which is reminiscent of Yom Kippur. The Moslems observe five periods of prayer which are based on the three daily prayers of *Shacharis, Mincha* and *Ma'ariv* in Judaism. Originally,

34

Mohammed instructed his followers to face Jerusalem in their devotions. The pilgrimage to Mecca which was obligatory upon every Moslem followed the biblical command which was enjoined upon every Israelite: "Three times a year shall all thy males appear before the Lord thy God in the place which He shall choose; on the feast of unleavened bread, and on the feast of weeks, and on the feast of tabernacles, and they shall not appear before the Lord empty" (Deut. 16:16). The absolute unity of God was scrupulously maintained by Mohammed, who did not claim any of the divine attributes which are associated with the founder of Christianity, as indicated in the Moslem declaration of faith: "There is no God but Allah, and Mohammed is His prophet."

However, there was a complete reversal of Mohammed's attitude toward the Jews and Judaism when the Jews of his day refused to accept his appeal. Hate ran riot. While he formerly admonished his people to respect the "People of the (Sacred) Books" (*Am el-Kitab*), he proclaimed the basic doctrine of *Jihad*, the Holy War, which was directed against all unbelievers who did not accept Islam. The sword was used as a means of convincing the infidels of their sin in repudiating the offer of Moslem salvation, and the pages of history are saturated with the blood of the Holy Wars which were waged against the Jews and others. Even to this day there is the threat of a holy war which the Arabs would unleash against Israel.

Many changes were made in the ritual of Islam, originally based on biblical laws, in spite of the admonition: "All this word which I command you, that shall ye observe to do; thou shalt not add thereto, nor diminish from it" (Deuteronomy 13:1). Instead of turning to Jerusalem in prayer, the Moslems turn to Mecca. A radical change was made in the observance of the Sabbath, which was changed to Friday, as a day of assembly for divine worship. In the same spirit as the Nicean Creed in Christianity, which made many changes in the observance of the holidays—such as Passover to Easter, Islam changed its fast day to the celebration of Ramadan, when fasting is maintained from morning to evening every day during the month.

The relationship between the Jews and the Moslems during the Golden Age of Spanish-Jewry in the 10th and 11th centuries constituted one of the most glorious periods in Jewish history. There was a close affinity between the Jews and Arabs which was reflected in the influence which one exerted upon the other. The Jewish scholars of that period used the Arabic language in writing their books on medicine, astronomy, mathematics, astrology, philology and grammar. The Mishna was translated into Arabic and the works in Jewish philosophy by Saadia, Ibn Gabirol, Bahya Ibn Pekuda, Judah Halevi, Abraham Ibn Daud, and Maimonides were originally written in Arabic. Many valuable Greek philosophic and scientific works have been preserved in Arabic translations, and thereby became more accessible to the scholarly world. Biblical translations and commentaries served to keep the Arabic-speaking Jews acquainted with Hebrew literature. Academies flourished in the principle cities in Spain, in Cordova, Lucena, Granada, Toledo, and Seville. Jews were very active in public life. They were appointed to serve as the physicians to the kings and caliphs, and many attained the position of vizier, which was the highest office in the land.

Arabic culture was a challenge to Judaism which the Jewish scholars of that period faced courageously. The conquests of Caliph Omar II (582-644), who subdued Egypt, Syria, Palestine and Persia, and of Walid I, who extended his power into North Africa and Spain, brought Arabic culture to the two continents and made Arabic almost a universal language. The Jews welcomed the dynamic influence of the new intellectualism which the Arab scholars exhibited in every branch of scholastic endeavor. The Arabs were particularly proud of their language, with special emphasis on exact grammatical forms. Saadia was the first who made Hebrew philological studies a special science, although there were others before him who wrote Hebrew grammars, and attempted a comparative study of Semitic

36

languages. Only fragments of Saadia's *Agron*, which was partly lexicographical and partly grammatical, have been preserved. But in his other works, especially in his commentary to the *Sefer Yetzira*, there are several grammatical paragraphs.

Arabic seemed to be felicitously suitable for poetic composition, and there are many Arabic *piyutim* embodied in the prayer books of the Oriental and African communities. Jewish scholars were more concerned with *Halacha* and less with literary endeavors, such as poetry, novels, dramas, the entire field of linguistics, belle-lettres and humanities. But the rich *piyutim* in our prayer books, written in a classical Hebrew with rhythmic style and a metric flow, were stimulated by Arabic poetry. The poems of Yehuda Halevi, called the "Zionides," read on Tisha B'ab in the *Kinot*, are lamentations commemorating the great tragedy of the destruction of Jerusalem and the Holy Temple, and are regarded as some of the most sublime outpourings of the human heart. While the writing of poetry was not a new phenomenon among Jews—the Psalms of David and the many poetic passages in the Bible are still incomparable literary creations—from the end of the biblical era to the Spanish-Jewish Golden Age, there were no Jewish writers of literary compositions.

Arabic culture's greatest influence upon Judaism was manifest in the realm of Jewish philosophy. After the death of Mohammed, many religious schisms developed. The Motazilites, or Dissenters, were independent minds who sought to find confirmation of the teachings of the Koran in the philosophy of Aristotle and the Greek scholars. Their works were translated first into Arabic, and became the subjects of study and discussion. The dialectics of the Motakalamin, in analyzing the doctrines of the creation of matter, the unity of God, divine attributes, the nature of the soul, the creation of the world, and similar theological and philosophical subjects, were transplanted to Jewish soil. Saadia Gaon, who is known as the father of Jewish philosophy, followed the methods of the Motazilites in his major work,

Emunot v'Deot (*Beliefs and Opinions*), in which he endeavored to bring Judaism into harmony with the philosophic postulates of his day. But not all scholars were sympathetic to this seeming infiltration of foreignisms into Judaism. They feared the effect upon the rank and file who might lose their Jewish moorings. However, Abraham Ibn Daud came to the defense of philosophy. He declared that philosophy not only did not harm religion, but confirmed it and strengthened it. The Arab philosophic works were translated into Hebrew by Tibbon, Narboni and Gersonides. The one outstanding scholar whose gigantic intellect could cope with the challenging arguments of Aristotle, the Greek philosophers and the Arabic scholars, was Maimonides in his monumental work, *More Nebuchim* (*The Guide for the Perplexed*). He also became the greatest authority in Jewish law not only for his generation, but even until this day.

X

THE KARAITES

The Karaitic sect of Judaism, founded by Anan in 780, relied upon Sadducean and Essene principles, and built a rival religion by attacking the tradition of the Rabbinites and repudiating the basic laws of the Talmud. The Karaites claimed to adhere to the Bible exclusively, and their name is derived from the term, *B'nai Mikra*, the "Followers of the Bible." Others believe that the name Karaite is taken from the root, *Kara*, "to call." The Karaites were the "callers of a new faith." The conditions at that period in Jewish history were ripe for the emergence of new sects that were influenced by the spiritual upheaval caused by the heterodox movements in Islam. The Motazila school favored a rational approach to religion and questioned the validity of many of the traditions which were regarded as sacred. Once the floodgates of rationalism were opened, there was an outpouring of polemical literature causing internecine struggles and the splintering of innumerable schisms among the dissenters, to the extent that Al Kirkisani, a noted Karaite scholar, exclaimed that it was impossible to find two Karaites who were in complete agreement with each other. It is similar to conditions today in Judaism which have prompted the remark that "wherever you find two Jews you will find three opinions."

Influenced by the political success which Islam attained, Karaism drew closer to the new faith than to rabbinism, and borrowed from Islam many of the principles which afforded the ammunition to fight the talmudic interpretation of the Halacha. Karaism, therefore, was a mixture of all the defunct ideologies with which traditional Judaism had come to grips throughout the ages and triumphantly subdued. Karaism borrowed from Samaritan theology, as well as from the allegorical method of the Hellenistic school which flourished in Alexandria, Egypt. Philo's doctrine of the Logos intrigued the Karaite scholars, and their speculation led them far astray, to asceticism and to bizarre and rigorous practices which almost brought them to race suicide. Some emigrated to Palestine and lived like Essene hermits, as mourners of Zion. But the later Karaite leaders realized that a continuation of rigorous observance was incompatible with normal living, and the ascetic aspect of the original Ananite Karaism was modified.

Karaism flourished because of the general dissatisfaction with the stagnation of the Babylonian academies as the center of gravity of Jewish life began shifting to other parts of the world. The sun was setting in Babylon, and rising again in Spain. In this transition period new forces were brought into action, and new ideas asserted themselves. It has also been noted that the Gaonim were out of touch with the scientific approach to theology and philosophy, and were unwilling to cope with the new intellectual interests, thinking that by ignoring the new awakening they could defeat

the rebellion. For the most part, the arguments and interpretations of Karaism were not sufficiently refuted, until
Saadia took them on. By his forceful intellect and his scientific attainments he was able to demolish the very foundation upon which Karaism based its theology and its biblical
interpretations. Yet, the new faith continued to produce
learned men who fought rabbinic Judaism until they were
challenged most effectively by Maimonides. Then Karaism
began to disintegrate. Communities in Egypt, Palestine,
Syria, Babylonia, Persia and North Africa disappeared
entirely. Many were converted to Islam, and others were
annexed to rabbinism. In 1313 there was a wholesale conversion of Karaites in Egypt to rabbinism.

The Karaites settled in Crimea in the 12th century, and
there established a flourishing community, which endured
for many centuries. The story of the Crimean Karaites has
an interesting chapter. Czar Nicholas I came to visit Crimea
to restore an ancient castle in Bakchiserai. Representatives
of the Rabbinites came to him to plead for exemption from
military service. He asked them if they believed in the Talmud. Receiving an affirmative answer, he denied their
petition. Bobowich who was helpful in the restoration of
the castle, and who represented the Karaite community,
declared that his people never had anything to do with the
Talmud, and furthermore that since the Karaites had been
living in the Crimea since the time of Shalmanesser, in the
7th century, B.C.E., they had not taken part in the cruci-
fixion of the founder of Christianity. When the Czar asked
for proof, Abraham Firkovitch, one of the most famous
Karaite scholars, forged documents and produced other fantastic evidence that had no basis in fact, pointing to the
alleged antiquity of the Karaites. Furthermore, he maintained that the rabbinites received all their culture from
the Karaites. As a result the Karaites were granted full
civil liberties and were exempted from military duties.

The Karaites disassociated themselves from the rest of
the Jewish people and did not regard themselves in the same
category as Jews. The Karaites in Poland also applied to

the Polish government to exempt them from the restrictions which were placed on the Jewish population, on the basis that the Karaites are not Jews. For that reason the rabbis instituted rigid prohibitions which restrained intimate association between the Rabbinites and the Karaites. The Karaites were regarded as heathens, because of their failure to adhere to the regulations which are embodied in the Jewish codes of law.

Intermarriage with a Karaite was forbidden, because they violated the rules of forbidden marriages as interpreted by the Rabbinites, based on the laws of incest in the Bible (Leviticus, ch. 18). Their children were regarded as illegitimate as the Karaite sanctification rite at marriage was not according to law, and the *kiddushin* (marriage) was not binding. It was as if no marriage had taken place.

The ceremony of circumcision also was not performed properly because the Karaites omitted the *periah*, which is an essential part of the operation according to the rabbis. The Karaites were therefore placed in the same class as the uncircumcised, which would preclude any possibility of a marriage between a Karaite and a Jew. With regard to the slaughter of animals (*Shechita*), they did not have the same tradition as the Rabbinites who base the laws of slaughter on the passage: "Thou shalt kill of thy herd any of thy flock, which the Lord hath given thee, as I have commanded thee" (Deut. 12:21). The rabbis adhered to the principle of *Kabala,* the transmission of rules, customs and practices from generation to generation. The Karaites entirely repudiated the principle of *Kabala,* tradition, and maintained that only that which is written in the Bible, explicitly, is valid—without the use of the hermeneutical rules and without reliance upon oral transference. The Karaites, furthermore, did not recognize the five requirements of a kosher slaughter, *Shehia* (pausing), *Derasha,* (pressure), *H'lada* (burrowing), *Hagrama* (deviating) and *Ikkur* (tearing), as well as the other laws concerning the post mortem examination (*Bedika*) of the animals, to determine the presence of any physical defects or pathological

41

conditions which would have shortened the life of the animal, and therefore rendered it unfit for human consumption. Likewise there were many variations in the observance of the Jewish dietary laws which distinguished the Karaites from the Rabbinic Jews. The prohibition of the mixture of meat and dairy foods and the separation of the dishes and utensils of the two categories, is based on the biblical passage, mentioned three times: "Thou shalt not seethe a kid in its mother's milk (Exodus 23:19, 34:26, and Deuteronomy 14:21). The rabbis contend that the biblical injunction applies to all mixtures of milk and meat. The Karaites who take the Bible literally for the most part, although they have their own traditions, maintain that the prohibition only refers to a kid in its mother's milk, and it does not apply to any other mixture of the diverse foods. Therefore, a Jew was forbidden to eat of the slaughtered animals of a Karaite and also to partake of his food, which is not classed as kosher.

The Karaites were looked upon as worse than the Marranos, the Jews who were forced to abjure their faith publicly during the Inquisition in Spain, but who inwardly and in secret would practice Jewish rites. In the event that a Marrano repented and asked to be restored to his status as a Jew, he was accepted by the community. Not so with respect to a Karaite. Even if a Karaite repented he was not trusted, and he was rejected as a member of the Jewish congregation. However, there were some rabbis who were lenient in this respect. Rabbi Ezekiel Landau, the author of *Node B'yehuda,* would receive a Karaite who sincerely did penance, and petitioned to be enrolled as a Rabbinic Jew. In some respects the Karaites were treated as Jews; they were not to be asked to do work on *Yom Tov* even though they did not regard the work as a violation of the law, likewise it was forbidden to loan them money on interest, in keeping with the injunction: "Thou shalt not lend to thy brother on interest" (Deut. 23:20). If a *Sefer Torah* is written by a Karaite it cannot be used in the synagogue for the reading of the weekly portion, but it is regarded as a Torah that is *posul* (unfit), which is not to be burnt, but hidden like torn prayer books and other holy paraphernalia.

XI

THE MYSTERIES OF KABBALAH

Kabbalah, the mystic lore concerning God and the universe, and its powerful impact on Jewish thought, had its staunch votaries for whom it was vested with the greatest sanctity; but it also met with strong opposition. It would take us far afield to delve fully into the origin of the esoteric doctrines of the Kabbalah, and to present in detail the system of the theoretic speculation (*Kabbalah Iyunis*), and practical formulae (*Kabbalah Ma'asis*). In our study of the factors which contribute to the formulation of One Judaism and the movements which create divisiveness in our ranks, we must consider all the influences, appraising their value to the enrichment of our faith, and likewise indicating the imperilment of foreignism to the integrity and stability of our heritage.

Kabbalah, as its name implies, was a traditional transmission from master to disciple of the divine secrets of cosmology and theosophy, which vested the possessor with the power of creation, with the ability to conquer the terrestrial world and redeem mankind from all its ailments and its problems. The secrets were at first to be confined to the privileged few, as indicated in the Pirke Avot (6:1): "R. Meir said: Whosoever labors in the Torah for its own sake merits many things." And among them he includes the *Raze Torah*, "the secrets of the Torah." The powers which they conferred were not to be entrusted to those who were unworthy, because not everyone was able to endure the mental stress which they engendered. It is related in the Talmud (Hagiga 14b), that R. Eliezer b. Arak asked R. Yohanan b. Zakkai: "Master, teach me a chapter of the "Work of the Divine Chariot" (Ma'ase Merkavah), referring to the vision of Ezekiel (ch. 1 and 10). He answered: "Have I not taught you thus: Nor the work of the chariot in the presence of one, unless he is a sage and understands of his own knowledge." We read further of the experience of the four sages who entered the "Garden," interpreted by some that they entered Paradise, by others that they were immersed in the mystic speculation of theosophy. Ben Azzi cast a look and died; Ben Zoma became demented; Elisha b. Abuyah turned apostate. Only R. Akiva entered and departed unhurt.

However, just as the Torah Shebe'al Peh, the Oral Law, which was not to be written but passed on from one generation to another, was finally recorded as the only safeguard for its perpetuation, likewise, the Kabbalah was published in a voluminous literature, the most famous of which are the Sefer Yetzira, the "Book of Creation," and the Zohar, the "Book of Splendor." Unheeded went the warning not to exert the mind in occult thought, with its conjuration of angels and demons and the manipulation of the names of God, the letters of the alphabet, the mystic numbers, and the contemplation of the coming of the Messiah. Ben Sira admonished his disciple: "En lecha esek b'nistoros, Do not traffic with mysteries." The Psalmist long before declared: "The heavens are the heavens of the Lord, but the earth hath He given to the children of men" (Ps. 115:16). That means that we cannot "play God," and seek to control the forces of nature and change the course of events by miracles. We think of the pathetic plea of Daniel, who at the end of his book, after beholding the divine visions, admits: "I heard but I understand not. Then said I: 'O my lord, what shall be the latter end of these things?' He said: 'Go thy way Daniel, for the words are shut up and sealed until the time of the end'" (Daniel 12:8, 9).

44

But the human mind cannot be curbed. Kabbalah exerted a powerful influence not only upon Jews, but upon Christians and other peoples as well. For the Jews, it was more than a speculative pursuit; it served as a tranquilizer in times of impending crisis, when all avenues of escape from the "slings of outrageous fortune," seemed to be closed. Mysticism had its upsurge in the periods of Jewish history when doom seemed imminent, and the anguished cry for deliverance was heard in the land. The vision of Ezekiel and Daniel; the hundreds of references in the Talmud dealing with angelology, demonology, cosmogeny, and other branches of occult science; the Alexandrian schools that comingled Egyptian, Chaldean, Judean and Greek culture; the esoteric works of the Gaonim and the magic literature of the Spanish and Italian mystics, which culminated, it seems, in the Safed school, headed by Isaac Luria and his disciples, Hayim Vital and Israel Saruk, and was continued by the Hasidic *rebbeim,* all point to the heightened emotionalism which was induced by the persecution and affliction which "the people of the wandering foot and weary breast" endured. This is not said in disparagement of the role that Kabbalah played in the preservation of Judaism and the Jewish people. It served a beneficent purpose, despite the excesses to which it led.

While the followers of the Kabbalah have been legion throughout the centuries and even in modern times, many Jewish authorities opposed the excesses that resulted from the exuberant emotion which the bizarre concepts evoked. Both in ideology and in practice, the excessive study of the Kabbalah channeled the stream of Judaism in a direction which was contrary to the teachings of the Bible. While not unmindful of the ideals Kabbalah promulgated, Jewish magic, demonology, astrology, numerology, the manipulation and permutation of Hebrew letters, the use of mystical symbols in writing amulets, were practices which were forbidden in the Bible. We read in Deuteronomy (18:10): "There shall not be found among you any one who maketh his son or his daughter to pass through the fire, one that useth divination, a soothsayer, or an enchanter, a sorceror, or a charmer, or one that consulteth a ghost or a familiar spirit, or a necromancer. For whosoever doeth these things is an abomination unto the Lord; and because of these abominations the Lord thy God is driving them out from before you." All of these superstitions were the result of pagan influence, the *darke ha-Emori*, "the ways of the Amorites," which were forbidden to the Jews. It is explicitly stated: "Ye shall not walk in the customs of the nations, which I am casting out before you; for they did all these things and therefore I abhorred them" (Lev. 20:23).

Many strange customs infiltrated into the observances and way of life of our people during the Middle Ages: if you leave a house do not return to live there before seven years have elapsed; do not put on two garments at once; Monday and Wednesday are unlucky days; do not begin on Monday and end on Wednesday. The reason offered for this notion is that *Gehinom* (Hell) was created on the second day, and the luminaries were penalized on the fourth day. Some of these beliefs still exist among some Jews.

The rabbis in the Talmud who were opposed to superstitious practices were nevertheless influenced by the spirit of the times, and that accounts for the numerous passages in the *aggadic* portion of the Talmud which contain the magical formulae common to all the peoples with whom they came into contact. The populace demanded quick cures for their troubles, and in view of the fact that they afforded temporary relief and bolstered their courage, sanction was given for their usage. However, the rabbis instituted a restraining prohibition, realizing that excessive indulgence in eccentric exercises could become an obsession, and result in drifting away from the moorings of Judaism. They forbade many of the superstitious practices on the basis that they constitute the "Ways of the Amorites." The Mishna in Sabbath 67a indicates the two points of views of the rabbis with reference to the heathen magic. "One may go out with the *Hargol's* egg, a fox's tooth, and the nail from

46

the gallows of an impaled convict, as a prophylactic. This is R. Meir's view; but the sages forbid this even on weekdays, on account of the ways of the Amorites." Man's helplessness when afflicted by the numerous diseases for which no remedy was known, led to quackery in ancient days, not unlike the deception and the frauds which are perpetrated on a gullible public today. The pernicious influence of Gnostic literature which captivated the minds of the rank and file by its fantastic promises, was reflected in the multiplication of the Apocalyptic works and prompted the proscription of the non-canonical books. The people were urged to rely solely on the Canon which the rabbis approved, and on the rabbinical literature. Not only were the people led astray from the Jewish way of life, away from the concept of pure monotheism, but were led to intemperate and unbridled orgies of conduct which undermined the very foundations of Judaism. The Mishna condemns the practice of "one who whispers (a charm) over a wound and says: 'I will bring none of these diseases upon thee which I brought upon the Egyptians, for I am the Lord that healeth thee' " (Sanhedrin 90a). The practitioners relied upon charms for cures, and not upon faith in the Lord, the Healer of all flesh. Those who were engaged in these unholy deeds had no portion in the world to come. They are classed with those who deny that the resurrection is not a biblical doctrine and that the Torah is not divinely revealed, and with an *apikoros*, a heretic, or one who is an adherent of the Epicurean philosophy, as well as with the three kings, Jeroboam, Ahab and Menasseh, and the commoners, Balaam, Doeg, Ahitophel and Gehazi (Sanhedrin 90a).

Gershom Scholem, in his magnum opus, *Major Trends in Jewish Mysticism,* has defended Kabbalism and indicated its influence on the course of Jewish history, and its profound imprint on Judaism. One is impressed with the fact that in expounding his theorem, Scholem seems to make mysticism and Kabbalism synonymous. But they are not synonymous all along the line. Of course, the Kabbalah is based on mysticism, as is every religious order from the most primitive to the great religious denominations of today. In truth, Scholem declares that "all religion is based on mysticism," because "religion is unthinkable without an immediate awareness of God." But a religious devotee can experience "an awareness of God" without going off into the *En Sof,* without the ascent into the *Ten Sefirot* with the galaxy of angels and demons, the myriad of magical formulae and techniques for controlling the course of human events. Without a recognition of the mystic experience, that ineffable feeling that exudes from the inner being and which is beyond logic and philosophic speculation, we cannot begin to understand the intuitive wisdom of a Moses, the inspiration of the prophets, and the creative genius of all the saints and seers among our own people, as well as among the peoples of the world. There is no way to account for their superlative gifts of mind and heart other than some mystical power that they were endowed with. The Kabbalists were men of profound religious emotion. They infused into the heart of religion an elixir which made it vibrate and pulsate with life. It cannot be gainsaid that Kabbalah, as Scholem has masterfully interpreted, was instrumental in steering Judaism into the straight channel, avoiding the reefs of speculative philosophy on the one side and the rocks of *pilpulistic* legalism on the other. Classical Judaism had to contend with these two rivals. The philosophers endeavored to solve the riddle of the universe with cold rationalization, resorting to the working of the mind, and not to the promptings of the heart. They sought to prove by logical deduction that pantheism and mythical theology were wrong. But logic is a two-edged sword. It cuts both ways. By relying on dialectics, it is possible to prove white, black and day, night. The danger that is involved in depending solely on ratiocination, reaching conclusions based on premises which are assumed to be correct, but which may be altogether wrong, was sensed by the author of the book of Proverbs, who declared: "Trust in the Lord with all thy heart, and lean not upon thine own understanding" (3:5).

48

It is well to put the emphasis upon the heart. The heart may know the answers which the intellect cannot comprehend.

Gershom Scholem underscores the fact that where philosophy ends, Kabbalism begins. By that he means that philosophy does not have all the answers. There must come a time when philosophy reaches a dead end, a cul-de-sac, and finds itself helpless in solving the perplexing problems which baffle the human mind. The Kabbalists have been characterized as standing on the shoulders of the philosophers and viewing the world from a wider horizon. While philosophy ignored the fears of mankind, the fears of life and the fears of death, and dismissed them as mere figments of the imagination, Kabbalism taught its votaries how to cope with these phobias and master them. It is reminiscent of the saying attributed to the late Franklin D. Roosevelt: "We have nothing to fear but fear itself." This saying may well be a Kabbalistic doctrine, expressed unintentionally.

Kabbalah succeeded, where philosophy failed, in the acquisition of spiritual authority, because it spoke in the language which the masses could understand. Philosophy had a tendency to alienate the intelligentsia from religion. Their intellectual appetites were satisfied, and religion found no place in the regimen of their thinking. On the other hand, while Kabbalah aimed to scale the heights of the most fantastic upreaching of the human mind, it was the response of the heart that pointed the way "to discover the hidden life beneath the external shapes of reality and to make visible that abyss in which the symbolic nature of all that exists reveals itself." The Torah became a living organism. Every verse, every letter of holy script was vested with mystic potency, by which acts of creation could be achieved.

To the intellectual and prosaic among us, Kabbalism is looked upon as an aberration of the mind, and unbecoming to the normal and rational *Homo sapiens*. Indeed, objective students of the Kabbalah admit that when we turn to the writings of the great Kabbalists we are torn between alter-

nate admiration and disgust. However, there is a great deal
to be admired in the teachings of the Kabbalah and in its
ability to perpetuate its uninterrupted existence during the
millenia of the exile. There is no reason for feeling disgust,
even at the exuberance of the emotions which the votaries
of the Kabbalah have displayed in their beliefs and practices. We need not subscribe to membership in the mystic
order, but it must be evident to the student of Jewish history, for whom history means more than the chronicle of
events, that there are trends, an ebb and a flow in the
currents of historic movements, that serve a purpose which
cannot be discerned on the surface, but which must be
studied under submergible conditions. While it is true that
many unbalanced students of Kabbalah were lost in the
obsessions which overpowered their mental processes, it
is equally true that there were many Jews, like Rabbi Phin-
eas of Koretz, who declared that the Zohar *"hot mich der-
halten bei Yiddishkeit,* The Zohar helped me maintain my
Jewishness."

Kabbalah served a purpose at a time when Israel required its stimulation and support to help it cope with ad-
verse circumstances which might have resulted in Israel's
utter annihilation without its support. When we contemplate the black pages of Israel's martyrology, we must stand
in awe when honoring the memory of our ancestors who
withstood the onslaught, and did not flinch or bow their
heads in ignominious defeat. In Henley's memorable words:

> *In the fell clutch of circumstance*
> *I have not whined nor cried aloud;*
> *Under the bludgeonings of chance*
> *My head is bloody, but unbowed.*
> *It matters not how strait the gate*
> *How charged with punishment the scroll,*
> *I am the master of my fate*
> *I am the captain of my soul.*

These words may not be expressed in Kabbalistic language, but the spirit is that of a Kabbalist who felt that

with the technique of the ineffable name at his command, he could shape his own destiny. In fact, the true saint was not worried about his destiny. There is a legend that Dov Ber of Meseritz had a vision in which he heard a voice from heaven saying that he had lost *Gan Eden* (Paradise). Dov Ber was happy, for now he could serve his Creator without the prospect of gaining reward. The Rabbi of Ladi declared: "It is not *Gan Eden* that I want, but I want You." The merging of self into a higher union was the transcendent form of perfection to which the Kabbalists aspired. "He who is full of himself has no room for God," is a cardinal Kabbalistic doctrine. The analysis of the ethical teachings of the *Zohar* reveals a lofty conception of God which must be taken into account when we evaluate the role which Kabbalism has played in the development of Judaism. The fear of God, the love of God, purity of thought, chastity, charity, study of the Torah, penitence and prayer are some of the doctrines which the followers of the mystic lore have scrupulously sanctified in their thoughts and actions.

Graetz declared that Kabbalism has brought great harm to Judaism, from which it could not be liberated until this day. He branded the *Zohar* as a "book of lies," and looked askance at the veneration in which it was regarded, by those who placed it on a par with the Talmud. He felt that a new Judaism had been created which was outside of the rabbinic Judaism of the Talmud. It is against that danger which we must be on guard. Any movement, whether on the extreme right or on the extreme left, which tends to militate against the rabbinic authorities of classical Judaism renders a disservice to Judaism, and leads to one form of fanaticism or another. We take full cognizance of the dominating influence which Kabbalism exerted upon its sincere devotees, the comfort which it afforded its believers, the full rich life with which it endowed its practitioners, as contrasted with the vacuity of the masses who were devoid of any religious feeling. However, we must likewise view with misgiving the excesses and perversions which it unleashed, and which brought confusion within our ranks, at times.

51

XII

THE SHABBATAI ZEVI MOVEMENT

The Kabbalah purported to reveal the mysteries of the universe, but the greatest mystery of all is the working of the human mind, which is yet a "dark Africa" of unexplored territory. The story of the pseudo-Messiah Shabbatai Zevi, constituted one of the most dramatic epics in the history of Judaism. This man has been described as a manic-depressive character, afflicted with mental derangement, torn between fits of deepest gloom, depression and melancholia and uncontrollable exuberance and joy, haunted by hallucinations that he was pursued by demons, that he was the Messiah and the King of the Jews, and divinely appointed as the Redeemer to overthrow the nations of the world and to restore Israel to Jerusalem. The Shabbatai Zevi movement spread like wild fire throughout Europe and Palestine, and attracted some of the greatest scholars, whom he hypnotized by his personality, by his acts of self-inflicted penance, his fasting, his praying at graves and the saintly mode of life which he displayed. He was exalted to the extent that prayers were inserted in the prayer book with a special blessing: "Bless our Lord and King, the holy and righteous Shabbatai Zevi, the Messiah of the God of Jacob." He was hailed as "the first begotten son of God, the Messiah and the Redeemer of Israel." The atmosphere was charged with the hysteria of overwrought desperation as a result of the expulsion from Spain and later of the massacre of the Jews in the Ukraine at the hands of the bloody tyrant, Chmielnicki, the year 1648, known in Jewish history as the *G'zeras Tach*, "the evil decree of 5408," the corresponding Hebrew date.

The similarities between Shabbatai Zevi and the founder of Christianity are striking. Shabbatai Zevi had his John the Baptist or Paul of Tarsus in the person of Nathan of Gaza, who regarded himself as the incarnation of Elijah, who, according to tradition, will appear as the forerunner of the Messiah when he will arrive "at the end of time," as predicted by the biblical prophets. It was Nathan the Gazzite who promoted Shabbatai Zevi and placed him upon his throne of glory. Nathan was a student of the *Zohar* and was deeply immersed in Kabbalistic lore. He followed the ritual of *tikkun*, which was the purification of the human soul in preparation for the Redemption.

There were many mystical references which were interpreted to apply to definite dates of the period in which Shabbatai Zevi lived. A passage was found in the *Zohar* which seemed to indicate that the Messiah would come in the year 1648; and the Kabbalists accepted this as the authentic date of deliverance. The sufferings of Chmielnicki were the birthpangs of the Messiah, the *chevle d'mashiach*. But, the Jews were not alone in their calculation of the *ketz*, the end of the *galut* and the beginning of the Messianic age. Christians also believed that according to the Book of Revelation, the year 1666 was the fateful year of Redemption, which would be marked by the second appearance of the Messiah. Menasseh ben Israel appealed to Cromwell to readmit the Jews to England on that basis. The Kabbalist, Abraham Yakini, claimed that he found a manuscript which contained a prediction that a son would be born to Mordecai Zevi, who would be called Shabbatai and that he would be the Redeemer of Israel.

It was in Smyrna that Shabbatai proclaimed himself as the Messiah. There was great rejoicing, and dancing in the streets to the sound of music. Shabbatai Zevi raised the spirits of the dejected Jews who were ready for the least ray of hope that might bring them out of the valley of despondency. But the Orthodox rabbis looked with misgiving upon the strange antics of the pretender. They recoiled from the acts of desecration which he performed. He dared to pronounce the ineffable name of God, the four-lettered symbol which only the High Priest uttered on the Day of Atonement, as described vividly in all its detail in the Yom Kippur *Machzor*. "And when the priest and the people that stood in the court heard the glorious and revered name pronounced out of the mouth of the High Priest, in holiness and in purity, they knelt and prostrated themselves and made acknowledgement, falling on their faces and saying: 'Blessed be His glorious Name forever and ever.' " Shabbatai Zevi aimed to stir the same emotion in the hearts of the populace. He succeeded, but he incurred the disdain of the rabbis who excommunicated him. Shabbatai left Smyrna and went to Salonika, but even there he was not welcomed; and he thereupon left for Constantinople. His great ambition was to make Jerusalem the center of his movement, but even there he met with opposition by the local rabbis. He traveled to Cairo and finally returned to his native city of Smyrna together with his wife, Sarah, an ambitious woman who had dreams of becoming the destined bride of the Messiah. The ban against him had been lifted in the meanwhile, and he was welcomed in the city with ecstatic celebrations.

The human mind cannot be relied upon to make decisions without some form of checks and balances. Many factors are involved in the process of reasoning, which sway our conclusions like a pendulum from one extreme to another. That is why every well organized group has a stabilizer, from a small club with its by-laws to a government with its Constitution and the United Nations with its Charter. Shabbataism, like other sectarian movements in Judaism, displayed an unchecked and unbalanced distortion of logic and common sense which led its followers into the swamps of unreason, to absurdities and fanaticism. We often wonder how seemingly sane people of great repute, scholars and leaders of communities, could become involved in such strange ideas and practices. But the story of Shabbatai Zevi is a classical illustration of the dangers which lurk in allowing the mind to run riot.

The proclamation of Shabbatai Zevi as the Messiah and

54

the King of the Jews was disturbing to the Turkish government, which feared the power which Shabbatai had attained
among his host of followers, as a result of the pamphlets
which Nathan of Gaza had sent all over the world. When
Shabbatai came to Constantinople he was imprisoned by
order of the grand vizier, Ahmed Koprili, and chained hand
and foot. But the mystics had a ready explanation of the
turn of events. His imprisonment was merely a link in the
chain of events which proved his claim to be the Messiah.
Shabbatai himself gave a new twist to his predicament. He
had come on the scene as the Messiah in order to purify
the people of their sins. But the sins were not entirely expiated, and the Messiah had to suffer on that account. The
prison was given a fanciful name. It was called *Migdal Oz,*
the "Tower of Strength." He was treated royally in prison.
He held court there and received leaders of his party from
all parts of the world. They came with their complaints of
the suffering of the Jews, particularly in Poland, as a result
of the holocaust unleashed by the tyrant, Chmielnicki. Shabbatai assured the delegates that the day of redemption was
near when God would take vengeance on the enemies of His
people.

The Sultan at Adrianopol was informed that Shabbatai
Zevi had high ambitions to arouse the Jews to rebellion,
and he was brought to the royal court. The Sultan was
alarmed by the powerful influence which the pseudo-Messiah
seemed to exert upon the thousands of devotees who worshipped him throughout the world, and he came to the conclusion that the death sentence was the only way to put an
end to the aspirations of the self-crowned King of the Jews.
However, through the intercession of the court physician,
a Jew who had converted to Islam, Shabbatai saved his life
by abjuring his Jewish faith. He changed his name to Meh-
med Effendi and became a devout Moslem, at least out-
wardly. How far he truly believed in the tenets of Islam
cannot be ascertained, because he still kept his contacts
with the Jewish people and attended services in the synagogue. When the Sultan was apprised of this faithlessness

he put him in exile in Dulcigno, where he died on Yom Kippur in 1676.

The strange phenomenon concerning the unshaking belief of the Shabbatians in the Messianic claims of their leader is a subject for psychiatrists to study and appraise. All of Shabbati's experiences, his imprisonment as well as his conversion to Islam, served only to heighten their fanatic belief that he was the true Messiah. Every fanciful explanation was given for the defection. His apostacy was a sacred mystery. It was the way to salvation. He was converted to Islam in order to bring the Moslems nearer to Judaism. The popular use of *gematriot*, the manipulation of numbers, was relied upon to prove that Messiah must suffer until the day of final redemption. *Moshiah* (Messiah), and *nachash* (serpent), have the same numerical value of 358, which proves that the Messiah will have to fight the dragons of darkness, which in time he will conquer. The Messiah may sink to the lowest abyss, and commit the gravest sins, but that does not mean that he has failed. It merely means that he is undergoing a process which is a step in the direction of the final deliverance. "He who sinks to the lowest is bound to see the light," was the watchword. A virtue was made of sin, which was vested with a degree of holiness. There is no sin, it was claimed. Sin is not to be condemned, but rather to be viewed in the nature of the seed which must rot in the ground in order to produce fruit and provide the sustenance for the welfare of man.

XIII

THE FRANKIST MOVEMENT

We now turn to the Frankist movement, one of the many sects in Judaism which completely disappeared after a stormy period of intrigue, deceit and duplicity. Jacob Leibovicz Frank was born about 1726 in Korolowka, on the Volhynian and Podolian border in the Ukraine. He organized a movement after the conversion and death of Shabbatai Zevi, and inherited from his predecessor the prestige and power of leadership which the latter had attained. The conversion of Shabbatai Zevi to Islam was a shock to his votaries. Frank capitalized upon this feeling of disillusionment and despair by filling the vacuum which had been created. The people were forlorn; it seemed that the very foundation upon which they stood had collapsed, and they looked yearningly for a redeemer, to whom they could entrust their burdensome hearts. The time was opportune for any crank or charlatan to play upon the emotions of the populace. There was no time to think and to weigh the preposterous claims that were being made by a score of imposters and mythomaniacs who came with quack cures for their sufferings and tribulations. The furor which was detonated by the Chmielnicki massacre threw the helpless people into a panic. They needed some form of tranquilization for their jaded and lacerated nerves, and protection from their plight. A drowning man will hang on to a straw in a vain effort to save his life. And Frank, who had the magic potion, was welcomed by the mass of gullible dupes with wide acclaim. He had all the answers to their problems. He took the load off their hearts. He brought them the only ray of hope. They had nothing to lose.

The Shabbatian and Frankist movements constitute chapters in Jewish history which we would like to forget, because they represent a pathological period in the chronicle of Jewish life. They undoubtedly left scars and wounds which have not yet been healed. Like a sickness which afflicts a person, a nation likewise must undergo experiences of distemper and disorder, either from internal invalidism or from external attack. That the intrinsic stability of the Jewish body politic enabled our people to overcome the shocks which they endured throughout the ages has been a miracle, and the miracle of Jewish survival has been the source of great wonderment for the nations of the world.

Frankism was an affliction from which, fortunately, Judaism recovered, but the experience is only of importance to indicate that we must be on guard at all times to prevent a similar outbreak and its calamitous consequences. The extreme to which Frank led his flock was revolting. His sessions were held in secrecy, and they were characterized by orgiastic excitement, which was induced by song and dance, calculated to rouse the rabble to a state of frenzy. They broke all bounds of decency. Not only did they flout the rabbinic laws, violate every law in the codes, and scoff at Jewish tradition, but they also indulged in erotic excesses, breaking all family ties. They boasted of being anti-Talmudists, and preferred to be called Zoharists, because the *Zohar* was their Bible. Finally, the rabbis became alarmed at the menace which the Frankists posed in polluting the communal life of the Jews, and a ban was proclaimed on January 18, 1756, after they were brought into the rabbinical courts, and charged with heresy, adultery and profanation of the faith.

But the Frankists were undaunted. They challenged the rabbis to a debate in the presence of the Catholic Bishops. Frank avowedly had become a Catholic convert. His conversion was marked by a great deal of pomp and ceremony. The Frankists won the first debate, because the rabbis were too cautious in refuting the argument that the teachings of the *Zohar* were in agreement with the doctrines of the trin-

58

ity and the Messiah. The Frankists also charged that the Talmud teaches that the Jews use Christian blood for Passover. They made use of the symbols of the *Haggada* to prove the accusation. Jewish homes were ransacked for copies of the Talmud which were burnt. But the Frankists went too far, and soon the Bishops saw the insincerity of Frank, who posed as a Mohammedan in Turkey to win the Moslems. He was again thrown into prison, but was released by the Russian General Bibikov in 1772. He gained favor in the court of Vienna where Maria Theresa regarded him as a disseminator of Christianity. From Vienna he went to Offenbach where he lived like a wealthy nobleman, and received pilgrims from all parts of the world. He finally died of apoplexy in 1791. His daughter Eve took over as the "Holy Mistress." After her death the entire movement dissolved.

XIV

HASIDISM

Hasidism at one time encompassed half of world Jewry, who followed its teachings and was governed by its regimen of daily living. The movement is still active in many circles. There are still *rebbeim,* or *zaddikim,* who command the loyalty and devotion of their votaries. However, Hasidism has dwindled and become somewhat discredited due to petty quarrels, family feuds, and the worldly ambitions of its leaders. An attempt is being made to revitalize the Hasidic movement with a neo-Hasidic perspective, notably in the work of Martin Buber, who has popularized the Hasidic tales, interpreted Hasidism to the modern world, and declared that there can be no redemption of humanity without the Hasidic elements. Even Ahad Ha-Am, the protagonist of cultural Zionism admits that in Hasidic literature, and not in the literature of the Haskalah, one occasionally encounters, in addition to much that is purely fanciful, true profundity of thoughts which bears the mark of original Jewish genius (Scholem, *Jewish Mysticism*, p. 326).

What is the nature of the mystic philosophy of life which has captivated the minds of millions of people, and has inspired novelists, dramatists, romanticists and artists? Even today the *Dibbuk*, the *Golem*, the Hasidic legends, dances and songs, and the quaint costumes have a fascination even for Misnagdim (opponents of Hasidism) and Maskilim (enlightened Jews) who ridiculed the Hasidim for their opposition to every form of European culture. Not only Jews, but prominent non-Jews, have been influenced by the esoteric doctrines of Hasidism. In the wreckage of the plane in which Dag Hammarskjold died, there were two copies of a book by Martin Buber, one in the original German, called *Ich Und Du,* and its English translation, *I and Thou.* There were also twelve typewritten pages, the beginning of Dag Hammarskjold's translation into Swedish.

The former Secretary General of the United Nations shared Buber's philosophy of life. He was inspired by the lives of the medieval mystics, and deeply impressed with the idealism which they exemplified. "Love for them was a surplus of power that they felt completely filled them when they began to live in self-forgetfulness."

Hasidism had its paternity in a deep religious impulse. It stemmed from a period in Jewish history which was surcharged with high emotional tensions that clamored for articulation. The background of Hasidism was prepared by the Lurianic Kabbalism of the Safed School and the defunct Shabbatian travesty. Hasidism is the third stage of the same process, but the course it followed and the goals it reached were entirely different. Israel Baal Shem, the "Master of the Name," or the "Besht," as he was popularly known, found the fertile ground had been thoroughly plowed, richly seeded and in full bloom, ready for him to reap a rich harvest in disseminating the doctrines which he espoused. He succeeded in mobilizing a strong following, and he became the master spirit of a movement which brought healing to bleeding hearts and gave new zest and meaning to living. Hasidism would have been doomed to the same fate as Shabbataism and Frankism, but its essential difference in cosmic outlook saved the movement from degeneration.

The reason for the continued vitality of Hasidism must be found in the additional factors which were embodied in the system and which were absent from the other esoteric perversions. While Kabbalah, particularly the *Zohar*, formed the basis of the Hasidic theology, and mysticism gave it its rationale and its status, the strength of the movement can be explained in terms of mass appeal. In the beginning, before the institution of the *zaddik*, who was vested with unlimited powers, and was the source of all blessing and the fountain of grace, the individual Jew was given status. By exercising the three virtues of *shiflut*, "humility," *simcha*, "joy" and *hislahavut*, "enthusiasm," anyone could rise to the highest realms and attain redemption. The Kabbalah was restricted to the "illuminates," to the chosen few who felt vested with supernatural powers, and to whom the secret formulae were revealed by dreams, by visions, by visitation of celestial beings, the angels and the demons. Not everyone could aspire to be a Kabbalist or magical practitioner. By the same token, not every commoner could hope to be a scholar and master the talmudic lore. This inferiority complex was nullified by the example of the Baal Shem, who taught that man lives in a wonderful world, that God is everywhere, in the woods, the trees, the flowers and the birds. Call nothing common or profane; for God's presence is in all things and all things are holy, was a cardinal Hasidic dogma.

The Gaon Elijah of Vilna was vehement in his denunciation of the Hasidim. He issued the decree of excommunication, and opposed any association with the "Godless sect" as he stigmatized them. He accused them of pantheistic leanings. He went to the extent of forbidding marriage with Hasidic families. His opposition was prompted by the fear that Hasidism would lead to the same direful consequences as the Shabbatai Zevi and Frankist movements, and the Hasidim were accused of having intimate connections with these sects that proved so disastrous to Judaism. The Orthodox rabbis looked askance at the *zaddik*, whom the Hasidim venerated and had vested with supernatural powers. The rabbis regarded the *zaddik* as a sort of reincarnation of the priestly order of ancient days, like the Sadducees. The role of the *zaddik* was different from that of the rabbi, or spiritual guide of the community. The rabbi was honored and revered for his great scholarship, and the wisdom which he manifested was the result of his supreme mental acumen. Not so the *zaddik*. His strength lay in his mystical powers which had nothing to do with wisdom. The mere touch of his hand had necromantic potency. The writing of a *kamea,* an amulet, containing the magic words from Holy Script, was sufficient to perform miracles, to cure diseases, to fight enemies and fulfill every fantastic wish. A strong antagonism arose between the rabbis and the *zaddikim,* and attacks and counter-attacks followed in rapid succession. Hasidism attacked rabbinism and the rabbis went even further; they indulged in cruel persecutions, arresting the leaders of the sect and excommunicating the followers. The Mitnagdim (opponents) and the Hasidim formed two sects in Judaism that were at loggerheads; and only in recent days has the bitterness subsided, although a feeling of estrangement still remains, due to the variations in ritual and customs.

The enthronement of the *zaddik* was criticized by the rabbis as a form of man-worship which struck at the very foundation of Judaism. The rabbis saw in this exaltation of a human being an atavism from ancient days, and feared the return to the abuses which were perpetrated by the high priests in the time of the Hasmoneans. The *zaddik* became the embodiment of the Torah. He was regarded by the Hasidim as the true child of God. He was the connecting link between God and man, a sort of liaison officer who had direct communications with the deity, and through whom only the deity could be reached. The idea of an intermediary between God and man was foreign to Jewish religious thinking. In Judaism there is no agency. God can be reached directly: "God is near to all who call upon Him, to all who call upon Him in truth" (Psalms 145:18). Personality takes the place of doctrine in Hasidism, and personality was never idolized in any period in Jewish history. A human being, regardless how great he may be, was not infallible. "For there is no man, a *zaddik* on earth, who doeth good and sinneth not" (Ecc. 7:20). Even Moses, the greatest personality in Judaism, was buried in an unknown grave in order to avoid his deification.

The basic teachings of Hasidism hold a fascination for its adherents which, to an extent, must command our admiration. There are excesses and fanatics in every dispensation, from the most reactionary to the most radical. The so-called liberals are often more prejudiced and obsessed with their views than the sects which they attack. Hasidism was a protest against excessive intellectualism at the expense of the emotions. The Hasidim set out on an adventure in search of God, and when man met God and God met man, there was a spiritual ecstasy in the communion which elevated the soul to higher spheres, and enabled the devotee to endure his trials with courage. The Hasid literally followed the admonition: "Serve the Lord with gladness, come before His presence with singing" (Ps. 100:22). In a way, we may say that Hasidism aimed to merge the natural and the supernatural Jew. Nothing in the natural world must be despised. Eating and drinking become *mitzvot*. The flesh must not be penalized with self-emolation.

The branch of the Hasidim which succeeded in avoiding the Cylla of intemperate mysticism and the Carybdis of the miracle worker was the *Habad*, founded by Shneur Zalman of Ladi. He combined Talmudic learning with the mystic doctrines of Hasidism. Dedicated to *hochma*, "wisdom," *binah*, "understanding" and *da'at*, "knowledge," the initial letters forming the name *Habad,* the movement has succeeded in establishing a chain of *yeshivot* throughout the world, and building up a strong organization.

XV

THE HASKALAH MOVEMENT

The Haskalah movement represents another tributary from the stream of classical Judaism, which led many followers into the wasteland of conversion and assimilation. We are not unmindful of the voluminous output of literary endeavor which resulted from the spirit of "enlightenment," stimulated by the study of the classics in many foreign languages, German, Russian, Polish, French, and the revival of Hebrew. Haskalah was responsible for the moment of Jewish nationalism and the birth of political Zionism. But, the cost was colossal and disillusionment came only after we lost a generation of Jews who had drifted away from the moorings of their ancestors. Haskalah left scars and wounds that have not healed until this day.

The Maskilim were blinded by the promise of the millenium of "liberty, equality and fraternity." The Edict of Toleration which was issued by King Joseph II of Austria in 1782 proved to be a trap into which the Jews living at that time fell without realizing that the cure which was offered was worse than the disease. The disabilities which the Jews were suffering were unbearable. The pogroms and the blood libels which have darkened the pages of medieval Jewish history embittered the lives of our people and any promise of relief was welcome. The reason for the persecution of the Jews was misunderstood. It was believed that the hatred was due to the fact that the Jews were different. It was the old cry of Haman to King Ahasuerus: "There is a certain people scattered abroad and dispersed among the peoples in all the provinces of thy kingdom; and their laws are diverse from those of every people; neither keep they the king's laws; therefore it profiteth not the king to suffer them" (Esther 3:8). The Jews believed that by becoming like the nations of the world they would gain esteem, and anti-Semitism would vanish. "Be learned, lest the nations deny us the respect and especially the equality which we covet." This was the cry of the German Maskilim. Therefore, the *hedarim* were abandoned, and new schools were established, with the curriculum destitute of Hebrew and Jewish cultural subjects.

The younger generation was hungry for the new culture which they suddenly discovered, and the process of Germanization moved ahead at an accelerated pace. German *Kultur* was idolized, and the young people turned to Kant and Hegel, Schiller and Goethe, for their inspiration rather than to the prophets of the Bible, and the wisdom of the Talmudic sages. In many respects the movement was similar to the Hellenization craze at the time of the Hasmoneans about 2000 years before. The translation of the Pentateuch into German and the publication of the *Biur* by Moses Mendelsohn gave an added stimulus to the Haskalah movement. It had an effect contrary to that which was anticipated. Instead of bringing the beauties of Shem into the tents of Japheth, instead of inspiring the non-Jews with the exalted teachings of the Scriptures, it opened up a new reservoir of "living waters" to the young Jewish students. Jewish customs were attacked. Books were written to demonstrate that even according to the Talmud, prohibited foods were kosher. By the use of casuistry and the distortion of logic, 150 arguments were presented to prove that a "reptile is clean according to the Bible." The abolition of ritual observances and even prayer was advocated. There was a general feeling that all the old encumbrances of Judaism interfered with the new awakening of the era of brotherhood which would integrate all mankind and abolish forever all prejudices and hatreds. That morality could be inculcated without religion, was a dominant theme in those days. Some of the more daring went even further. They preached actual conversion to a liberal form of Christianity. Mendelsohn's children became Christians, as did many of the sons of the Maskilim.

Assimilation became the order of the day. Lured by the slogan which was avowed in the words of Gordon: "Be a Jew at home and a man in the street," an inferiority complex was developed with respect to one's Jewishness. *"Ma yomru ha-goyim?* What will the nations say?" was a source of great worry to the assimilationists, as it was to the Hellenists in ancient days. By obliterating one's Jewishness, the nations will learn to love you more, it was felt. It was a terrible mistake; the worst pogroms were unleashed in the cities where the Jews were like their neighbors in every respect. The most diabolic massacre in history took place in Germany where the process of assimilation was most complete.

The Hasidim and Mitnagdim, although they were opposed to each other, nevertheless joined hands and closed ranks against the Maskilim, whom they regarded as a common enemy. Both were menaced by its disintegrating tendencies which would have resulted in the complete liquidation of Judaism as a religion. Some rabbinic leaders endeavored to combat Haskalah by going to the other extreme. We are told that when Rabbi Israel Salanter was informed that his son had gone to Berlin to study medicine, he removed his shoes and sat on the ground to observe *shivah,* (the seven days of mourning). The famous Mark Antokolsky, who was noted for his wood carvings, was beaten in his childhood by his father because he ran away from *heder* to carve figures, which was a violation of the second commandment.

However, there were other eminent figures whose mental equilibrium kept them on an even keel and who followed the *derech ha-memutza,* "the middle course." The rabbis have admonished us against going to extremes, according to a Talmudic dictum: "The Torah consists of two paths, one of fire and the other of snow. If you turn to one extreme you will perish in the fire, and if you turn to the other extreme you will die in the snow. What shall man do? Walk in the middle" (Y. Hag. II,77a). Mention can be made only of a few who endeavored to reconcile the Hasidim and the Mitnagdim and also make a place for the favorable features of the Maskilim. Menashe Ilyer (1767-1831) was known as a *talmid vosik*, one of the most erudite disciples of the Gaon of Vilna. He was a great Talmudist, and yet an admirer of the founder of *Habad* Hasidism, Shneur Zalman of Ladi. But, he was a lover of the truth, and he did not hesitate to criticize Rashi and the Shulchan Aruch, if he had evidence that the facts did not harmonize with the opinions embodied in their writings. He applied himself to the study of secular subjects, and realizing that the sages of old and the sages of every generation were well versed in the scientific knowledge of their day, which is important for a true understanding of Jewish laws and rituals, he likewise aimed to perfect himself in natural philosophy and in the languages of the people among whom he lived.

The great leader who stemmed the tide of Haskalah and checked the flood of assimilation and reform which threatened to engulf our people was Perez ben Moshe Smolenskin (1842-1885). He was a man of firm resolution who did not hesitate to articulate his convictions in no uncertain terms. He published *Ha-Shachar* (The Dawn) which was dedicated to the totality of Jewish learning, unrestricted by the fanatics on both sides of the fence, the extreme Orthodox and the opinionated Maskilim. He hailed the disillusionment of the latter in the following words: "Now that they, who have hitherto walked in darkness, are beginning to discern the error of their ways, lo and behold, those who have seen the light are closing their eyes against it. . . . Therefore, let them know beforehand that, as I have stretched out my hand against those who under the cloak of holiness, endeavor to exclude enlightenment from the house of Jacob, even so will I lift up my hand against the hypocrites, who under the pretext of tolerance, strive to alienate the children of Israel from the heritage of their fathers." He was the pioneer, by a decade, of the Zionist movement, before Pinsker wrote his *Auto-Emancipation* and Herzl began thinking of the *Judenstadt*. Jacob Raisin described the role which Smolenskin played in the resurrection of the national hope: "He was the first to remove the shroud."

Smolenskin saw that the only hope of salvation for the Jewish people was a renationalization. The Jew was the pariah of the nations because he had no address. He was therefore looked upon as a fugitive and a vagabond. The church viewed the exile of the Jew as a punishment for his refusal to accept the Nazarene as the Messiah. There was only one way to prove to the Christian world that the theological doctrine of the curse was false, and that was, to regain *Eretz Yisrael* as the Jewish homeland. The Jewish people must become like the nations of the world, but not in terms of imitating the *goyim*, which was advocated by the assimilationists. Smolenskin expressed it: "Yes, be like the other peoples, proud of your literature, jealous of your self-respect, hopeful, even as all persecuted peoples are hopeful, of a speedy arrival of the day when we too shall inhabit the land which once was, and still is, our own." He looked askance at the Russian Jew, the Polish Jew, without any hyphen. Perhaps, this is a lesson to those who speak in terms of the American Jew. In all our love for America and Americanism, with its roots in the Old Testament, we still must regard Judaism as universal, and not dominated by or patterned after any particular foreign ideology.

XVI

THE ZIONIST MOVEMENT

In our study of the divisive groupings among our people in modern times, we come now to the Zionist movement. Before the establishment of the State of Israel, there was a wide cleavage between the Zionists who labored in behalf of a Jewish national homeland and the non-Zionists and anti-Zionists who were opposed to the racial and national categorization of Israel. The rebirth of the new state has served to cement the bonds of unity among our people, as never before in the two thousand year history of the *Galut*. With the exception of the two extremes, the American Council for Judaism which is still an outspoken enemy of Zionism, and the Neture Karta in Israel, the extreme Orthodox wing that opposes the Jewish state, the bulk of the Jewish people in the United States and throughout the world support Israel either by active affiliation with the Zionist Organization, or by contributing to the United Jewish Appeal, buying Israel Bonds, investing in Israeli enterprises, tourism, and by cooperating in other projects dedicated to the enrichment of the Jewish State. We hear less today of the debatable question of yesteryear whether the Jewish people is a nation or a religious group. The United Nations gave the definitive answer on November 29, 1947, when the resolution was adopted by the General Assembly, voting 33 to 13, approving the plan for the creation of Jewish and Arab states in Palestine.

Fears were formerly expressed that the political factor in Zionism "is bound to work mischief not only for the Jews in Palestine, but for those who are living and will continue to live in other countries," and the bug-a-boo of dual loyalty aimed to scare away timid souls from the movement of self-emancipation. Of course, the battle with the Arab states has not yet been won, and the evil machinations of Soviet Russia against its Jewish citizens and against the state of Israel are a serious worry. Nevertheless, the majority of the nations of the world recognize Israel as a sovereign state which is on earth to stay. Time alone will determine the fate of Israel, which is tied up with the fate of all humanity. If the international climate is settled, and instead of frigid temperature, storms and tempests raging in one part of the world or the other, we will have fair weather, and the sun of universal peace will shine forth, Israel will also enjoy the blessings of that messianic day, and sing with the Psalmist: "This is the day that the Lord hath appointed, we shall rejoice and be glad thereon."

But the internal struggle within Judaism will have to subside first. And there are many controversial questions which have caused considerable disturbance and heated debate. We cannot curb or eliminate differences of opinion, which have always existed in human relationships, but there are some clashes which serve no purpose except to create cleavage and a dissipation of energy. The very Zionist movement in the Diaspora is on trial for its life. There are some who are ready to pronounce the *Kaddish Rabbonon* over its final demise. The *shelilat hagalut,* the liquidation of the Galut, has been adopted, it seems, as a platform upon which to build a stable Jewish State, in the firm conviction that Judaism in the Galut is bound to disappear, and the sooner the Jews abandon the land of their present sojourn the stronger will Israel become. Ben-Gurion has expressed this fantastic notion with great emphasis, exciting the ire of Zionists throughout the world. He would have all Jews pack bag and baggage and settle in Israel. A Zionist is one who lives in Israel. All others who profess to be Zionists are pseudo-Zionists, he maintains.

This damaging concept of Zionism has exerted a deleterious influence in two directions. It has weakened the

Zionism movement in the Diaspora, alienated many ardent workers from taking no more than a philanthropic interest in Israel, on the one hand, and instilling a feeling of estrangement in the hearts of the "Sabras" and those who become integrated into the Israeli way of life on the other. They regard themselves as Israelis and not as Jews. They have set up an iron curtain between themselves and the Jews living *hutz l'aretz,* outside of Israel. This stratification in the ranks of Israel runs counter to the dream of every Zionist in the Galut who has worked indefatigably for the realization of the dream of Zion rebuilt. For one of the chief objectives of the Zionist movement was to unify all Jews and create in them a "consciousness of kind" which was impossible while the Jews were scattered throughout the world. Zion was to be the *briach hatichon,* "the middle bar in the midst of the boards, which shall pass through from end to end" (Exodus 26:28). The middle bar served as the coupling devise to join the boards of the tabernacle which was built in the wilderness according to the instructions in the Bible. This was to be the role of the Zionist organization, vis-à-vis the Jews in the Diaspora and the Jews in the land of Israel. There should be no argumentation in Zionist circles with regard to the fundamental doctrine of the integrity and the solidarity of the Jewish people wherever they may live. The bridge between the two camps of Israel and the Diaspora must bring world Jewry in closer contact, like the boards of the Tabernacles in the wilderness. We are one people, as Herzl expressed it: *"Wir sind ein folk, Ein Folk.* We are a people, One People." We cannot afford to shut out of consciousness the fundamental principle of the Oneness of the Jewish people, regardless of where they live, in any part of the world. We must clear away the black smoke which is caused by the bitter recriminations bursting forth from time to time. It is only in the light of this dynamic that the Zionist movement can find its *raison d'etre* which is challenged today in many quarters—not only by the American Council for Judaism but also by government officials in Israel and by leaders of the Zionist movement

71

in the Diaspora. We should ignore the American Council and not engage in any debate with them, but conserve our our energy for the constructive program to which the Zionist organization should dedicate itself. Declarations like those that have been repeatedly uttered by Premier Ben-Gurion on the one hand and Dr. Joachim Prinz, president of the American Jewish Congress on the other, must not be repeated. Ben-Gurion quoted the dictum on Ketubot, 100b, that "whoever lives outside of the Land (of Israel) may be regarded as one who has no God." The statement was unfortunate for many reasons. In the first place, there is an exception made in folio 111a with reference to Babylon. "R. Judah said: 'Whoever lives in Babylon is accounted as though he lived in the land of Israel; for it is said in Scripture: Ho, Zion, escape, thou dwellest with the daughter of Babylon'" (Zech. 2:11).

The first quotation from the Talmud could not have been meant to be taken literally. That would condemn as idolators all the saints, seers and scholars who have lived throughout the Galut in almost every part of the civilized world. It is evident that the intention of the rabbis was to stimulate living in Israel as the most effective means of fostering godliness in thought and deed. Belief in God, therefore, is the *summum bonum*. The state is the most effective means of achieving that end, but the state is not an end in itself. Judaism is bigger than the state. The communist concept that the interests of the individual are subordinate to the state and that the state has the power to deprive the individual of his rights, is contrary to the fundamental teachings of our sages, who declare: "We do not impose a hardship on the community which the majority cannot endure" (Baba Bathra, 60b). One of the chief reasons for the continued existence of the Jewish people even after the commonwealth was abolished (and we have been stateless for about two thousand years), is that we have not made the state the *sine qua non* of Jewish existence and survival. In this respect we are unique among the nations of the world. The universality of Judaism has been stressed in

72

Scripture and in the sayings of the sages. "In every place where I cause My Name to be mentioned I will come unto thee and bless thee" (Ex. 20:21). That means that God can be found everywhere in the universe, not only in Israel, but in every country on the face of the globe. The concept is made more explicit by the dictum, "The whole earth is full of His glory" (Is. 6:3).

The prophet Jeremiah, who witnessed the destruction of the Temple and the exile of the people to Babylon, sensed the feelings of frustration and despair which the people experienced at the calamity which had befallen them. The end of the state meant to them the end of the Jewish people, even as they bemoaned their fate to the prophet Ezekiel: "Our bones are dried up, and our hope is lost: we are clean cut off" (Ez. 37:11). Ezekiel prophesied the eventual rebirth of Israel and the resurrection of the dry bones, but Jeremiah gave them wise council in the interim: "Thus saith the Lord of hosts, the God of Israel, unto all the captivity, whom I have caused to be carried away captive from Jerusalem unto Babylon. Build ye houses, and dwell in them, and plant gardens, and eat the fruit thereof . . . and multiply ye there and be not diminished. And seek the peace of the city whither I have caused you to be carried away captive, and pray unto the Lord for it; for in the peace thereof shall ye have peace" (Jeremiah 29:4-7).

Zionism is like the scaffold of a building which is dismantled and discarded as soon as the building is completed, it has been argued. Similarly, now that the state has been established, we do not need Zionism anymore, according to the view of Ben-Gurion. The simile is completely irrelevant. Zionism has never been the scaffold for the building of the Jewish state. Zionism is the foundation upon which the Jewish state has been erected. Take away Zionism, and the state is bound to collapse. And Israel needs Zionism as much as Diaspora. It is a mistake to feel that Zionism is only applicable in the Galut. The reason why the lot of Zionism has fallen in "unlovely places" (to paraphrase the expression in Psalms 16:6), is that it has been equated only with political ends. The Basel Program which was adopted at the First Zionist Congress in 1897, convened by Theodor Herzl, stated: "The aim of Zionism is to create for the Jewish people a home in Palestine secured by public law." The term Zionism was coined by Nathan Birnbaum in 1893 and put the *trop*, the accent, upon Jewish nationalism, divorcing the movement, in the eyes of many of its leaders, from the religious traditions which the Jews have kept inviolate throughout the ages. That was a big mistake. And that is why Zionism has lost its glamor for the thousands of adherents who worked so indefatigably for an implementation of the Basel Program and the Balfour Declaration which likewise speaks in political terms: "His Majesty's government view with favor the establishment in Palestine of a national home for the Jewish people." But what has been entirely forgotten is that Zionism, first of all, did not begin with Theodor Herzl. Its roots are deeply imbedded in the soil of ancient Jewish history. The prophets dreamed of Zion rebuilt.

"For out of Zion shall go forth the law and the word of God from Jerusalem." How often is this verse quoted with pride and dignity, but like a cliche, it is given lip service and its real intent is entirely ignored. It is true that modern political Zionism speaks in terms of the need of a Jewish homeland for an oppressed people, and was sparked by the humiliations, the massacres, the pogroms, the blood libels, which our people have suffered. But it must also be remembered that during the Middle Ages, the ideal of Zionism was inspired by the yearning for the coming of the Messianic age, the age which will mark the end of Israel's wandering, the realization of the final redemption, and the establishment of universal peace for all the nations of the world. That was the dream of the prophets of Israel, as expressed in the oft-repeated words of Isaiah: "It shall come to pass in the end of days that the mountain of the Lord's house shall be established as the top of the mountains, and shall be exalted above the hills, and all the nations shall flow unto it" (Isaiah 2:2), "and they shall beat their swords into ploughshares" (2:4).

The Torah is the *vis vitae* of the Zionist movement; this is its keystone, this is its motivation and this is its ultimate goal. What has been said of the Sabbath can be paraphrased with the words: "More than Israel has kept Zionism, Zionism has kept Israel." The secret of Israel's survival throughout the centuries can be found in the hope that eventually the Holy Land will be returned to the Holy People in order to disseminate the teachings of the Holy Torah among the nations. In the light of this charge which has been imposed upon the Jewish people by divine decree: "I will give thee for a light of the nations, that My salvation may be unto the end of the earth" (Isaiah 49:6), there can be no talk of liquidating Zionism. The work of Zionism has now really begun. It is only the first stage that has been accomplished by the rebirth of Israel. But the purpose for which the State has been recreated is still remote from implementation. Even if all the enemies of Israel that are hounding its borders and threatening to destroy it, were vanquished, and peace were established in the Middle East, it would still be incumbent upon the Jews everywhere, not only in Israel, to serve as a priestly people, to exemplify the ideals of the Torah by precept and practice, and hasten the coming of the millenium. The Holy Land has waited during the centuries of the exile for the landless people to come back to the peopleless land. No other people on earth could have rebuilt the Promised Land with the same spirit of devotion and sacrifice as the people of Israel. This is one of the greatest miracles of our time. But we cannot allow our exuberant emotions to run riot and forget that the greatest gift which the Lord has bestowed upon His people must be regarded as a sacred trust which the Chosen People must assume in an effort to reach the goals which have been outlined in the Torah. And this is a task which devolves upon Jews everywhere. It is only through cooperative effort, by Jews in Israel and Jews in the Diaspora, that success will be achieved.

75

One of the strangest paradoxes in Jewish life today, which is hard to comprehend, is the downgrading of Zionism in the eyes of the sabras and the confusion which is working havoc in the Zionist Organization in America and in the World Zionist Organization. Today we need unity in the Jewish ranks. There should be no question as to the role which Zionism should play in the strengthening of Judaism and the Jews in these perilous times. There is no more potent Jewish organization in the world than Zionism, which is capable of showing the way toward Jewish unity and Jewish creativity. Zionism has shown its strength by the realization of the dream of Zion rebuilt, which perhaps the most sanguine prophet of our people could not presage. It is true that Herzl, as a visionary, saw the establishment of the Jewish state in fifty years. But no one really believed that we would live to see its achievement in our day. However, whatever explanation we may offer for the miracle that took place in 1947 at the United Nations, if there were no Zionist organization ready to function when the new state was born, and if there had not been a background of two thousand years of suffering and praying and yearning for the redemption, there would have been no follow-through. We would have been called—and found wanting.

The organization that was able to galvanize world public opinion and at the same time mobilize the forces of world Jewry toward a recognition of Israel's claim on the Promised Land, and toward freeing the Jewish people from Galut, must take the leadership in freeing the *Shechina* also from Galut. We read in Tractate Megilla 29a: R. Simon b. Yohai said: "Come and see how beloved are Israel in the sight of God, in that to every place to which they were exiled the *Shechina* went with them." What more exalted task can Zionism assume than "to restore the Crown to its former condition" (Yoma 69b). Zionism must do for the Jewish soul that which it has done for the Jewish body politic. The physical emancipation of our people must be followed by the liberation of the Jewish spirit which is still in Galut. Just as the deliverance of the Israelites from Egyptian

76

bondage was only a prelude to the revelation on Mt. Sinai, when spiritual freedom was achieved, likewise the victory over the Egyptian and Arab hordes in the War of Independence did not mark the culmination of Israel's upreaching and upsurging, not only because the last battle has not yet been fought, but because the final goal is far short of attainment.

We have thus far outlined the task of post-Israel Zionism in general terms. What specifically are the duties which devolve upon the Zionist Organization of America and the World Zionist Organization? First: The air must be cleared of all the misunderstandings which have arisen within the ranks of the Zionists themselves. All talk of reconstruction must cease; the formation of a new organization might prove suicidal. There is nothing in the present set-up that a good dose of honest exertion cannot cure. If the same technique and the same fervor and enthusiasm would be dedicated to the work that is urgently needed in every community in the United States as well as throughout the world—both in countries where the Jewish people enjoy constitutional rights and in countries where the rights are denied—the Zionist movement would be rendering vital service and would find its rightful place in Jewish life.

Secondly, the Zionist Organization should outline a definite program of activities to be sponsored by the local districts, which would reactivate and revitalize them. There is no reason why the community Zionist lodge cannot be made as popular as the chapters of the many national organizations and the fraternal lodges that function successfully and seem to command the support of the membership. Certainly, the Zionist movement has a dynamic which appeals to the people. Zionists should keep abreast of all that is happening in the Middle East. We still must mobilize public opinion in order to secure American support for the protection of the state which is surrounded by enemies on all sides. In order to determine what steps should be recommended, every Zionist should be informed in detail, as much as possible, of the dangers facing Israel, as well as the dangers threatening our people in Russia and in other parts of the world. While other national organizations are likewise concerned with the plight of our people on the domestic and global level, there is no organization that is better qualified for effective service and can contribute to the amelioration of the many problems that confront Jewry than the Zionist organization.

Thirdly, since Zionism has succeeded in establishing an address for world Jewry, and has removed the stigma of the vagabond people, it is time to give world Judaism an address, which will perform the same miracle for the Jewish soul which it did for the Jewish body politic. In other words, Zionism has taken the Jew out of Galut, by giving every Jew an opportunity, if he so desires, to live in Israel instead of the Diaspora. Now Zionism should go a step further and take the Galut out of the Jew. It is evident that throughout the ages, the Jew has been encrusted with many foreignisms which have clung to him. He has been influenced by his environment in every country in which he has sojourned. It is amazing that the hard core of the Jew has not been affected. But the fragmentation and the divergencies which have recently become pronounced in Jewish life in the *Galut,* and which also are being projected into Israel, have worked havoc with our people, and a unification of forces must be formulated in order to bring about stability within our ranks.

There is no other body which can be instrumental in effecting that consolidation than Zionism. Without attempting to take sides in the issues which confront our people today, considering the diverse movements of Orthodoxy, Conservatism, Reform, Reconstructionism and the shades of opinion within the ranks of the denominations themselves, Zionism can bring them together and seek to find, first a common denominator, a common platform, upon which they can all stand, and then eventually work out a code of practice and a philosophy of Judaism which all will endorse and follow in its essentials. This may seem utopian and unattainable, because the vested interests have become so entrenched and so ingrained, that they may be impervious to any attempt to merge forces. However, any observer must admit that there are many controversial issues which have set up iron curtains between one sect and the other which are inconsequential and expendable. For the sake of Jewish unity, it becomes necessary to give up so-called "sovereign rights" to be free, even as a citizen must, at times, curb his own idiosyncrasies and comply with the law of the land.

This brings us to the crux of one of the main issues facing world Jewry today: that is, the establishment of a Sanhedrin, or Supreme Court, which will give world Judaism the address we mentioned before. There is a great deal of opposition to the implementation of such a project, both on the part of the Orthodox rabbinate in the Diaspora, as well as the leaders of the other denominations in Judaism. The idea was favored by the late Chief Rabbi of Israel, Isaac Herzog, who had to give up the venture because of pressure. But, eventually, an authority in Jewish law will have to be established which will bring order out of the confusion which exists at the present time, due not only to the diversity which has segmented Jewish life, but also because of the many new discoveries and inventions which have revolutionized modern living, posing new problems which were unknown to our ancestors. Of course, Zionism cannot and must not be involved in matters of *halacha* which is the exclusive province of the rabbinate. But Zionism can help create the climate which will bring the hearts of our people closer together not only in the fields of philanthropy and defense against anti-Semitism but also in religious and cultural projects. Dedication to the ideal of Jewish unity should be Zionism's chief goal, and we can think of no other organization that can cross the lines which separate Jew from Jew in ideology and status, and appeal to them to close ranks.

Fourthly, Zionism in Israel and in the Diaspora must help bring about a synthesis of Jewish nationalism and the Jewish religion. The questions: "What is a Jew?" and

"What is Judaism?" have not yet been clearly answered, and while some attempts have been made to clear the atmosphere, as in the case of the convert, "Brother Daniel," who sought recognition as a Jew despite his conversion, there are many issues still unresolved. Further study should be made of the problem to determine the line of demarcation between Jewish nationalism and religion, where they separate and where they approach one another, the extent and the nature of the relationship between the Jew in the Diaspora and the Jew in Israel, the theocratic character of the Jewish state, and the demand for the separation of religion and the state.

In an article published on August 7, 1945, entitled, "Judaism and Zionism," Bernard A. Rosenblatt made the following declaration: "The restoration of Zion is a solemn obligation enjoined upon us by our ancestors and voiced in every page of the Hebrew Prayer Book, so that it constitutes a religious principle; a spiritual force that is comparable only to the allegiance of the Roman Catholics to the Vatican State and Papal supremacy." These words were written before the Jewish State was established, when very little thought was devoted to the fundamental concept of the state of which the prophets of old dreamed and for which the people of Israel have been praying and yearning throughout the ages. The comparison made by Rosenblatt between the Jews and the Catholics, the State of Israel and the Vatican, must be further explored today in the face of the confusion which prevails in the ranks of the Zionists, the stagnation and paralysis afflicting the movement, which was so vibrant and pulsating with emotional ecstasy prior to Israel's Proclamation of Independence. Perhaps we can find a new dynamic which will revitalize the seeming dry bones of the Zionist movement by invoking the spirit of Ezekiel who performed the miracle in his day. We read in Chapter 37, "The bones came together, bone to its bone; there were sinews upon them; and flesh came up, and skin covered them above, but there was no breath in them. Thus saith the Lord, God: Come from the four winds, O breath, and breathe upon these slain, that they may live."

The resurrection of Israel is a re-enactment of the prophecy of Ezekiel: "Thus saith the Lord, God: Behold, I will open your graves, and cause you to come out of your graves, O My people; and I will bring you into the Land of Israel. And ye shall know that I am the Lord." But the prophecy did not end there. It continues: "And thou son of man, take thee one stick and write upon it: for Judah and for the children of Israel, his companions; then take another stick, and write upon it: for Joseph, the stick of Ephraim, and of all the house of Israel, his companions; and join them for thee one to another into one stick, that they may become one in thy hand."

The message of Ezekiel enjoining Jewish unity, which must follow upon the rejuvenation of the Jewish people and upon their return to the land of Israel, was echoed by Solomon Schechter who defined the center of authority in Judaism, as a "living body, not represented by any section of the nation, or any corporate priesthood, or Rabbihood, but by the collective conscience of Catholic Israel as embodied in the Universal Synagogue." There can be no more potent dynamic to which the Zionist organization can be dedicated than the mobilization of all forces in Judaism, to create that universal synagogue with headquarters in the Holy Land. That would mean the integration of all the dismembered bones of the body of Israel, so that they might become an exceeding great host.

We ought to conjure up the souls of the early pioneers of the Zionist movement, visionaries like Zvi Hirsch Kalischer, for whom the return to Zion meant the resumption of religious life at the point at which it had been cut off when the exile began. To maintain the continuity with the past, and to proceed with the further development of the Jewish law, philosophy and theology which was interrupted by two thousand years of Jewish persecution and humiliation —that should be the goal to which the Zionist should strive.

Under the present circumstances, with the splintering

of Judaism into many factions pulling in opposite directions, it is impossible to achieve the goal of Jewish unity, which will lead to the Messianic era envisioned by the ancient prophets, and which even the modern "prophets" and leaders of the Zionist movement have likewise characterized as the culmination of their fervent hopes and sanguine prospects. Zionism must adopt as its slogan the ancient rabbinic declaration that "Israel, the Torah and the Holy One blessed be He are one." We teach our children the familiar song, which is often glibly repeated without realizing its significance, *"Eretz Yisroel bli Tora, hi k'goof bli neshama.* The Land of Israel without Torah is like a body without a soul." To look upon Israel as just another small Levantine state robs it of its universal character. Jerusalem has been waiting throughout the centuries for the people of Israel to come and re-establish it as the headquarters of Judaism. It is an act of Providence that the major faiths have chosen other locales for their sanctum sanctorum, Rome for the Christians and Mecca for the Moslems.

That Jerusalem has waited two thousand years for the Jews to reclaim it and reestablish the new capital of Israel, is one of the miracles of all time. For two thousand years the land remained desolate in its primitive state, and nothing was done to make it pulsate with life until the Jews came on the scene. Why has it waited all these years? Why has no other people or religion taken advantage of the passing centuries, captured the city and the land, and built up the waste places. The Arabs did nothing to make the Holy Land throb with religious fervor or to make it the center of the religious world. The "finger of God" must have directed the course of human events. The time was not ripe for the resurrection of Jerusalem. It took the slaying of 6,000,000 Jews and the devastation caused by two world wars to rouse mankind from its stupor and to gird the loins of the Jews, particularly those who have been the victims of Nazi brutality, in order to fight for the right of the Jew to live an independent life in his ancient homeland.

Jerusalem must become not only the political capital of

the State of Israel but the capital of the religious world. And the Jew must begin to play the role assigned him by divine mandate. The biblical dictum: "And ye shall be unto Me a kingdom of priests and a holy people," gives the best definition of what a Jew is, and also indicates his place among the nations of the world. Politically, the state of Israel is small, one of the smallest nations on the globe. For that reason its voice is weak and it does not command the respect and the prestige claimed by the mighty powers. But when Israel speaks in the name of the Father of mankind, in the name of all the prophets, the saints and seers that have marched across the stage of four millennia of Jewish history, in the name of all the Jews wherever they may live, then the voice becomes all powerful. That voice of authority can hold sway in the face of the ranting of tyrants and dictators. The voice of God that commanded Pharaoh to free Israel; the voice that was heard through the spokesmanship of the prophets when they exclaimed, "Thus spoke the Lord"; the "still small voice" that defied the priests of Baal; that is the only voice which can challenge the blustering, bullying, arrogant despots who boast that they will bury those who refuse to be subjugated.

As a member of a world religion, the Jew has status, and is on a level with any man living in the world. When properly understood, his claim that he is a member of God's chosen people has meaning, for he was chosen at the beginning of civilization, when man was emerging from idolatry and paganism, to bring the message of the One God to all mankind. And the message of the One God means One Humanity, One World, One Law, the law of justice for all the children of the One Father. That message also includes all the prophetic ideals of universal peace, integrity of character, honor and faithfulness.

The World Zionist Organization can make the voice of Judaism reverberate from one end of the globe to the other. And there must be *one voice*, which alone can be effective. If we aim to be like the other peoples of the world, let us take a lesson from their *modus operandi*. The recent encyclical of Pope John XXIII, "Pacem in Terra," found an echo in the hearts of men, regardless of race or creed, because he spoke in the name of the millions of his followers. How impressive and majestic would be the voice emanating from the Holy Land, from the Chief Rabbi of Israel, speaking in the name of the millions of Jews, as well as in the name of the God of Israel, as did Isaiah, Jeremiah or Ezekiel! But, *ba'avonosenu harabim*, unfortunately, the Chief Rabbi does not speak in the name of all the Jews in the world. Because of the fragmentation of Judaism into numerous sects, and the vast numbers who belong to no sect, his voice is like a *kol kore bamidbar*, a voice crying in the wilderness. Here is a task which devolves upon the Zionist Organization— to cement the bonds of unity among the Jews, to reduce the areas in which the sectarians differ, and bring all Jews together under one roof.

The Zionist organization must serve as the liaison officer between the Jews in Israel and the Jews in the Diaspora, and attempt to preserve the integrity of world Jewry. The Israelis are increasingly inclined, it seems, to disregard the name, Jew, and prefer to be known as Israelis, to indicate that they are different from their brethren in the rest of the world. They know very little about the Jews in America. When Ben-Gurion's attention was called to the fact that there is very little news published in the Israeli press concerning Jewish life in America, he replied: "What is there to tell about the Jews in America?" This feeling of estrangement must be corrected, because it runs counter to the entire philosophy of Zionism, which has its basis in the unity of the Jewish people everywhere. Although scattered to the four corners of the globe, their eyes and hearts are still directed toward the Holy Land. *Kibbutz Galuyot* has been taken by the Israelis to mean, the physical "Gathering of the Exiles," into the Promised Land. The daily prayer, "Sound the great trumpet for our freedom; lift up the ensign to gather our exiles, and gather us from the four corners of the earth," has been taken literally. *Kibbutz Galuyot* has been realized by the two million Jews who have settled in Israel since the establishment of the State. And there is no doubt that many exiles who are being driven from the countries where they had sojourned for generations, will continue to stream into Israel. But regardless of how many Jews will be absorbed into Israel, even if its absorptive capacity is stretched to the limit, a Jew who lives in the remotest corner of the earth is still a brother to every other Jew, particularly to the Jews in Israel.

Now, why do the Israelis feel alienated from the Jews in the rest of the world? The answer must be found in the fact that they do not seem to share a deep, rooted, common bond which would instill a sense of kinship and a "consciousness of kind." Many suggestions have been offered to bring about that affinity of spirit and homogeneity of soul which will make Jewish hearts beat as one. All of these recommendations are indeed worthy, but they will not produce the result which we anticipate. What are some of the suggestions?

1. Cultural exchange. Hundreds of Israeli students have come to the United States to study in our universities, and brought back with them techniques which have been developed by the American scientists, and knowledge which has been acquired through experiments in the American laboratories, equipped with the most advanced apparatus which Israel does not possess as yet. Many American students have gone to Israel to study in the Hebrew University and the other higher institutions of learning, and have returned to the United States inspired by their rich experience in the land of the Bible, and the dynamism of the pioneers who are building a new civilization. Nevertheless, this exchange has not brought about a closer relationship of kindred. It is like those who go to a strange land, learn of its culture, and return enriched no doubt, but not having made that culture their own.

2. The development of Israeli culture—dance, music, drama, artistic creations—must win our admiration, and we must do everything we can to encourage Israel's continued progress in every field of human endeavor. Never-

theless, even these developments serve only to accentuate the difference between the Jews in Israel and the Jews in America. The art is known as Israeli art, not Jewish art, because the Jews in other parts of the world have not, throughout the ages, directed their minds and hearts toward a unique Jewish culture, as the Israelis have done.

3. The study of Hebrew which has made tremendous strides in the United States, due to the spread of the Day School and the *Chug Ivri* is not the bond which will bring the hearts of the Jews together to pulsate as a united people. In Israel, there are thousands of Moslems and Christians who speak Hebrew fluently, and yet there is no feeling of kinship with the Jews, even though they are citizens of the same land.

What, then, is the bond that will unite all Jewry, and prevent Jewish assimilation, a possibility which is feared now, even more than before the State of Israel was established? There can be but one answer. Look at Jewish history and the answer can be found. It was *Judaism* which safeguarded the Jews from disappearing in the maelstrom of the onrushing cultures in which they were engulfed as they were driven from one country to another. And *Judaism* —in whatever form it may assume in the Holy Land— must continue to play the dominant role in Jewish life.

The religious elements in the Jewish community must combine to propagandize aggressively for Jewish unity on the basis of "a common religious and cultural tradition." The religionists are outnumbered by the secularists, and for that reason Jewish life has become secularized to the extent that religion must bow obsequiously to the "unafflliated," and give them status in "the organic Jewish community." The time has come when religion must assert itself in the administration of communal affairs, in every field of philanthropic, educational and civic activities. Jewish life in the Diaspora as well as in Israel must be synagogue-centered. But it is useless to speak of the synagogue as the hub about which all Jewish activities must rotate, unless the term has the same meaning for all the members of the community.

Of course, we cannot expect all Jews to be in accord with our conviction. There will always be Jews who will not submit to the regimen of Jewish ritual as prescribed in the Codes. But Zionism must lend its full support to the religious forces, for its own preservation and for the survival of the entire people of Israel. Every Zionist must become a member of a synagogue, and every synagogue must become a member of the local and World Zionist Organization. We must draw into the circle of the religious community all Jewish men and women, in the conviction that a strong religious body will also sustain segments of the Jewish population who are interested in other aspects of Jewish culture.

For example, there is still a large contingent of our people who are avowed Yiddishists, who firmly adhere to the Yiddish language and culture which were developed in Europe before the Nazi holocaust and served to inspire millions of our people with a unique literature, folklore, drama, song, and humor. With the liquidation of European Jewry, the decline of the Yiddish speaking and reading public in the United States, the future of Yiddish, despite heroic efforts is very precarious. Nevertheless, there will always be a coterie of devotees who will find in Yiddish a medium of cultural enrichment. However, it is doubtful that Yiddish would enjoy its current longevity without the use of that language in the Yeshivot, in the study of Bible and Talmud, and in the synagogue where the *maggidim*, the old time preachers, quickened the hearts of the congregants in a language and intonation which delighted and inspired them. Secular Yiddish culture will continue to appeal only to a chosen few; Hebrew, English and languages spoken by Jews in other lands, are strong competitors. Just as in the past, Yiddish will only survive if its use is also continued in the religious circles.

Ben-Gurion has stated that "the State has been established by the power of the Messianic vision and by constructive pioneering." His concept of the "Messianic vision" is spelled out in terms of the new social patterns which are founded on mutual assistance and cooperation without discrimination, guaranteeing the maximum degree of civic freedom. But all of these ideas are derived from the Bible and Jewish religious tradition. If the ultimate goal of the state is the redemption of all mankind, not only of Israel, it can only be achieved by promoting the spiritual values for which the Jewish people have suffered martyrdom throughout the ages.

The world needs, not a new revelation, but a renewal of the Revelation on Mt. Sinai, a rededication to the Ten Commandments and to all that is embraced in those fundamental doctrines. The greatest crimes in human history were committed by a Christian country, in an age when Christian civilization dominated the world. During the last two decades, Islam has embarked upon a campaign of vengeful hatred toward Israel. The philosophy of communism has intensified its anti-Semitic policies in Soviet Russia. All this points to the conclusion that the world needs a rejuvenation of the spirit, which must come from the original Divine source of spiritual dispensation. It is more important today, perhaps, than at any other time in human civilization that the voice of Judaism be heard. Zionism and the Universal Synagogue must join hands in a world-wide movement for the redemption of mankind.

XVII

CONTEMPORARY JEWISH SECTS

Until Reform Judaism appeared on the scene, the term "Orthodox Judaism" did not exist. Judaism had never borne any adjectival labels, regardless of differences in ideology. The various sects which arose during the centuries, such as the Samaritans, Sadducees, and Karaites, who drifted away from the main stream of Judaism, the Hasidim and Mitnagdim in more recent times, never limited Judaism with an adjective. There was *One Judaism,* characterized by a variety of interpretations. Similarly we do not speak in terms of Republican Americanism or Democratic Americanism. There is only one Americanism, and the constituent elements of the pluralistic American population vary in customs and habits, political and religious thinking.

Many religious leaders in Orthodox Judaism would welcome the elimination of the qualifying adjective from the vocabulary of Judaism. In the words of Rabbi Leo Jung: "It would be more just to term "Orthodox" Judaism unlabeled, and to use the qualifying and designating adjectives to define its dissenting branches." We would even go a step further, and remove the "trade-mark" from all the sectarian movements in Judaism! That does not mean that we would stifle debate on the vital issues which confront our people in modern times. Discussion and argumentation have marked the study of the Talmud in the Yeshivot throughout the ages, from the very creation of the Talmud, which is basically the documentation of the pros and cons of the controversial legal questions presented by the rabbis in the academies of Palestine and Babylonia.

Homogeneity in practice and thought never existed in Israel, and yet diversity never led to the disintegration or dismemberment of Judaism. Except in the case of the sects that definitely made a break with the authorities, severing all ties, the bulk of world Jewry maintained contact with each other, and always felt the "consciousness of kind." When they were forced to take the wanderer's staff and move on to more hospitable climes they always found a friendly reception. Moses Ben Enoch was one of the four scholars who left Sura in Babylonia on a mission to collect funds for the academy shortly before it closed its doors. He was taken captive to Cordova, Spain, by a Moorish admiral, and was ransomed by that community in 945. There he founded a school with the cooperation of Hasdai Ibn

Shaprut. Coming from the opposite ends of the then-known world, they nevertheless felt a close kinship, and continuity was maintained in advancing Jewish scholarship in the new environment, without a radical break or change.

The variety of customs which were observed by the Jews who were scattered, so to speak, to the four winds, indicates that so-called Orthodox Judaism was not a stereotyped religion with a rigid regimen of living. Dr. Judah Bergman, in his volume, *Hayahadut,* devotes a chapter to the diversity and unity of Jewish life, and describes in detail the diverse customs which characterized the Jewish communities living in many lands in ancient as well as in modern times. For example, in the city of Nahardea, portions of the Hagiographa, the Sacred Writings, were read at the *Mincha* service on Sabbath, but the practice was not observed in any other city. The purpose was to include all the three categories of the Jewish canon (the Pentateuch and the Prophets were read during the morning service). In Cyprus the Jews did not observe Friday night but included Saturday night as the Shabbat. In Greece, they offered the *Shacharis* service before sunrise. In Italy, on Simchat Torah, crowns were placed on the heads of the worshippers who received the honor of ascending the *Bima* during the reading of the *Sidra* of the week. And on Tisha B'Ab, a Torah was placed on the bent back of a congregant who stood bowed before the ark, while the portion of the Torah was read, as a symbolic interpretation of the "yoke of the Torah," the burden which the Jew must carry. In Kurdistan, the Jews did more than go to *Tashlich* on Rosh Hashanah, and empty their pockets into a body of water to get rid of their sins. They dipped into the waters bodily as a purifying process to wash away their sins. In Alkush, the community leaders went up to the nearest mountain on Shavuot to simulate the ascent of Moses to Mt. Sinai, and there the Ten Commandments were read to the people who were assembled at the foot of the mountain. Then they descended, and a mock battle took place to represent the battle

of Gog and Magog, destined to take place before the coming
of the Messiah.

The differences in observances between the Jewish communities in Israel and in exile in Babylonia during talmudic
times were notable. And even in Israel, the customs of the
provinces varied in many respects. For example, in Judah,
daily work was continued until noon *erev Pesach;* but in
Galilee, they did not work all day in preparation for the
Passover. In Babylonia *chol hamo-ed* Passover and Succoth
were regarded as week days, and they attended to business
as usual. But in Israel the days retained their sacred
character as the holidays, and no labors were conducted.
In Babylon, there were nineteen benedictions in the *Shemone Esre;* in Israel, only eighteen. The *Kaddish* before
Borechu could be recited only with a *Minyan* of ten worshippers in Babylon; but in Israel, a quorum of seven suf-
ficed. The *Kedusha* of the *Shemone Esre* was recited daily
in Babylon; but in Israel only on Sabbaths and Holidays.
When the *Shma Yisroel* was proclaimed during the services,
the congregation stood up in Israel as a recognition of the
fundamental doctrine of Judaism; but in Babylon, they
did not move from their seats. (The discussion of the varying opinions of Beth Hillel and Beth Shammai is found in
Berachot 10b-11a.) The cycle of the reading of the *Sidrot*
of the Torah was completed annually in Babylon; but in
Israel, a tri-annual cycle was observed, and it took three
and a half years to complete the reading of the Pentateuch.
Three blasts of a *shofar* announced the advent of the Sabbath in Israel; but in Babylon, the *shofar* was not blown.
During the three-fold benediction, the priests (*kohanim*)
faced the congregation in Babylon; but in Israel, their
faces turned toward the ark. In the eastern countries, the
Duchan was held every day during the *Shacharis* service,
which is the custom today in Israel and as it was in Yemen;
but in Spain, the priestly blessings are pronounced only
on Sabbaths and holidays, during the *Musaf* prayers; and
the custom is omitted on the Sabbaths, or when a holiday
occurs on the Sabbath in western countries. In the syna-

gogues of the Eastern lands, the women did not go to the synagogue to participate in the prayers, but this restriction was removed by the establishment of an *Ezras Nashim,* a section of the synagogue which was separated by a *mechitza,* a curtained partition which concealed their presence.

There were many variations in customs between the Jews of Spain and the Jews of France, despite their proximity. When the Jews of Spain came to a French community, there were twenty-four *minhagim* which they brought with them, and which they insisted upon observing, causing considerable strife and misunderstanding. In some respects there were radical differences. For example, the Jews coming from Spain relaxed the prohibition against playing musical instruments on the Sabbath, to which the Jews in France were strongly opposed. The Jews of Spain observed the Sabbatical year, and included a clause in their contracts which included the Sabbatical restrictions. In order to quell any communal conflicts, R. Menachem Meiri ruled that the Jews of every community should "observe the *minhag* of their sainted ancestors, and of the former sages, and no future sage shall come and protest against them. Every community should maintain its own integrity, every people according to its language and every country according to its script." The Talmud declares: "Everything goes according to the custom of the land."

The differences in the prayer books in use by the Sefardim, the Spanish-Portuguese *Nusach,* the *Nusach Ari* of the Lubavich Hasidim, and the Ashkenazim, indicate that Orthodox Judaism is flexible in matters of custom which are not in violation of the basic teachings of the Bible and Talmud. There are variations in interpretation which the rabbis have offered from time to time in the Responsa and in the voluminous treatises which fill the shelves of our libraries.

Many compilations of Jewish customs have been published, among the earliest, the *Minhag Olam,* of Abraham ben Nathan Hayarki of Lunel, who traveled extensively. Among the more important works, are the *Shibole Haleket* by Zedekiah ben Abraham Anaw of Rome, and the *Orachot Hayim* of Aaron ben Jacob Hakohen, known more popularly as the *Kol Bo*.

Throughout our history there were two movements in Israel, the centrifugal, tending away from the center, the splintering of the ranks into a multiplicity of customs, and the centripetal, the drawing toward the center. As the Jews have been dispersed throughout the world, the danger has arisen that in the end there will be complete disintegration if the fragmentation of religious life remains uncontrolled.

The conflicting theological interpretations of Judaism which exist today have created a condition which is confusing to our young people who need spiritual guidance, and who are very little concerned with the fine-spun arguments which the sectarians offer to attract followers. We will endeavor in the following chapters to analyze the claims of the current divergent sects in Judaism, expound their philosophy of Judaism, underscore their points of agreement, and, hopefully, indicate that the differences are expendable. They are hardly worthwhile fighting about, and serve no purpose except to militate against the unity and solidarity of the Jewish people.

XVIII

SECULARISM

As the barriers of the ghetto were lowered, the Jews came into contact with their neighbors. The effect of the confrontation varied with the cultural character of the Jews, extending from complete absorption into the general society by conversion and intermarriage, to a greater intensification of religious loyalty, as exemplified by the Hasidic movement. In between the two extremes there were segments of the population who sought to fulfill their cultural requirements in the Haskalah movement, in the development of Yiddish and Hebrew literature and art, in Zionism, and in pursuing studies in the sciences and the humanities. The Jewish religion, its traditional customs, lost all meaning for the secularists. Nevertheless, they did not forsake their people, and still considered themselves part of the Jewish community, supporting every philanthropic endeavor. But secularization and assimilation spurred the development of the Reform movement which felt that the only way to preserve the faith was to bring it up-to-date, to modernize it, and make it approximate the character of the religious institutions of the environment. To what extent Reform Judaism checked secularized Jews from abjuring their faith is a conjecture which would be difficult to prove statistically. With the exception of a small number of German Jews who constituted the Reform congregations, the great mass of the Jewish people either ignored the Emancipation and the Enlightenment and adhered to their religious practices as their elders had done for generations, or they drifted from the Jewish religious moorings completely. There was no half way. Reform enjoyed its greatest success in the United States, where assimilation was no problem at all!

Assimilation has been a problem which Judaism has faced from time immemorial. From the time of the worship of the Golden Calf until today, the spiritual leaders of every generation have exhorted the masses to ignore the pagan Sirenes which beckon and allure by their seductive voices. A lesson can be derived from the Greek legend of Orpheus who received a lyre from Apollo, upon which he played with such consummate skill, that even the most rapid rivers ceased to flow, the beasts forgot their wildness, and the mountains moved to listen to his song. He alone was able to escape the Sirenes, the sea nymphs, who charmed seafarers with their voices so that they forgot their work to listen and at last died from want of food. Ulysses escaped by blocking his ears with wax. But Orpheus outplayed and outsang the Sirenes, and made them listen to his music. By the same token, classical Judaism, the Judaism of the sages, seers and prophets of old, plays a religious rhapsody which has inspired mankind throughout the ages and still continues to outcharm all the Sirenes, all the distracting serenades which have enchanted and ensnared some of our sophisticates and intellectuals.

Throughout Jewish history, the Jews never stood aloof when they came into contact with the cultures of the peoples among whom they sojourned. They accepted and assimilated all the worthwhile cultural values of their neighbors—without surrendering and compromising any of the ideals which they held inviolate and sacred. The Babylonian Talmud contains numerous Greek terms, and the rabbis willingly embodied these concepts of the Greek philosophers which did not conflict with Jewish teachings but which helped rather to strengthen their validity. The liberal spirit was expressed by the rabbis in the dictum: "Let the chief beauties of Japhet (Greece) be in the tents of Shem" (Meg 9b). The *Guide for the Perplexed* of Maimonides is an attempt to reconcile the philosophy of Aristotle with the doctrines of Judaism as expounded in the Torah. Aristotle was held in high veneration, and was known as "the philosopher." His works were quoted by all the medieval Jewish philosophers.

There is perhaps no people on the face of the earth, going back to the earliest chronicles of the history of civilization, who came into contact with more cultures and locked horns with more ideologies than the Jews. And yet, there is no culture that has withstood the acid test of time and maintained its integrity more than the Jewish religion. Blown about by the winds of persecution and hate, caught in the maelstrom of titanic forces, as the international scene was rocked by the currents and cross-currents of world-shaking events, the Jews never lost their religious anchorage, and maintained an even keel as they sailed the stormy seas.

In the Jewish struggle for survival throughout the ages,

the admonition of the prophet Micah was followed as a compass and the sextant: "For let all peoples walk each one in the name of its god, but we will walk in the name of the Lord our God forever" (Micah 4:5). The Jews fought against assimilation. It was a wrestling match reminiscent of the combat between Jacob and the spirit of Esau. Jacob's name was changed to Israel which meant, "for thou hast striven with God and with men, and hast prevailed" (Gen. 32:29). This was interpreted to mean that Jacob had vanquished celestial beings, and also emerged victorious in his encounters with human beings. If Judaism had yielded to the enticement of all the cultures it met, there would be no Judaism today.

Assimilation is a greater threat to the survival of the Jewish people today than ever before in the history of our people. There are many renegades from the traditional discipline. The ranks of Christian Science, Ethical Culture and the numerous other sectarian groups are recruited from the seed of Abraham, Isaac and Jacob, and the numbers that have turned their backs on *all* religion have reached alarming magnitude. How to cope with this problem is the concern of all segments of Judaism—Orthodox, Conservative and Reform. While it is true that there always were, there are today, and perhaps there always will be, adherents of every form of religious persuasion who are convinced that they hold the only key to salvation, it must be evident to all that assimilation can be tackled only by a pooling of all forces for attack upon the common enemy. The Jew who has become infected with the virus of assimilation cannot find his cure with less Judaism, with a watered-down Judaism, with a Judaism from which all color has been bleached. A good dose of strong Judaism, undoctored and unsugared, may be the most effective medication for his spiritual ailment.

Without the conviction that the Judaism which we have inherited from our forefathers embodies the highest concepts of civilization which will regenerate mankind and bring about the realization of the dreams of universal peace,

Judaism will not prevail. The only form of assimilation which Judaism will accept is the assimilation to Judaism of all contributions to wisdom from any source whatsoever. And Judaism in every generation has done just that. The rabbis in the Talmud laid down the rule: "Whosoever says a wise thing, even if he is of the nations of the world, is called wise" (Megilla 16a). There is a passage in Tractate Pesachim 94b, in which problems of astronomy are discussed, and the opinions of Jewish scholars are presented together with a quotation from the "scholars of the nations of the world." And the rabbis admit: "Their view is preferable to ours." That seems to indicate that the rabbis and the Jewish scholars of every age did not fear the opinions and theories of gentile scholars in subjects of scientific interest or philosophy. With their mental acumen the rabbis have always succeeded in finding support in the Torah for new concepts coming from non-Jewish scholars. In the firm belief that the "seal of the Holy One is truth," they followed the dictum of Ben Bag Bag who declared: "Turn it (the Torah) and turn it over again, for everything is in it" (Perek 5, 27), and heeded the warnings: "Neither shall you walk in their statutes" (Lev. 18:3), and "Know what answer to give to an *epikoros*" (Perek 2, 19).

Judaism has thus far been able to overcome opposition and competition, not by surrender and compromise, but by continuing to hold up the Torah as a mirror to man, to reveal to him the hideousness of his features in the face of all the crimes which have been committed. The salvation of the human race does not depend upon a new religion or a reformulation of the old religion, but in the contriteness of the spirit, in the reform of man's own heart. Man must pray in the language of the Psalmist, who implored the Almighty in pathetic terms: "Create in me a clean heart, O God, and renew a steadfast spirit within me" (Ps. 51:12). And in the words of the Prophet Ezekiel: "Make ye a new heart and a new spirit, for why shall ye die, O house of Israel" (Ez. 18:31).

XIX

ORTHODOX JUDAISM

What is the basic thesis of Orthodox Judaism? We have indicated already that it is *not* an inflexible regimen of Jewish belief and practice, as it is commonly understood. With all the codes that have been formulated by Maimonides, Joseph Caro, and others, there are many variations in so-called Orthodox practice. And yet that there has been cohesiveness within Jewish ranks must be acknowledged, otherwise the continuity of the Jewish people would not have been maintained. In spite of the fact that the various denominations in Judaism boast of their numerical strength, and each claims to hold the exclusive key to Israel's future, none can foretell what the Jew a hundred years from now will be like (if civilization will then exist), or what form of Judaism he will practice. The evidence seems to indicate that a new type of Jew will emerge, who will embody valuable features contributed by many practices and viewpoints. He will be a resultant of all the forces in Judaism that act and react upon each other.

Basically, all sects in Judaism derive from the historic religion of Israel which dates back to Moses at Sinai, and by tradition even to more ancient days. The distinguishing feature of Orthodox Judaism is the firm conviction that there is an unbroken chain from primordial times which must not be severed in our day. The fear that the continuity of Judaism will be impaired by any unwarranted change in precept and practice has prompted resistance to any reforms which have been advocated by modern sectarians. The protagonists of Orthodox Judaism affirm that there is nothing in modern life which is incompatible with the ancient faith. It is for that reason that the men of the Great Synagogue enjoined: "Make a fence around the Torah," to prevent trampling upon the "vineyards of the Lord" and destroying the fruits thereof. The many restrictions that were instituted by the rabbis were designed for the purpose of preserving the integrity of the faith and preventing dissolution. These prohibitions are not *per se* in violation of any basic law, but are made obligatory in order to forestall any infraction of the law. It was for that reason, for example, that the Sabbath was declared to begin not at the moment of sunset, but eighteen minutes before; and the Sabbath was to continue after sunset on Saturday until three stars were visible in the sky, and not end at the exact time of the setting sun.

There are many devoted souls among our people who keep the Sabbath, the dietary laws and as many of the *taryag mitzvot* as are applicable to the *Galut*, and still keep abreast of all the modern developments, inventions and discoveries. Yeshivah University, which is under the auspices of the Rabbi Isaac Elhanan Theological Seminary, the training academy for Orthodox rabbis, maintains many departments for the study of secular subjects, and its Einstein Medical School takes its place among the finest institutions of higher learning in the country and the world. Samson Raphael Hirsch has expressed the Orthodox attitude toward modernity: "If the spirit of the times does not agree with the Torah, all the worse for the times." The word of God must be accepted as the eternal mandate which must be observed under all circumstances. Indeed, throughout the centuries, the Jews have suffered martyrdom and displayed a constancy of faith which has defied all the tyrants in history. It is for that reason that the loyal Jew has developed an aversion to "modern civilization," which is anything but civilized. What is there in modern life, he asks in effect, which is superior to the ideals of the prophets, that we should bow before them in humility and capitulation?

The Orthodox Jew refuses to be influenced by the pressure of modern civilization, because modern civilization has brought him nothing but sorrow and misfortune. The Orthodox Jew who lived in the ghettos of Russia, Poland and the countries in Eastern Europe, was not attracted to the literature, art, science, or philosophy of the Gentiles; he did not appreciate these treasures, because he could not understand how anything good could be created by men who were depraved and who were guilty of the most unspeakable crimes of rapine, massacre and murder. He knew that the Torah condemned persecution and and hate. It must be that "their Torah," which they called their "culture," inculcated into their hearts the feelings which prompted the iniquity and the cruelty which they displayed. His Torah preached love; their "culture" preached hate. His Torah taught justice and truth; their "culture" taught them to inflict unjust laws incited by false doctrines. His Torah taught peace; their "culture" inflamed the passions to wage war against neighbors whom they looked upon as enemies. In his Torah it is written: "Not by might nor by power, but by My Spirit saith the Lord" (Zechariah 4:6); their "philosophy" of life was motivated by the creed: "By thy sword shalt thou live," which they inherited from their ancestors, Ishmael, Esau and Amalek. All of this will give us an understanding why the Orthodox Jew, not only in medieval days and throughout the entire modern period in pre-Nazi days, but also today, still clings tenaciously to his ancestral faith. He sees no improvement in the moral status of mankind. The same hatreds and the same evils continue to tyrannize the world. We see flashes here and there of an attempt to humanize society in accordance with the primary tenets of the Bible, but mankind is far removed from their full realization.

Let us seek to understand the spirit of the Orthodox Jew, particularly the saintly religious leaders who feel the pulse of the world and, like physicians who take the temperature of a patient, realize that mankind is afflicted with serious spiritual ailments, and needs spiritual medication to restore the social organism to sound mental and physical health. The Orthodox Jew believes that he knows where to find the cure and prescriptions—in the Torah. That will explain the intransigence of the Orthodox rabbis against any tampering with the *Halacha* or with the traditions of the faith.

Maimonides formulated the "Thirteen Principles of the Faith" which may be regarded as a summary of the philosophy of Orthodox Judaism. Among them is the doctrine of the unchangeability of the law. "I believe with a perfect faith that the whole law, now in our possession, is the same that was given to Moses, our teacher, peace be unto him. I believe with a perfect faith that the Law will not be changed, and that there will never be any other law from the Creator blessed be His Name." Of course, there have been amendments to Jewish law, promulgated by the rabbis to meet extraordinary occasions as they arose. They were called *hora'at sha'a* "a decision under an emergency," and were not to be regarded as precedents. But these were official acts which were accepted by the entire people, and not the decision of a dissenting group. Orthodoxy has strenuously fought against dissident groups within Judaism who unilaterally assumed authority to make changes in the *Halacha*. This, the rabbis felt, was undermining to the integrity of the faith.

The excuse has repeatedly been made that modern life required a new dispensation, a new interpretation and a new revision of Jewish law. Times change and Judaism must keep in step with modernity, was the argument advanced for the adoption of radical changes within the religious body. But throughout the ages, Judaism has fought against prophets who promised a new salvation which could be achieved only by making deep incisions into the body of the traditional code. Orthodox Jews claim that when new conditions arise it is possible to find applicable precedents in the rabbinic literature, in the Talmud, in the writings and commentaries of the sages and scholars of every generation, and in the recorded responsa which have

Judaism, lest it lead to apostacy and assimilation. The fundamentalist would not admit that Aristotle was right and that Judaism must be harmonized with the doctrines which he expounded. Judaism need not be apologetic before any culture in the world. The Torah was the truth, and every other concept which seemed to contradict the Torah must be studied on the basis of "Know what answer to give an *apikoros* (an unbeliever)" (Perek 2:19). There can be no contradiction between the Torah and the philosophies which have arisen from generation to generation, and still new ones which will appear on the scene in the future.

Orthodoxy can be understood and appreciated only in terms of the pre-eminence and pre-dominance of the Torah. When we start with the premise that the Torah is holy, a direct revelation from God, inviolable and eternal, the conclusions which the Orthodox reach are inevitable. If the Bible is a man-made book and the result of progressive stages of man's development, it must follow that the laws therein contained are subject to man's frailties, and for that reason not binding and changeable at will. Here is the fundamental difference between Orthodoxy and the present sectarians. For the Orthodox, the Torah expresses the will of God, and we must curb our will to correspond to His: "Do His will as if it were thy will, that He may do thy will as if it were His will. Nullify thy will before His will, that He may nullify the will of others before thy will" (Perek 2:4). The rabbis were not disturbed by the seeming discrepancies in the Bible, the seeming contradictions which have led our Bible critics to deny its authenticity and its sacred character. In the first place, the attitude which the Orthodox have assumed is the natural reaction of an impassioned lover who adores his mate with all her imperfections and faults. He resents any criticism or condemnation of her. The Torah is dear to the Orthodox Jew, and every affront against its integrity which is expressed in a spirit of contentiousness, is viewed with alarm and is resisted vehemently.

The rabbis were cognizant of the many problems to be found within the Bible and the tenets of the Jewish faith. They made every effort to interpret the controversial questions, creating a voluminous literature which has accumulated throughout the ages. The commentaries upon commentaries on the Bible, the Talmud, the sermonic material, the responsa, the questions and answers, all are calculated to furnish an explanation of textual incongruities. The dialectical ingenuity which was displayed by the sages in their attempt to solve the problems in biblical exegesis, and their talmudic inductive and deductive reasoning, may not please modern sophisticates and intellectuals, but if we can put ourselves in their place and view Judaism from their angle of vision, we must be convinced that our venerable rabbis who carried the "yoke of the Torah" throughout the ages, have been loyal to the oath of allegiance which they pledged when they assumed spiritual leadership. The ancient faith was regarded as a sacred heirloom, a rich heritage handed down by our forefathers for safekeeping, to be transmitted to our children and to posterity for their edification and spiritual guidance. Our ancestral religion is at least as precious as the masterpieces created by men who were endowed with unusual spiritual power, the invaluable works of art that have been preserved throughout the ages, the paintings, sculpture, classical literature, musical compositions—the entire gamut of creative endeavor. We would not think of altering a painting by Rembrandt, for example, or substituting a chord in one of Beethoven's symphonies, or adding an aphorism or phrase to a play by Shakespeare. That does not preclude anyone who is inspired by the "muse" to indulge in self-expression, to give his fellowmen the benefit of his talents, and to enrich the treasury of scholarship and art by his wisdom. Jewish scholars have always prided themselves upon the *chidushim*, novellae, which gave new illumination to a difficult discussion in the Talmud or a passage in the Bible. Students in the yeshivot were encouraged to offer a *chidush*; often it would be in the nature of a *pilpul*, a fantastic twist of logic, of which many rabbis disapproved, because of the excesses to which it would lead. Nevertheless it served to sharpen the intellect, and stimulated the study of our sacred lore. The *pilpulistic* era which prevailed in the European yeshivot in the pre-Hitler period has passed, but whatever its faults it must be admitted that it kept the flame of Jewish scholarship ever ablaze.

In the same spirit we must look with sympathy and not condemnation upon the doctrines which the Orthodox have espoused, and which they continue to harbor even to this day. One of the basic issues is the dogma, *Torah min hashamayim*, divine revelation. According to the Orthodox point of view there was, literally, divine transmission of the Ten Commandments to Moses on Mount Sinai. *Torah min hashamayim* is regarded as the quintessence of Judaism. The rabbis declare: "The following have no portion in the world to come; he who says that the Torah is not from heaven, or that the resurrection is not taught in the Torah" (Avoda Zara 18a).

An Orthodox Jew does not speculate with reference to the phenomenon of the divine revelation at Mt. Sinai. It was a supernatural event, and yet as real as any visual or auditory experience in life. Supernaturalism is no problem to the Orthodox Jew. He is conscious that the whole of life is a miracle, which his finite mind cannot grasp. We do not begin to understand the secret of life. What makes a blade of grass grow? What power produces the flowers in the fields and the fruits on the trees? What regulates the time of day and night, and the seasons, with mathematical accuracy? What is life and what is death? From where is the wisdom derived which enables man to think, to become creative, and to produce the miraculous inventions before which man is lost in wonder? The questions can be multiplied *ad infinitum*, and mankind is no closer to the answer today than the day the Psalmist declared: "The heavens recount the glory of God, and the firmament declareth His handiwork." The more discoveries that are made in the realm of science, the more mystifying the universe becomes, and the more problems come to the fore. What and where is the power that orbits the space capsules at the speed of about 18,000 miles an hour and enables man to circle the globe in about 81 minutes? We know how it works; but we do not know the secret of the power that makes it work.

It is in this spirit that the Orthodox approach the dogma of *Torah min hashamayim,* divine revelation. It cannot be explained in scientific terms. Nor do the ancient sages attempt to fathom the secret of its propulsion. We can go no further than the science professor in the laboratory who conducted the elementary experiment in physics by placing a piece of steel between two magnets, one on the table and one suspended from the ceiling. When equidistant from both magnets, the piece of steel hung in midair without visible support. "What is the secret?" asked the professor. "To say 'magnetism' is to beg the question. There is but one answer: The will of God," he said. He was no theologian; he was a physicist, a scientist who faced reality.

Supernaturalism, therefore, need not be equated with mythology and superstition. To confess that we do not understand the bewildering richness of nature; to admit that there is a higher power which governs the operation of all the movements in our earthly existence is, after all, the basis of faith and religion. That power is God, who is supernatural; and mankind, as yet, has not reached the status of supreme intelligence to comprehend His deep mysteries. Perhaps, in "the end of days," as presaged by our prophets, the secrets which man has been yearning to fathom, will be revealed. But until then, we must follow the admonition of the sage: "Trust in the Lord with all thy heart, and lean not upon thine own understanding" (Prov. 3:5).

Attempts have been made to rationalize the event that took place at Sinai and to question the authenticity of revelation. According to the Bible, the divine voice was not only heard by Moses, but by the entire assemblage that stood at the foot of the mountain. As we read in Scripture: "Did ever a people hear the voice of God speaking out of the midst of the fire, as thou hast heard, and live?" (Deut. 4:34).

"These words the Lord spoke unto all your assembly in the mount out of the midst of the fire, of the cloud, and of the thickness, with a great voice" (Deut. 5:19).

According to the rabbis, God revealed His will to the other nations of the world: "R. Yohanan said: It was one voice that divided itself into seven voices, and these into seventy languages. R. Shimon b. Lakish said: (It was the voice) from which all the subsequent prophets received their prophesy" (Exodus Rabba 28:6). The rabbis implied that the revelation was not only horizontal, embracing the whole universe, but also vertical, echoing down the corridor of time to all future generations. In fact, revelation antedated the giving of the Ten Commandments at Sinai. God made known His will to previous generations by the establishment of the so-called seven commandments of the sons of Noah. Six of the basic commandments were enjoined upon Adam, as implied in the words: "And the Lord commanded Adam" (Gen. 2:16). They include: idolatry, theft, blasphemy, authority of judges, bloodshed, and incest. The seventh was the injunction against eating flesh torn from a living animal, which Noah was admonished to observe since he was the first to receive permission to eat meat (Genesis Rabba 16:6; 34:8). It is God's will that is revealed to man, who is conscious of what is good and what is evil, by the "still small voice" which is heard in his conscience. In this respect man is different from the beast, who operates and functions from instinct and not from consciousness. To humanize revelation is to negate its authority and effectiveness as the eternal standard of human conduct.

Respect for authority is a fundamental principle of Orthodox Judaism. It is, in fact, the basis for all civilized society. Law and order require that the laws must be observed whether they are established by custom and tradition, or instituted by legislators who are empowered to make the laws. The legislative branch of the government enacts the laws, and the police department and the judiciary enforce their obedience. While a law is on the statute books, no one dares flaunt it, whether it is acceptable or not. It is the privilege of every citizen, however, to express his dissent and labor for its nullification if he believes that the law is unjust or objectionable. But only by legislative act can a law be abolished and a new law substituted in its place.

Jewish law, or the *halacha* as it is known in rabbinic circles, as formulated in the Talmud and the Codes, has been developed in the same manner as the laws of any government or group in human society. There are customs and traditions which have been the accepted norms of practice and observance throughout the years, and there have been special enactments by the rabbis which were embodied in the codes to serve as guides for Jewish living. The Shulchan Aruch of Joseph Caro has been accepted by Orthodox Jews as the code to follow in the regimen of daily life, in the celebration of the Sabbath and holidays and the solemnization of the major events in the life of the Jew. In the Diaspora, there was no police power to enforce compliance with the law, other than the conscience of every person. But public opinion was strong in the Jewish community, to the extent that anyone who attempted to deviate from the accepted mode of conduct, was ostracised from society, even without an official edict or ban of excommunication. There were times when the *cherem,* or ban, was imposed upon a sinner or transgressor, but they were rare occasions, because the environment was strong enough to restrain insubordination.

Without the firmness of faith with which Orthodox Jewry has clung tenaciously to the *halacha* as it has been handed down from one generation to the other, it is quite possible that Judaism would not have survived the attacks from the outside and corrosion from the non-conformist groups within who objected to the *halachic* restrictions. Adherence to the law required self-restraint and self-discipline, and the denial of pleasures which others enjoyed. Not everyone had the courage and the strength to withstand temptation. The rabbis were cognizant of the foibles of mankind, and by means of a fable they explain why the righteous are able to bear the burden of the *mitzvot* and endure the afflictions they often experience. In commenting upon the verse: "The Lord trieth the righteous; but the wicked and him that loveth violence His soul hateth" (Ps. 11:5), Rabbi Eliezar said: "When a man possesses two cows, one strong and the other feeble, upon which does he put the yoke? Surely upon the strong one. Similarly, the Lord tests none but the righteous" (Genesis Rabba 32:3). Further, we read in Tractate Berachot 32b: "Four things require to be done with vigor; namely, the study of the Torah, good deeds, praying and one's worldly occupation." To be different in the face of pressures from all sides requires courage, and whether we agree or not with the mannerisms which the extreme Orthodox display, we must admit that they have the courage of their convictions. On the basis of man's inalienable right to live his own life to his own satisfaction, even though we may not approve, we cannot condemn them. Man has the right to be different; and it is these differences which make life colorful, instead of drab and monotonous.

While the Orthodox Jew has unshakeable and unquestioning belief in the truth of the Torah, he is also aware, with the sage, that "the fool believeth everything" (Prov. 14:15). Every man must believe in something and follow someone as his guide. To avoid confusion of thought and the diversion of the mind toward the vagaries which an uncontrolled and undisciplined heart may arouse, the word of God serves as the compass to indicate the direction man should travel, the sextant to tell him where he stands, and the anchor which keeps his ship on an even keel as he sails the ocean of life.

Orthodox Judaism has recognized the need for changes in living patterns—but only as long as these changes do not deviate from *halacha*. Many habits acquired in the ghetto have no place in the social environment in which Jews live today. One marked change in the Jewish way of life even among the firm advocates of Orthodoxy has been the esthetic improvement in the synagogue services. They have become more decorous, and the buildings no longer

110

exhibit the dinginess and disorder which characterized the houses of worship and study in the European communities.

And yet, to follow the rabbinic mandate, *dan lechaf zechus,* "seek the positive aspects of that which is judged," it must be admitted that in spite of the unpleasant and oft repelling surroundings, the inner spirit of the *shul* in which our grandfathers worshipped reached heights of devotion and piety which will scarcely be found in the most magnificent temples in the United States. One thing is certain: religious fervor does not increase proportionately with the size and the splendor of the structure. The trend is most likely to go in reverse. While there can be no justification for lack of decorum, loud conversation, the ebb and flow of the worshippers as they come and go at will, and similar aspects of the Orthodox synagogue of a by-gone day, a *hasid* who has been accustomed to daven with *kavanah* and *hitlahavut,* calling upon every muscle and every nerve in his body as he intones his prayers, literally following the devotional outpour of the Psalmist, "All my bones shall say: 'Lord, who is like unto Thee'" (Ps. 35:10), such a Jew would feel confined in a straight jacket if he had to sit quietly and read from a prayer book in unison with the rest of the congregation. What an effort for an "old-timer" to keep in step during the recital of the *Kaddish* led by the rabbi, particularly when the mourners dutifully repeat it word by word, struggling with unintelligible syllables as strange as Chinese or Sanskrit!

An explanation has been offered for the lack of formality and dignity, for the levity and the abandon which governed the conduct of the worshippers in the old-time synagogue. The Jew feels perfectly at home in his house of worship. He speaks with his God in terms of familiarity, as one who approaches his father in time of need, with the hope that his wish will be granted. Modern man who rarely thinks of God, feels strange in His presence, and for that reason when he meets his Maker in communion face to face, he stands in awe and reverence, as a servant would approach a king or a celebrity, fearing that a *faux pas*

111

might lead to severe penalty. In spite of the fact that prayers in the old *siddur* speak of God in terms of the "King of kings" before whom the worshipper must tremble, and there are times when that feeling does dominate the heart of the truly pious, nevertheless, the Orthodox Jew has a feeling of intimacy and an awareness of nearness of the Creator which is apparent in his conduct and in his thoughts when at prayer, particularly in time of crisis when his soul cries out for help, in the knowledge that "the Lord is nigh unto them that are of a broken-heart" (Ps. 34:19).

The classical illustration is the legend of the conversation with God conducted by Rabbi Levi Yitzhak of Berditchev. The spirit of the conversation has been embodied in the hasidic songs which form part of the repertoire of all popular Jewish singers. Before the Day of Atonement, when the fate of every Jew is about to be sealed, whether he is destined to be inscribed in the Book of Life or in the Book of Death, the Berditchever Rabbi pleads with God for reconciliation on the following basis: "It is true, I must confess that Thy people, Israel, has sinned. They have not obeyed Thy commands. They have been guilty of every crime. They have not kept the Sabbath and they have fallen short of the observance of the *taryag mitzvot*. But, Thou too, Almighty Father, has made Thy people suffer many wrongs. Thou hast afflicted them with sickness, Thou hast deprived them of their livelihood, Thou hast caused them to be driven from their homes. Let us cancel their sins with your afflictions and let everything be forgotten and forgiven on the New Year."

The conditions under which the Jews lived in the European ghettos may have been responsible for the way of life of our people. The spirit of mind and heart of the Orthodox Jew in the ghetto was intensely religious, and he had a deeper appreciation of the spiritual life. The Jew had to show that there was a difference between him and his gentile neighbors. They showed hate; he must show love. They were guilty of ruthless brutality; he must be kind and charitable. They indulged in drunken orgies and debauchery; he must display dignity and honor in all his relations with his fellow man. However, because of the restrictions placed upon the Jew by his enemies, he could not live where he pleased, he was not free to wear the same garments as the rest of the population, he was limited in his choice of business, profession or occupation, and barred from holding public office. No other people in the world suffering similar indignities would have survived. The Jew, too, would long have disappeared from the face of the earth, if not for that inner intangible spirit which he acquired from his religion. The aim of his foes was to bring about a demoralization of character, which ultimately would lead to complete collapse. But, while many idiosyncrasies were acquired, nothing happened to the character of the Jew, except to strengthen his determination and stimulate in his heart a stronger will to live and outlive his tormentors and outshine his oppressors.

However, in one generation, all of this has changed in large measure. Although beards, long black *kapotes, streimels, tzitzis,* and *peos* still abound among hasidim, young American Jews in particular fall easily in line with the norms of their environment, sometimes all too easily. But, it is possible to keep inviolate the sacred traditions of Judaism and at the same time maintain a dignified bearing in the eyes of one's neighbors without going to extremes. There are difficulties due to economic pressures involved in keeping the Sabbath and observing the rituals, but these difficulties are not insurmountable. Although the spiritual climate in the Diaspora is not conducive to piety, there are brave souls who keep the Sabbath holy by selecting occupations which will enable them to rest on the day ordained by divine mandate. Where Jewish feeling is intense, and there is a full appreciation of Jewish values, sacrifices for the sake of the preservation of the Jewish religion do not seem burdensome. But the person who has little or no knowledge of the history of his people, nor feeling for the ceremonies and sanctities of his faith, finds it meaningless to exert any effort, exercise any self-restraint in the effort to preserve a Jewish way of life. *Selbsthass*, the feeling of frustration which was characteristic of many Jews who could not endure the ordeal of Nazi tyranny, can be attributed to their failure to understand the reason why they were being persecuted as Jews. They were not Jews in spirit. There was nothing Jewish in their way of life which distinguished them from their neighbors. It was a regrettable accident, they felt, that they were born from Jewish parents. Their Jewishness was an *unglick*, a misfortune.

There was a vast difference between the assimilated and dehydrated Jew in Germany and the valiant heroes of the Warsaw Ghetto. The Jews of Warsaw fought back with a power of the spirit which has become immortalized. Their defeat was their greatest triumph. The cannibalism of the Nazis will forever remain as a nightmare; the stigma of Cain will forever be branded upon their foreheads, but the denizens of the European ghettos will go down in history as the saints and martyrs who offered their lives as a burnt offering for the sins of mankind, and for the redemption of the human soul.

XX

REFORM JUDAISM

The Reform movement in Judaism traces its origin to Moses Mendelssohn, the philosopher and translator of the Bible. Mendelssohn himself did not advocate radical changes in Jewish religious practice, but his disciples, beginning with David Friedlander, accepted only that phase of Mendelssohn's rationalism which appealed to them, leading to a repudiation of the spirit of traditional, or as we may call it, "Orthodox" Judaism to which he was loyal. Mendelssohn sought to reconcile world culture with our ancestral faith. If his disciples and students had emulated his example, Judaism might have followed a different course.

It was Mendelssohn's aim to make the treasures of Jewish lore accessible to the masses, and he proceeded to translate the Bible into German. That catapulted the centrifugal forces into motion. Interest drifted toward the development of *Judische Wissenschaft*, the scientific approach to history of our people, its contribution in the fields of literature, art, science and the entire gamut of human knowledge, and away from ritual observances, from the study of the Torah as divine wisdom, and the exercise of piety which characterized the "old school."

The accomplishments in the spread of *Wissenschaft* were indeed lauditory on the part of the early scholars, but the cost was likewise heavy. In spite of the fact that it is claimed that "Reform Judaism came into being a half century after the impact of the Emancipation for the very purpose of halting the flow of Jews out of Judaism," there was a decided tendency to become enamoured of foreign culture which colored every phase of Jewish learning. Foreignisms influenced Judaism and threatened to change the entire character of the Jew, often resulting in complete assimilation.

The translation of the Bible into German did not serve the purpose which Mendelssohn hoped to attain. Instead of making the student of the Bible more Jewishly-minded, bringing him closer to original sources, the readers of the German version of the Scriptures were attracted to German *Kultur*, to the German philosophers and toward secular learning in general. The Torah became not a holy book, with a supernatural halo, but a "great literary masterpiece."

The hope that Judaism would influence German culture resulted in the reverse—German philosophy magnetized Jewish thought. This is reminiscent of the story of the Jewish father who lived on New York's lower East side. He had a son of whom he was very proud, and having en-

joyed outstanding success in his financial ventures, he was
desirous of providing the best possible education for his
heir. He decided to send the boy to Oxford University. There
he could acquire an ability to express himself in literary
English which becomes a polished gentleman and which, he
felt, was not possible in the environment in which he lived.
After a period of time had elapsed, the father went to visit
his son and met the professor, mentor and guide of the
young student. "How is my son doing?" the father asked
eagerly. "He must be speaking a poifect English by this
time." "Soitenly," answered the professor, "a poifect
English."

Why was the translation of the Bible regarded as a sin?
Not because translation into a foreign language is wrong
per se. The need for making the scriptures intelligible to
the populace was always an important project in the Jewish
educational endeavor. There is no other way to account
for the myriad of commentaries in every language which
scholars of every generation contributed to the advancement of biblical knowledge. The Talmud records the custom of placing the *meturgamon,* or translator, near the
reader of the weekly portion of the Torah, to interpret the
verses to the congregation, who knew little Hebrew. The
translation was in Aramaic, which is the language in which
the bulk of the Talmud is recorded. The Mishna is Hebrew,
but the Gemara, the exposition of the Mishnaic texts, is
for the most part in the vernacular, Aramaic, which was
the conversational language of the Jews in talmudic times.

Moreover, the Talmud contains scores of Greek terms,
and many of the Greek expressions became well ingrained
in the talmudic vocabulary, even as foreign terms are embodied today in English. Borrowing is a common practice
in all languages where contacts are close, and Hebrew is
no exception. That is why *synagogue, sanhedrin, prosbul,
apitropos, epistoli* and hundreds of other technical phrases
of non-Hebrew origin have become naturalized in talmudic
citizenship, as it were, without the slightest feeling that
they do not belong.

Nevertheless, the rabbis rejected the Septuagint because they feared that the effect would be entirely different from the anticipation. The hope of popularizing the Bible and the Hebraic treasures among the uninformed was frustrated. Instead, Greek and Greek culture in the time of the Septuagint, and German and German culture in the period following Mendelssohn were enthroned, while Judaism became the handmaid and was relegated to the background. To be "cultured" came to mean to speak the language of the land perfectly and be able to quote from the literary works of its writers and philosophers. The Hellenists in ancient days and the reformers in our day have followed the same pattern, with a similar divisive effect upon the traditions of the Jewish faith.

David Friedlander, the disciple of Mendelssohn and his immediate successor, led the movement of Jewish assimilation and the Germanization of Jewish life. He founded the Judische Freischule in Berlin in 1778, and translated the prayer book into German, believing that he was following the footsteps of the master. He exerted the full weight of his influence and ability to introduce radical changes in the rituals of Judaism, repudiating the authority of the rabbis and rejecting the codes which have guided Jewish religious conduct throughout the centuries. He showed the direction from which the Reform wind was blowing. The destination which he reached very early in his career and the new dispensation which he sought to institute, indicated the results which must ensue if reform were allowed free rein without control. He expressed his willingness to accept baptism and be converted to Christianity. Friedlander addressed an anonymous letter to the chief consistorial councillor in Berlin, in which he made application for admission into the Christian Church, with the condition that he would be free to deny the divinity of the Nazarene and be excused from participation in the rites of the Church. The answer was a sharp rebuff. The Church would have nothing to do with straddlers who "halt between two opinions."

Friedlander and his followers found it difficult to maintain an even keel, to live Jewishly in keeping with the traditions of their people, and at the same time keep abreast of the dominant cultural environment in which they lived. But the rebuke of the Church should have convinced them that it is not necessary to surrender Jewish religious principles to placate Christian neighbors, and that there is nothing in Judaism which conflicts in any way with the general cultural surroundings or prevents the Jew from becoming completely integrated into the community. Friedlander should have learned the lesson of religious honesty and consistency, which the Jew has maintained throughout all the years in which he has suffered indignities, rejecting with contempt all attempts to make him compromise his convictions.

How else can we explain the urge to join the church other than by the discomfort which the assimilationist experiences in bearing the burden of his Judaism? It would appear that Friedlander labored under an inferiority complex, and sought to free himself by affecting a complete change of religious affiliation, yet he still retained mental reservations and was restrained by an inhibition which could not be entirely conquered. If the chief consistorial councillor had accepted the terms which Friedlander presented, it is entirely probable that in time the terms would have been forgotten. The second generation might not have regarded the Christian doctrines and the rites of the Church as insuperable obstacles to interfere with a complete integration into the Christian community.

The Protestant Reformation was in the air, and in keeping with the familiar saying, *"wie es cristelt sich zo judelt es sich,"* imitating Christian example, Judaism likewise had to be reformed. The old-fashioned had to be discarded. New thought had to replace the old. It was a sign of progress to scoff at the ancient customs and traditions. The loyalist was looked down upon with disdain as a reactionary and a fanatic. Little did the reformers realize that in their own set ideas, there may, at times, be more fanaticism than in fundamentalist tenets.

118

The proponents of Reform Judaism found their rationale for radical changes they made unilaterally without consultation or conferences with rabbinic authorities, in the impact of the Emancipation which opened the gates of the ghettos for the Jews and brought them into contact with men of other religions and cultures. We have already seen how many Jews were blinded by the false rays of Emancipation, and began to break their ties to the Jewish religion and the Jewish past. They drifted in many directions. Some followed the line of the Haskalah movement, and substituted secular Yiddish and Hebrew culture for the Torah and rabbinic lore which the Jewish saints and scholars developed and nurtured during the nineteen centuries of the Diaspora. Many lost their moorings completely, repudiated their heritage, and forsook the fountain of living waters. The prophet Jeremiah complained in his day: "For my people have committed two evils: They have forsaken me, the fountain of living waters, and hewed them out cisterns, broken cisterns that can hold no water" (Jer. 2:13). The Jew who had been confined to the ghetto and who had suffered cruelly for his faith, was made ecstatic by the announcement that now the sun of freedom had arisen. He was blinded in the belief that at long last the Messiah had come, or at least the *"ikve hamashiach,* the footfalls of the Messiah" were audible in the distance. Comparing the dinginess of the ghetto with the "exhilarating cosmos" of western culture and enlightenment, a sense of inferiority possessed him to the extent that he was willing to barter his birthright for a mess of pottage. Some Jews took seriously the words of Comte Clemento Tonnere, the champion of Jewish Emancipation, who indicated the terms of the bargain which offered the Jews full human rights when he declared: "To Jews as Jews, nothing; to Jews as men, everything." It was the avowed purpose of Reform to stop this assimilation and halt the flow of Jews away from Judaism.

There were two goals which Friedlander attempted to achieve which were vital to the welfare of our people and worthy of full support. But, the methods he employed for their realization were questionable.

The first of these goals was political equality. Friedlander's great ambition was to fight for equal civic rights for a people that was just emerging from the darkness of the Middle Ages. The era of emancipation was dawning on the world. The Jew had endured more than his share of misery at the hands of a cruel destiny. He cried out for surcease from the humiliation which had been heaped upon him during the holocaust of the Galut. The enjoyment of equal rights and duties with all other human beings was one of the fundamental principles of Judaism, but the outside world gave little heed to the message of human oneness which the Bible sought to inculcate. But now, new winds were blowing. The Jew began to feel that perhaps there was hope of a new world in which he could find his allotted place. He was desperate in his longing to grasp the coveted prize of security and peace.

For the Jew who was immersed in his Jewish religious life and in the spiritual world in which he lived, who found his satisfaction in the glorious past, who felt close to the great masters of yesteryear, and who had the unconquerable hope that ultimately the Messiah would arrive through the grace of God, the new promise of emancipation held no attraction whatsoever. He was convinced that a change of heart could not be effected over night, that the thin veneer of social refinement which was manifest in the circles of the elite and the growing fraternization between Christians and Jews was not based upon a solid foundation. It was only on the surface; deep down there were still the same hatreds, prejudices and brutality. The pious Jew would wait. He had waited for two thousand years. He could afford to wait longer. As a member of an eternal people time had no significance. He found solace in the words of Maimonides, contained in one of the articles of creed: "I believe with a perfect heart in the coming of the Messiah, and though he tarry, I will wait daily for his coming." At any rate, the genuine, tradition-minded Jew would never think of compromising with his sacred ideals, which to him meant perfidy and treachery.

However, to the weaklings who could not withstand the strain, the means justified the end. Life meant nothing to them, if misery and suffering must be their lot. After all, Judaism must bring a measure of happiness. And if it fails to do so, there must be something wrong with Judaism. They began to reflect upon the persecutions which the devotees of Judaism had to endure in every age and land. Was it possible that the whole world was wrong and the Jew, who numbered but a small segment of the global population, right? Living as a Jew brought only frustration and blighted hopes. The Jew was beginning to lose faith in himself and to lose the faith which was the essential part of himself. Perhaps the Jew himself was to blame for the enmity which he aroused. There must be something about the Jew which arouses resentment and antagonism! If the Jew would remove the objectionable features which set him apart from his neighbor, and live his life in a closer approximation to the general environment, he would be unnoticed and unmolested.

There are two means which the world of nature surrounding us employs to meet the challenge of hostile neighbors. One is by fortification through sheer physical strength, weapons, or defense, to ward off attack. Another, is to escape detection by means of camouflage. Various creatures succeed in thwarting the enemy by developing a covering of hair, skin or feathers which matches the foliage or the haunts in which they live. The survival of the species has been achieved by the animals which succeeded in secreting themselves most effectively. By the same token, the art of camouflage is an integral part of modern military strategy.

The effectiveness of escape by means of camouflage cannot be denied. But there comes a time when direct confrontation takes place and when it is necessary to meet face to face with the adversary. Today, when the danger of starting a war hangs on a hair and threatens every area of human habitation and not merely the battlefield, when the atomic bomb brings its total destruction to those who are exposed as well as to those who may hide in secrecy, camouflage becomes a travesty.

Friedlander seemed to have adopted a policy of camouflage and escapism in the reforms which he championed. The passing of the equality law of 1812, which he interpreted as the culmination of his efforts, induced him to publish a declaration calling upon the Jews to show their appreciation for the gift which they had received at the hands of the state. The program is indicated in the long title of his work: "Concerning the necessity of changing the form of divine worship in the synagogue as a result of the new organization of Jewry in the Prussian states." But disillusionment had to set in. The willingness of the Jews, as expressed by Friedlander, to capitulate to the Christian world was interpreted as a sign of weakness. Jewish emancipation was not realized because of the political reaction which followed the War of Liberation. But the Christians capitalized upon the opportunity to engage in missionary activities and to capture the Jewish soul. Friedlander saw his mistake, and endeavored to combat the forces which were arrayed against his people. He used his literary talents to argue against the attempt to convert the Jew and endeavored to plead for tolerance, on the basis of liberal thought which the period of Enlightenment, for a time, seemed to espouse. But it was all in vain. Emancipation could never be gained by endeavoring to placate the enemy, by apologetics, by reasoning, by an appeal for clemency and mercy. Appeasement, by which Friedlander hoped to gain his objective, has proven time and again to be a step toward humiliation. Appeasement has never won an honorable peace. There is an old saying: "Never explain or apologize. Your friends do not need it, and your enemies will not believe you anyway." We do not please our Christian neighbors by emasculating our Jewishness and indicating our approval of their condemnation of our way of life. True Christians who are our friends and who truly appreciate what the Jewish contribution has meant to the advancement of civilization are provoked when the sanctities of our traditions are brazenly flouted. Pious Christians expect Jews to be loyal to the teaching of the Bible and the codes which have been hallowed by universal adoption.

Some years ago, the great educator and humanitarian, Dr. Charles W. Eliot, one time President of Harvard, was invited to address the Harvard Menorah Society at the Hotel Lenox in Boston (May 5, 1913). He took occasion at the time to speak frankly and with utter candor as a friend of our people, and revealed a sore spot in Judaism as a doctor would diagnose an ailment. It hurts, but it is true. The following is a portion of the address as it was published at the time.

"I was taking luncheon with a friend at Columbia University one day, and just as we were having a quiet and enjoyable luncheon, suddenly, hurriedly, six young Jews and Jewesses, three of each sort, very noisily came up to the table adjoining the one at which my friend and I were sitting and proceeded to give orders for their luncheon, each giving his own, all so very loudly, that I could not help hearing every word that they said to the waiter. Their lunches seemed to be selected rather on purpose to show that they were no longer conforming to Jewish methods and ceremonials. One of the dishes ordered, I remember, was pork, for instance. I could hardly describe how painful that process was. It is a bad example for all of us, all the other people, that young Jewish people are falling away from the practices of their fathers."

There was no animus in the words of the Dr. Eliot. He was concerned with the effect that violation of *any* law, wherever manifest, would exert upon society in general. As an educator he knew the imperative need for discipline. The break down of discipline in one phase of human life must be followed by a concomitant degeneration of all of life. It was that phase of religious lawlessness which distressed the president of Harvard University.

Even though Christians may themselves be guilty of

laxity and indifference toward their own religious obligations, they expect more of the Jew. For the Jews are regarded as God's chosen people, in spite of the protestations of some of our theologians who repudiate that doctrine. Christians expect the Jews to set the example of piety and religious integrity, and when religion is trampled under foot their reaction may be articulated in various forms. For some, the feeling of ill will may express itself in every conceivable act of violence and persecution. Others may adopt a different course of action. In the eyes of many Christians, the decline in Jewish observances is an indication that there is something radically wrong with Judaism and the Jew. Hence, missionary work is conducted in an effort to "capture the souls." Missions to the Jews are still active in our larger cities. Their effectiveness may not be too serious and the number of souls which they conquer may be insignificant. They may succeed in converting a bad Jew to a worse Christian. However, there are other agencies at work which may not be avowedly devoted to a proselyting program, but which have made grave inroads into Jewish ranks, giving cause for grave concern. The defection to Christian Science, Ethical Culturalism, and other new dispensations which compete with and militate against Judaism, must be attributed to the defiance of Jewish traditional discipline which is condoned by the spiritual leaders themselves.

Jewish lawlessness may result in yet more serious consequences than the intrigue to effect conversion. The Reform movement in Germany aimed to gain for the Jewish people the full rights of citizenship; it was not prompted by desire to improve Judaism as such. Judaism was looked upon as a hindrance to the achievement of social, political and economic ambitions. But, what was the result? In no country in the world has the hatred for the Jew exploded with more violence than in Germany. Even the Spanish Inquisition and the *auto-da-fé* and its horrors did not measure up to the orgy of cannibalism which plunged Nazism into the lowest abyss of human depravity. The experience of the Jews in Germany should serve as a warning that appeasement is not a means of gaining a victory, but is rather a sign of weakness, of which the enemy will take advantage. And when the attack comes, the appeaser has no will to fight back. The hope which David Friedlander entertained was blasted, not only in his day, but more so in the days of horror which followed.

The second objective of Friedlander's radicalism was to harmonize Judaism with the culture of his day. The new movement was predicated on the admission that the dominant culture was the criterion by which to judge the merits or the shortcomings of our ancient faith. Jewish apologetics was reaching a "new low." German culture was right and Judaism was wrong. Judaism must be patterned and molded to conform with the new philosophy, it was declared. Otherwise, the Jews will stagnate. German philosophers began to compete with the wisdom of the sages of Israel. Kant, Fichte, Hegel, Goethe and Schopenhauer eclipsed (*lehavdil*) Isaiah, Jeremiah, Hillel, Rabbi Akiva, Maimonides and the Gaon of Vilna.

Now, no one will deny that many of the philosophers of Germany, and for that matter among all the peoples of the world, have important concepts which every cultured man should learn and understand. The Jew has never closed his mind to the contributions of the philosophers of the nations of the world, nor despised wise counsel from any source. Moses listened to the recommendations of Jethro, the priest of Midian, as recorded in the Bible. The Talmud describes the friendly relations and the interchange of ideas between Rabbi Judah Hanasi and the Roman Emperor, Antoninus. Every school child knows the legend of Rabbi Johanan Ben Zakkai and the Emperor, Vespasian, who granted the rabbi permission to erect a talmudic academy at Jamnia when he escaped from the siege of Jerusalem, even as the Roman soldiers were burning the city.

What a strange paradox! While Christians were turning to the Bible and Jewish traditions for their inspiration,

125

the Jews, blinded by the fake flame of cosmopolitanism, were repudiating their ancient heritage.

The inspiration of the Exodus from Egyptian bondage, was constantly mentioned by the preachers of Washington's day, and the story of the prophet Samuel, who protested against the popular demand for a king, served as the precedent for the liberation of the American colonists from British bondage. The extent to which biblical influence enkindled the hearts of the founders of the United States of America can be discerned in the design of the first seal which was adopted by the government.

The seal was drawn up by Franklin, Adams and Jefferson, and depicted Pharaoh sitting in an open chariot, a crown on his head and a sword in his hand, passing through the dividing waters of the Red Sea in pursuit of the Israelites. Rays from a pillar of fire illuminate Moses, who is represented as standing on the shore, his hand extending over the sea, in which the hosts of Pharaoh are drowning. Underneath is the motto, "Rebellion to tyrants is obedience to God."

The Old Testament teachings had deep influence upon the course of the American Revolution. The Puritans in England who fled their native land to enjoy religious liberty in the new world felt close kinship with the Jewish people. Their bitter experiences were but a repetition of the plight of the "tribe of the wandering foot and weary breast." Puritanism has been described as "the rebirth of the Hebrew spirit in the Christian conscience." The language which they spoke, the phrases which they employed to express their yearning for liberty, the communal life which they sought to establish, all were Hebraic in spirit. The Hebrew language was the "sacred tongue" because it unlocked the secret of God's will. The list of the New England Hebraists is a catalogue of the leading citizens of that period. Henry Duster, the first president of Harvard College, and his immediate successors, John Cotton and the Mathers, were Hebrew scholars, and expressed great delight in the knowledge of the sacred tongue. Elder William

Brewster revered Hebrew to the extent that his name was perpetuated on his tombstone in the language of Israel. The early American colleges included Hebrew in the curriculum and the popularity of the course among the students constitutes an inspiring chapter in American Jewish history.

The very structure of the communal organization of the early Puritans followed Jewish precedent. The meeting house paralleled the synagogue instead of the church. The elder resembled the rabbi in the performance of his pastoral duties, and the Sabbath spirit followed the injunctions of the Holy Sabbath which prevailed in Jewish homes.

However, the most potent Jewish influence on the mind of the early American settlers was manifest in their concepts of government and the administration of the laws of the land. It is to the Old Testament that they turned for guidance. Law was not man-made. Law was divinely revealed in the Bible, and the Bible was the foundation upon which the government was based. The entire civilization of America stems from the Holy Scriptures, and all of its political and social institutions can be understood only in the light of the Torah. The Biblical Commonwealth established by Moses was the pattern followed in organizing the three branches of the government of the United States: The Chief Executive was the *Nasi* of the community; the *eda,* a smaller assembly, and the *kahal,* or larger assembly, were the prototypes of the Senate and House of Representatives, respectively; and the judiciary derived its inspiration from Moses, who "Sat to judge between man and his neighbor, to make them know the statutes of God and His laws" (Ex. 18:16).

Greater service would have been rendered to the cause of human liberty if we were dedicated to the Judaization of civilization, and if we had capitalized on the intense interest in biblical lore which was manifest in the communal life in New England. Instead, Reform went off on a tangent, to discredit the Jewish tradition, in the belief that progress was being achieved. The Jews in Germany who found that they were oppressed and persecuted, should have emulated the example of the early settlers who left England to embark upon a great spiritual adventure in "the land of the free." But the Germanic influence, not the Hebraic spirit, dominated the minds of the early reformers who came to America.

The epoch-making events of our day have emphatically negated the two basic principles upon which Reform Judaism was founded. Reform was based on the false assumption that the utopia of human brotherhood had arrived, and the dreams of the prophets had finally been achieved. The naive belief that at long last the prophetic dream had been realized and that the Jew would be accepted by his neighbors on the basis of social equality was forever exploded by the Nazi holocaust. And the anti-Zionist doctrine that "Germany is our Zion and Berlin our Jerusalem," which many German leaders adopted as their slogan, was repudiated by the rebirth of Israel. Nazism and its horrors will forever be a warning that equality cannot be guaranteed to any minority in any state, while human passions, ungoverned by God's laws, still dominate the human heart. The salvation of the Jew rests, not in less Jewishness, but in a firm stand, in integrity, in loyalty to the pledge made at Sinai. The establishment of the Jewish State and the elevation of Jewish status in the eyes of the world surprised all Jews, especially the reformers who did not believe in Jewish nationalism and who fought the upbuilding of a homeland in Eretz Yisrael. That many Reform rabbis have been leaders in the Zionist movement does not alter the fact that "orthodox" Reform was opposed to nationalism.

* * *

The early founders of Reform Judaism in America came to these shores because they probably felt that radical reform would not flourish in Germany. America offered a fertile field. Here the traditions of Judaism were not firmly rooted among the Jewish population and they would encounter little opposition in comparison with the difficulties they encountered in the old country.

Reform had its American inception in 1824 at the Beth Elohim Congregation in Charleston, S.C. Forty-seven members of the congregation petitioned the vestry for the introduction of English prayers and for changes in the ritual. The inspiration came from the Reform Temple in Hamburg, Germany, which was used as the pattern for the formulation of the services and the emendation in Jewish observances.

But the real impetus came later when Isaac Meyer Wise and David Einhorn settled in the United States, the former in 1846 and the latter in 1855. There was a sharp clash of ideologies in their approach to Reform Judaism in America. Einhorn was pro-German to the extent of offering prayers in German on behalf of his *Vaterland*. He refused to preach in English. He had to leave Germany because his "liberalism" not only provoked the teacher who had ordained him, and who called him "an insolent and wicked infidel," but even alarmed the governmental authorities who viewed with apprehension the uncompromising and inflexible frame of mind in which he sought to introduce his radical changes. His temple in Budapest was ordered closed by the government, and he decided to settle in the United States. He became rabbi of the Har Sinai Congregation in Baltimore.

Isaac Mayer Wise saw the danger of the extreme reformism and the Germanic influence of his colleague and endeavored to combat the movement which Einhorn sought to prosecute with all the fervor of a crusader. Reform Judaism as it is practiced today in the congregations in America is patterned after the ideas of Einhorn and not those of Wise. If the ideas of Wise had prevailed there probably would not have been an off-shoot in the form of Conservatism. Wise was perhaps more Conservative in his day than many of the spiritual leaders of today who claim affiliation with that branch of Judaism.

Wise was opposed to sectarianism, and constantly preached the unity of Judaism. The two institutions which he founded, the Union of American Hebrew Congregations in 1873, and the Hebrew Union College in 1875, stressed the word "union," and not reform, because it was Wise's hope that the institutions would serve American Jewry at large, and not one segment or schism. "I do not wish to sever the bond of Synagogue unity," he exclaimed. Dr. Maurice N. Eisendrath of the Union of American Hebrew Congregations characterized the contribution of Isaac M. Wise to the development of Jewish life in America in the following terms: "'His (Wise) was no narrow, sectarian viewpoint. Long before the actual phrase was popularized by Schechter, Wise was a staunch advocate of 'Catholic Israel.' The solidarity of *K'lal Yisroel* was the burning passion of his being. Consequently, from the moment he set foot on the soil of the new world, he dreamt of a college of higher education in America that would serve and enrich the whole of American Jewry."

As we look back, we must admire the strong stand which Wise took in his denunciation of all the reforms which were being introduced, not as a positive contribution to Judaism, but in the spirit of negation. The quotation of a few passages from his writings will indicate that Wise fully understood the dangers which Reform held for the future of Judaism. He endeavored with all the vigor at his command to stem the tide. "Long enough Reform has been negative, saying what we do not believe, what should be abolished and changed . . . the community is tired of that everlasting spirit of negation . . . we need now a positive teaching, what we believe." Even more to the point is the following declaration:

"What would become of Judaism had we, like Acher, abrogated the whole law and thrown ourselves headlong into the embrace of the supposed spirit of our age and country? . . . The Jewish spirit in the body of modern Gentile forms is as farcical a deformation as it was eighteen centuries ago, and looks as foreign as it did then to the honest contemplative mind . . . all reforms with the tendency merely to abolish, to ape the style or fashion, or to innovate for innovation's sake, have met and shall always meet with our honest and efficient opposition."

He sought to steer the course of Jewish development along historic, traditional lines, in the same spirit which prevails in Conservative circles. He sought to avoid the chaos which must result from each congregation and each rabbi unilaterally instituting changes as the spirit moved them. There must be discipline in Jewish life. Wise was willing to cooperate with Orthodoxy and courted the Orthodox rabbis of his day, declaring that the Talmud should be the authority for the validity of any of the proposed innovations. He argued from talmudic precedents in the same spirit as the rabbis in the academies and yeshivoth, and endeavored to maintain the continuity of Jewish scholarly tradition.

It was for that reason that Wise was a strong advocate of two practices which Einhorn and Holdheim sought to abolish, namely, the Sabbath and the use of the Hebrew language. It is of interest to note that Isaac Meyer Wise conducted a campaign to revitalize the Sabbath in 1859, a century before the United Synagogue and the Rabbinical Assembly resolved to awaken American Jewry to the awareness of the Fourth Commandment. He urged his congregants to close their businesses on the Sabbath, because the "Sabbath is the corner stone of practical Judaism." His opponents were ready to substitute Sunday for the Jewish day of rest. Wise instituted the late Friday evening service on October 19, 1866, to check the growing movement to hold Sunday services. Today, almost all Conservative and even many Orthodox congregations hold late gatherings on Friday evening, the program varying from a complete service beginning with *Lechu neranena*, to a forum or an *Oneg Shabbat*, which is a compromise measure. We must view with praise the efforts of Wise to combat with vigor and firm resolution the modifications instigated by Einhorn and later by Kaufmann Kohler and others who were undermining the very foundation of Judaism. As Reform Judaism began to approach Christianity, Wise stood guard to stem the tide at this juncture in American Jewish history.

Wise was equally as emphatic in his insistence that the

language of prayer in the synagogue should be Hebrew. He condemned the ignorance of the pupils and the neglect of Hebrew studies. "Loudly and vehemently we protest against the unpardonable negligence of Hebrew instruction and the forgetfulness of our national literature. We protest against the new fangled Christian system because it is pregnant with the ruin of Judaism," he exclaimed.

He did not spare words in rebuffing a proud member of a Reform congregation who felt that Reform had reached the summit of its development with the complete elimination of Hebrew from the services. Wise was caustic in his reply: "Take away the Hebrew from the synagogue and the school and you take the liberty of conscience from the Israelites ... this is not the object of Reform—not on ignorance, but on knowledge the hope of your cause is based."

But all his efforts were in vain. Einhorn and his son-in-law, Kohler, were successful in denuding the synagogue and the Jewish school of the Hebraic spirit, and substituting an *ersatz* Judaism which was often identified with Unitarianism. Reform Judaism today reflects nothing of the spirit of Isaac M. Wise and his strong passion for historic Judaism. Like Moses Mendelssohn, who meant well when he began to modernize Judaism, but whose successors failed to follow up with respect to the goal which he had in mind, the good intentions of Wise were either misunderstood by his followers, or were deliberately distorted.

But there were men who trusted Wise and who felt that there was a great deal of merit in his efforts to strengthen Judaism in America. When Wise issued a call in an article printed in the "Occident," published by Rabbi Isaac Leeser, and invited the rabbis to join in a unification of all American Hebrew Congregations, Reform and Orthodox, he found sympathisers and supporters in the most eminent Jewish scholars of that day. Sabato Morais, Lewis N. Dembitz, Judge Meyer Sulzberger and others agreed to give him full cooperation. The word "union" was intriguing. The Philadelphia Jewish leaders accepted positions in the administration of the newly founded Hebrew Union College. Dembitz became the Chairman of the Committee on Curriculum, and Morais acted as one of the examiners at the college. In addition, Morais urged his congregation to join the Union of American Hebrew Congregations, which meant that he identified himself completely with purposes which Wise aimed to accomplish. Dr. Cyrus Adler hailed the spirit which prevailed among the promoters of the new movement, commending the willingness to cooperate, which was manifest among the leaders although they did not see eye to eye on issues of Jewish observances. In the words of Adler: "He (Morais) was willing to join hands with those of differing views, without giving assent to changes whatsoever in ritual practices."

What happened to the union which started auspiciously and which would have been of momentous importance to the development of Judaism, not only in America, but throughout the Jewish world? All efforts to bring about a reconciliation of divergent views were frustrated, because the radical elements were not satisfied with Wise's rightist tendencies, and the graduates of the Hebrew Union College, who were gathering strength, leaned toward a complete break with Israel's past. There was no foundation upon which to build a union, as Wise had hoped. The ideologies of the eastern European rabbis, who were reared in a traditional atmosphere, clashed sharply with the ideas of the rabbis who were inoculated with the germs of German culture and the new "enlightenment," beguiled by the sirens of internationalism, liberty and rationalism. The influence of Abraham Geiger and the German school of Jewish scholars was overpowering. The burden of Judaism with its restrictions hampered the movement toward the progress of civilization, as they saw it. Their philosophy can be summarized in the following observation: "Judaism requires merely the liberating breath in order to become rejuvenated from within." The false belief that science and philosophy would contribute more to the promotion of human happiness than the mystic teachings of the Torah and the ideals of the sages and seers

133

of Israel, colored their Jewish concepts and led to excesses in the violation of Jewish sanctities.

The "Pittsburgh Platform," which was adopted at the conference in November, 1885, constituted a turning point in the history of American Judaism. It meant that Jewish unity was guillotined and the dream of Wise turned into a soap bubble. The eyes of Dr. Morais were opened to full realization that Reform was destructive to Judaism, and that a movement must be inaugurated to check the flood gates before it was too late. All that Wise had feared, and against which he cried out at times in anguish of spirit, came to pass. Reform did become another "Protestant" movement in America. The Germanizing tendencies scored a victory over the true spirit of Americanism, which Wise aimed to inculcate into the hearts of American Jews. Reform became negative in character, and offered very little of positive Judaism to compensate for the radical changes which were effected. Hebrew was discarded from the curriculum of the Sunday Schools; daily Hebrew instruction was completely abandoned. The Sabbath became a farce. There was no Jewish spirit in the home to foster a Sabbath atmosphere, and no attempt to encourage abstention from business and labor on the Sabbath. The defense of the Talmud as the authority in Jewish law and practice, which Wise had championed, failed completely. Wise warned and stormed against Radical Reform, but he was snowed under by his opponents. It was Wise who characterized the movement as a "farcical deformation" instead of a reformation, but nothing could stem the breach which he himself had created by sanctioning many innovations unilaterally without conferring with his colleagues in the spirit of talmudic debate which he had advocated.

A new Karaism had come into being with the adoption of the Pittsburgh Platform which proclaimed the "Bible as the most potent instrument of religious and moral instruction." But even the Bible could be sidetracked if the doctrines enunciated therein did not square with the new spirit.

To quote from the Pittsburgh Platform:

"We recognize in the Mosaic legislation a system of training the Jewish people for its mission during the national life in Palestine, and today we accept as binding only its moral laws, and maintain only such ceremonies as elevate and sanctify our lives and reject all such as are not adapted to the views and habits of modern civilization.

"We hold that all such Mosaic and rabbinical laws as regulate diet, priestly purity, and dress, originated in ages and under influences of ideas entirely foreign to our present mental and spiritual state. They fail to impress the modern Jewish spirit of priestly holiness; their observance in our day is apt rather to obstruct than to further modern spiritual elevation.

"We recognize in the modern era of universal culture of heart and intellect the approaching realization of Israel's great Messianic hope for the establishment of the kingdom of truth, justice and peace among all men. We consider ourselves no longer a nation, but a religious community, and therefore expect neither a return to Palestine, nor a sacrificial worship under the sons of Aaron, nor the restoration of any of the laws concerning the Jewish state."

Morais was disillusioned by the heretical doctrines enunciated in the Platform, and he broke away from Wise and all the followers of the new protestant religion. There was no hope for a union with men who were blinded by the false rays of "enlightenment," who were unmindful of the admonition of the Psalmist: "Put not your trust in princes, in the son of man in whom there is no salvation" (Ps. 146:3). What a mockery to prate about the immediate approach of the "kingdom of truth, justice and peace," as a justification for the abolition of the Mosaic and rabbinic laws, and the abandonment of the age-old hope of Israel's return to its ancient homeland!

Morais and his colleagues revolted against the assertion that the Jewish way of life is foreign to modern man. It is a gross affront to imply that the Jew who maintains a kosher home, who observes the Sabbath according to the

135

rules of the Shulchan Aruch, who wears *talith* and *tefilin* daily, is guilty of acts not in keeping with the spirit of modern life. Are we to understand that the eating of bacon and other forbidden food will "further spiritual elevation?" If that were the case, the rest of humanity which is not bound by the laws of *kashrut* and priestly purity proclaimed in the Holy Bible would all be angels and paragons of virtue! It is a disparagement of the saintly character of Elijah Vilna, Akiva Eger and Chasam Sofer, to mention only a few of the spiritual giants of the past generation, and the thousands of rabbis and laymen who still adhere to the ancient Jewish code. They found no obstruction to "spiritual elevation" in Jewish practices. The presumption that modern rabbis are in a better position to attain a higher degree of sanctity by the elimination of the Mosaic and rabbinic laws is too brazen to deserve comment. The contrary seems to be nearer the truth. The spiritual life of an individual seems to diminish in the same ratio as religious observances are flagrantly desecrated.

There was no reasoning with the radical Reformers of a generation ago, although the Reformers of today are beginning to realize that Wise was a better guide to follow than Einhorn. This is apparent in the revision of the Pittsburgh Platform and the return to many of the traditional practices which were regarded as "antiquated." There is seeming atonement for the sins of the past, and it is indeed a hopeful sign that a closer approximation of the conflicting segments of Jewry will be effected.

It was the intention of Wise to "protect Judaism against the presumptuous innovations and the precipitation of rash and inconsiderate men," a fear which he entertained as he endeavored to establish some sort of authority at the Pittsburgh conference. But "authority" is foreign to reformism, because Reform was a revolt against the authority which has preserved Judaism throughout the long history of the Diaspora. On the subject of authority, there were two diametrically opposite views. Einhorn rejected the Talmud because of the fear that a hierarchy would be established

136

which would impede the progress of Reform Judaism in America. A code "would stifle free experimentation and transform a dynamic Judaism into a static and sterile formalism." This is the basic philosophy of Reform. On the other hand, there were those who saw danger in a *laissez-faire* policy, which encouraged a man to stand idly by and allow every vagary and whim to assume the status of sanctioned practice. Flexibility is effortless and convenient, while rigid discipline is disturbing and often hard to bear, demanding sacrifices and discomforts. To abide by a code means to be tied down to a routine, which may interfere with pleasure, and make demands upon time and energy.

But can society endure, or any group life function, on a voluntary basis, allowing each individual to do as he pleases? There must be rules and regulations for the collective welfare of the group. An individual all alone on an island does not need the laws and statutes enacted by city, state and nation, requiring inhabitants to obey or suffer the penalty which a court of law will enforce. Authority, however, must be respected as soon as two people live together. At once there must be a 'code' to govern their conduct vis à vis each other. If every human being were endowed with superior intelligence, would know exactly what to do at every given moment, and honesty and integrity would be universally harbored in every human heart, there would be no need for authority or for laws and governments. But, civilization has not reached utopia as yet, and perhaps never will, as long as human beings are human. The disembodied spirits, the angels, who inhabit the heavenly spheres may not be controlled by law as we understand it, but even they must obey the will of the Creator.

Anarchism was a political philosophy which had its day in the eighties and early nineties of the nineteenth century, attracting an army of intellectuals who threatened to overthrow every constituted state and government in the world. Anarchism was based on the theory that society can function without government or obedience to authority, but by free agreements among various groups. It was believed that man should not be limited in the free exercise of his powers, nor stifled by capitalist monopoly and by the dictates of the state. He should not be curbed in the expression of his will by the fear of punishment or by obedience to a chief, leader or metaphysical entity, which leads to depression of initiative and sterility of mind. His guide should be his own understanding, the action and reaction between his own self and the ethical conceptions of his surroundings.

The movement to enjoy greater freedom from oppression which was the motivation of the Anarchists gained momentum from the French Revolution, and its impact was felt in every field of human endeavor. Religion also was drawn into the vortex of the seething whirlpool of revolutionary ideas, as Jews and Christians alike looked for an opportunity to throw off the yoke of authority which was found to be too burdensome. Communism is today the most aggressive and the most potent expression of the revolutionary spirit which dominated the mind of men since the beginning of time. But communism has resulted in tyranny and abject subjection to a dictator.

However, anarchism as a movement is dead today, simply because it is impossible to conceive of any form of organized life without government, or authority. A revolution which overthrows one government or state does not eliminate authority, but merely substitutes one for another. The new government becomes more oppressive than its predecessor. Communist Russia rebelled against the tyranny of Czarism, but whether Russian citizens enjoy greater freedom under the Soviets than they did before is no longer a question. Absolutism may assume a different form, but it is despotic and cruel, nonetheless.

Democracy does not imply that "a man can do that which is pleasing in his eyes." A democratic society cannot endure unless there is a code, a definite formulation of the will of the group which is binding on every constituent member. The first project of the smallest club, which is the nucleus of group government, is the formulation of a constitution or a charter, defining clearly the objective, the *modus operandi,* and the rules without which nothing constructive can be accomplished. In the establishment of the United States of America, a constitution had to be adopted which was to serve as the foundation upon which the super-structure of the republic could be erected. In order to maintain collective security and communal stability, it is necessary for the individual to surrender some of his freedom and assume some obligation in sharing with his fellow man the responsibility of promoting the general welfare. Patriotism and loyalty are measured by the extent of a man's willingness to relinquish his personal comforts for the benefit of others, and for the benefit of the state. The recreant citizen is one who not only shirks his duties, but even goes further in undermining authority by engaging in all manner of corrupt practices, political scandals, and criminal acts of every description.

It is not easy to determine the areas of personal liberty and collective authority. Majority rule is a principle which governs parliamentary procedure, and is regarded as the basic doctrine of all democratic bodies. Without the operation of the majority rule, society would stagnate. If there can be no single minded conclusion with respect to a given project, nor a definite decision which way to turn, to the right or to the left, there can be no destination. To offer a simple illustration: If in a family, the father, mother, and children cannot agree whether to go to the mountains or the seashore, and each one will go in a different direction, and if the same disunity pertains to every aspect of family life, in the kind of food on the table, in their church affiliation, in their relationships with their fellow men, what will happen to family integrity?

Even in parliamentary rule, however, allowance is made for personal privilege, which is always in order. There are spheres of autonomy, personal conviction and unrestricted enjoyment of the right to live as one wishes—if one does not impinge upon the rights of others. There are many preferences which each person is entitled to enjoy, which enrich the mosaic of life, and which must be regarded as

139

sacred and inviolable. But these differences must not conflict with the general pattern. They must complement and make a valuable contribution to the sum total of communal welfare.

Liberty is a sweet sounding word, and the Jews, perhaps more than any other people on earth, appreciate the greatest gift which can come to any man, because the Jew has been the greatest victim of tyrants and taskmasters. And yet, "free experimentation in religion" cannot be included in the categories of the "four freedoms," any more than "free experimentation in law," or "free experimentation in marriage." Variations are permissible only to the extent that differences do not stir up conflicts. When two states are adjacent, and the laws concerning drinking, gambling, marriage and divorce, taxation, and other matters of human welfare vary in each state, the effect upon the citizen, who finds the same act lawful in the one state and a crime in the other, is confusing rather than salutary. He loses respect for all law, and this may account in large measure for the lawlessness, crime and corruption which prevail in society today.

Free experimentation in religion is still worse. Religion has an important role to play in society, in controlling the anarchistic, restive and ungovernable impulses in man. There can be no debate on the need for the discipline of law. Every organization must have some form of rules and by-laws, and every professional body must have an ethical code to govern the relationship between the constituent members and their individual and collective relationship with the community at large.

There is a vast difference between freedom and license, the spirit of *laissez faire* which would remove all inhibitions and restraints. No one as yet has found the formula which will strike the happy medium between freedom and discipline. There is always the danger that the scale may overbalance on one side or the other, and lead to extremes. Man in his impulsiveness follows the line of least resistance, either to extreme license where there is no discipline at all, or to tyranny and dictatorship where freedom is entirely non-existent. *Mirabile dictu,* even the most radical revolutionists who rebelled against oppression and exploitation and yearned for freedom, resorted to strict discipline when they gained controlling power. Witness the enslavement of the people in Soviet Russia, under the aegis of Communism, which was heralded as the champion of liberty and democracy, a "people's government" in which there were to be no restraints and no hierarchy or overlord. The frequent purges and severe penalties inflicted upon the rebellious individuals who do not keep to the party line, and the fanatic zeal with which fellow travelers justify every move of the Kremlin, is eloquent testimony to the fact that "free experimentation" is but a novelty which does not last long.

The Jew has been fighting for the recognition of minority rights in the practice of his religion and in the exercise of the opportunities which are vouchsafed to all the other members of the community. The Jew has been fighting dictatorship since the days of Pharaoh, and has been the greatest victim of oppression in the entire history of man's inhumanity to man. And yet, at the same time, the Jew has been willing to submit to authority in the regulation of every phase of his life from the moment his eyes are open in the morning to the time of retiring at night, and from the cradle to the grave. Every act of the Orthodox Jew is controlled by the specifications of the Shulchan Aruch. There are still thousands of Jews who endeavor to follow all the minutae of Jewish ritual, and think nothing of the hardships entailed. They arise early in the morning and attend services daily. They follow all the requirements for the daily prayer, before and after meals, observe the Sabbath in accordance with the talmudic rules, abstain from forbidden food, and endeavor to adhere to the *Taryag Mitzvot* with punctilious exactitude. There is no dictator that commands obedience. There are no police who will arrest the violators in our day, although the ancient tribunals did endeavor to enforce law and order in Jewish life by means of flagellation and other forms of punishment.

But, there is an inner authority, a conscience which impels every pious Jew to obey the Torah, and there is no evasion or secret dereliction of duties. We think of the legend of the heathen, king who claimed to possess power superior to the God of Israel. As proof, he issued a decree, but it required constant vigilance and police supervision to enforce its obedience. On the Sabbath day, the rabbi took the heathen potentate to a high elevation, and he pointed to the Jewish quarter, where all activity was at a stand-still. They observed that no smoke issued from the chimneys. "You see," said the rabbi, "Jews obey a higher authority and there are no soldiers nor police to check violations."

Such has been the spirit of the Jew throughout the ages. Respect for inner authority has been the key to Israel's survival and Israel's strength. It is because of the supreme command of God's laws that the Jew has been able to ward off all extraneous autocrats, refusing to obey the mandates of pagan and heathen tyrants. It is for that reason that Mordecai did not bow down to Haman, Judas Maccabeus did not fear Antiochus Epiphanes, and the martyrs of Israel defied Titus, Torquemada, Hitler and all other despots and inquisitors in their day.

The Pittsburgh Platform was replaced by a resolution adopted at a meeting of the Central Conference of American Rabbis held in Columbus, Ohio, in 1937. The preamble admits that a new declaration of the teachings of Reform Judaism is necessary. A comparative study of the two declarations indicates the change of heart which prevails today in Reform circles. The use of the term "Torah" instead of Bible demonstrates that there is a more sympathetic appreciation of the ancient traditions and a closer approximation to the ancestral vocabulary which had been regarded as outmoded and obsolete. The admission that the Torah, both written and oral, enshrines Israel's evergrowing consciousness of God and of the moral law, seems to be a reversal of the erstwhile repudiation of the authority of the Talmud as a guide for Jewish practice and Jewish thinking. The blunt statement in the Pittsburgh Platform, that the observance of some of the Mosaic and rabbinic laws "is apt rather to obstruct than to further spiritual elevation" has been omitted. Neither is there an exaltation of "modern civilization," which was always the trump card in the hand of reformers propagandising for radical changes in Jewish law and the rejection of the Jewish traditions. The "Columbus Platform" does not use the word "reject" which is found in the old Reform dispensation when referring to the laws of the Bible and Talmud as unacceptable, but rather the conciliatory expression "certain of its laws have lost their binding force with the passing of the conditions that called them forth."

But above all, the uncompromising anti-Zionist platform was discarded at the Columbus Conference. The new spirit which was undoubtedly influenced by the strong movement for the rebirth of Israel was made articulate in the statement: "In the rehabilitation of Palestine, the land hallowed by memories and hopes, we behold the promise of renewed life for many of our brethren. We affirm the obligations of all Jewry to aid in the upbuilding of a Jewish homeland by endeavoring to make it not only a haven or refuge for the oppressed, but also a center of Jewish culture and spiritual life."

Reform Judaism today is not the same as Reform Judaism of the past generation. Not only has there been a change of heart with respect to the attitude toward Zionism and the establishment of a Jewish State, but there has been modification of its position with regard to *halacha*. It was formerly held that Reform had repudiated *halacha* as no longer binding, but antiquated and obsolete. One of the provisions of the Pittsburgh Platform reads as follows: "We hold that all such Mosaic and rabbinic laws which regulate diet, priestly purity, and dress originated in ages and under the influence of ideas foreign to our present mental and spiritual state. We accept as binding only its moral laws, and maintain only such ceremonies as elevate and sanctify our lives, but reject all such as are not adapted to the views and habits of modern civilization."

But, a new spirit seems to hover over Reform Judaism as indicated in the pronouncements by the younger spokesmen of the movement. They took the liberal spirit of their elders literally, and began to think for themselves, unencumbered by the old shibboleth, which might have been radical in the early days of Reform, but which have become threadbare with the passing of time. One cannot live on a diet of sterile negations for too long. Spiritual hunger had to be satiated with a substantial meal consisting of recipes taken from the ancient books of spiritual foods.

The trend can be detected in a paper published by Professor Eugene Mihaly of Hebrew Union College, entitled: "Reform and Halacha—the Contemporary Relevance of the Mishneh Torah," in which he declared in language which seems to be so different from the "traditional" doctrines of the pioneers of Reform Judaism: "Halacha represents the totality of the demands of God as defined by Judaism and realized in Jewish experience. There is no Judaism without Halacha." It is indeed gratifying to know that Reform Judaism which has detoured from the *derech hamelech*, the royal road of Judaism, and from the tracks of *halacha*, has now been restored, and will continue on its way toward the goal and destiny of our people, together, it is hoped, with the votaries of the other segments of Judaism.

The recognition of *halacha* is in reality not a new orientation in Reform Judaism. The archives indicate that Rabbi Isaac Meyer Wise, one of the fathers of classical Reform, stated his position on *halacha* very clearly: "To be sure, I am a reformer as much as our age requires, because I am convinced that none can stop the stream of time; none can check the swift wheels of our age; but I always have the *halacha* for my basis; I never sanction a reform against the *din*." Even David Einhorn did not repudiate the Talmud: "Israel believes thee; thou art the medium through which the divine may be reached, but thou art not divine."

The question of merging the Reform and Conservative groups in Judaism has been discussed at conventions of the Reform movement. Rabbi Morris Liberman, leader of the

Baltimore Hebrew Congregation, speaking at the opening exercises of the 75th academic year of Hebrew Union College, was quoted in the public press to have said that "the differences between Conservatism and Reform are only chronological, quantitative and personal, not ideological." What has happened since Morais broke away from Hebrew Union College, where he was one of the examiners, and started the Jewish Theological Seminary as a protest against radical Reform? Reform has become more Conservative, and Conservatism has turned more to the left! Both movements have been approaching each other and at some point it is possible that the twain will meet, if vested interests and entrenched officialdom do not seriously obstruct unification on issues other than ideology.

Reform Judaism has come to feel that something more is needed for the spiritualization of Jewish life than mere external embellishment. The hue and cry had been heard for decades among the laymen that the service must be more interesting and attractive to bring the worshippers into the Temple. The onus is placed upon the officials to "do something" in order to induce the members to come and pray. It was and still is a challenge which every rabbi has to face, and his position is largely dependent upon the "gimmicks" which he must devise, like a producer of a television program or a director of a Broadway performance, to fill the pews. The rabbi is no longer a spiritual leader, but a "showman," and he must vie with the "showmanship" of the entertainment world for survival.

But many sincere leaders in the Reform camp have begun to realize that they are on the wrong track. The pronouncement by Rabbi Solomon Freehof, the scholarly mentor of the Reform movement, is an indication of the new orientation of Reform in its retreat from the radical approach to Jewish ritual, and its realization that mere ceremonials, regardless how spectacular they may be, are meaningless without an inner spirit. Prompted by an inner emotion, even a crude religious rite exerts a powerful impact upon the mind and heart. Where there is no soul-stirring *hitlahavut,* the religious fervor which Hasidism aims to inspire, even the most elaborate function is but a momentary effervescence.

To quote Rabbi Freehof: "As we consider the problem of Jewish public worship, we realize that in the breakdown of Jewish loyalty a century and a half ago, something was lost which we have been unable to recover. Historic Jewry looked upon worship, private and public, as a duty, a commandment, an obligation to God . . . It is this sense of obligation and inescapable duty which has vanished from Jewish life . . . In other words, the people ask the wrong question; will the service interest me? instead of asking; is it my obligation to be present? To have made Jewish services interesting and often, for those who come, inspiring, is not an inconsiderable achievement; but that is the whole achievement of the modernization of the worship, and it is not enough. We must work now to re-establish the sense of mandate, of mitzva, of unshakable obligation to prayer in the home and in the synagogue."

Rabbi Freehof is not the only one who realizes the danger that threatens Jewish religious life in the emptiness caused by the over-emphasis on over-awing the Jewish laity with the splendor of multi-million dollar structures, with dramatic performances in choral recitation, and flowing eloquence mouthing universalistic platitudes. There are others who have complained against the vacuum that exists not only in the Reform camp, but in the other denominations in Judaism as well. The sects feel the pinch of competition, as they rival each other in popularity and attempt to increase membership rolls and gain support in meeting the annual overburdening budget. A voice of lamentation was heard in a recent publication: "It (Reform) cared more for decorum and order in the synagogue than for *kavana,* the inner intention of prayer; it was more preoccupied with adapting Judaism to its surroundings than with affecting the quality of Jewish living. Much of this was necessary and constructive; but the other side of the coin is that this effort of adaptation also tended to convert Reform, in all

146

too many ways, into an easy and comfortable religion with a minimum of commitment."

Many suggestions have been offered to revitalize Judaism and bring it back to its pristine glory. First, the movement should cease to make Judaism a religion of accommodation, suiting itself to a pleasant family life. There is an imperative need for the shaping of a Jewish style of life in America, in which the terms *mitzva, kedusha* and *beracha* have significant meaning. We have been prating about Judaism in the abstract, Judaism for my neighbor, for the other fellow, and not Judaism for self. What promises most for the future of Judaism is to restore individual piety. We may criticize the garb, the crude mannerisms, of our fathers and grandfathers, but we must admit that we fall short of the degree of genuine religious feeling which they embodied. We are all beginning to realize that we have paid too high a price for the glittering tinsel which camouflages our vaunted civilization.

XXI

CONSERVATIVE JUDAISM

The beginnings of Conservative Judaism can be traced back to one of the most colorful figures in American Jewish history, Rabbi Isaac Leeser. He was born in Germany, but the character of his Jewish soul was molded in the city of Brotherly Love, Philadelphia, and quickened by the spirit of the American Sephardic environment. Believing that "an educated people is an invincible people," he organized schools for the study of Hebrew and the Jewish religion, wrote text books and issued publications. But his greatest ambition was to establish a college to train rabbis for the American pulpit. The Maimonides College came into being in 1867, dedicated to a three-fold purpose of 1) protecting the rights of the Jews; 2) providing a college of higher learning to train Jewish scholars; and 3) establishing a publication for the dissemination of Jewish literature.

The venture did not last long. It languished for want of financial support. But the seeds planted, later produced fruit. It is worth noting that the guiding principle which was the beacon light for the building of the college was the promotion of Jewish unity. The immortal words of Leeser may be regarded as the preamble for the movement of Universal Judaism which he endeavored to promulgate:

"Some may object to the movement, that it is not pledged to either Reform or Orthodoxy. These hateful words are always at hand when anything is being done, from the election of a secretary to a society, to printing a book, or establishing a college. The illiberal always asks: 'To what party does he or it belong?' For our part, strange as it may sound, we belong to no party. We commenced life with certain convictions and have not swerved from them. We know only Judaism; if you call it 'orthodox,' *you* do so, not we."

Here is a summation of sound Jewish philosophy, which should be emblazoned on the conscience of every Jew in every sect and faction.

Sabbato Morais was a member of the faculty of Maimonides College, and when it was closed he continued to hope that another institution would be opened for Jewish education. It is for that reason that at first he welcomed the efforts of Isaac Mayer Wise, the founder of Reform Judaism in America. However, shocked by the Reform proclamations, he called a meeting of the prominent rabbis of his day, including Mendes, Jastrow, Kohut, Szold, Drachman and others, in an effort to combat the corrosive tendencies of Reform. They saw the dangers of disintegration which were imminent if the reforms advocated at Pittsburgh were to go unchallenged and unchecked. It was indeed fortunate that men of vision held the lines of historic Judaism until reinforcements came from the masses of Russia, Poland and Galicia, and the ghettos of Central Europe.

Their call was issued in the following language:

"The undersigned, believing it imperative to make a strong effort for the perpetuation of historical Judaism in America, invite the cooperation of all Israelites who share their views."

An organization was created immediately. The urgency of a counter movement was felt keenly, and no time was lost in mobilizing the spiritual resources and proceeding to galvanize Jewish life in America in the spirit of historic and ancestral Judaism. They issued a clear statement of the purposes of the organization:

"The purpose of this organization being the preservation in America of the knowledge and practice of historic Judaism, as contained in the laws of Moses and as expounded by the prophets and sages of Israel in Biblical and Talmudic writings, it proposes in furtherance of its general aim, the following specific objects:

"1. The establishment and maintenance of a Jewish Theological Seminary for the training of rabbis and teachers.

"2. The attainment of such cognate purposes as may upon occasion be deemed appropriate."

Dr. Morais was very explicit in his interpretation of the platform of the new Seminary:

"At the basis of our Seminary lies the belief that Moses was in all truth inspired by the living God to promulgate the laws of government of a people sanctified to an imperishable mission; that the same laws embodied in the Pentateuch, have unavoidably a local and general application. Those comprised in the first category lose their force outside of Palestine, the others are obligatory elsewhere; but both the former and the latter, being of necessity broadly formulated, needed in all ages an oral interpretation. The traditions of the fathers are therefore coeval with the written status of the five Holy Books."

This declaration was aimed particularly against the Reform view that the Talmud was outmoded and had no binding force for the modern Jew. The new Karaism which Reform sought in a measure to revive was regarded as a

149

decided step backward in the development of Judaism. Karaism had failed, as Sadduceeism had failed at the beginning of the Talmudic period. Reform, it seemed, was merely a case of history repeating itself. There was every reason to believe that the same consequences would ensue.

Sectarianism was now on the march. The challenge of Morais spurred the leaders of Reform to erect barriers between Jew and Jew by introducing further radical changes in the Jewish rituals. It seemed a travesty to harmonize the actions of the Reform Jewish leaders with the statement made by Kaufmann Kohler that "Reform came not as a destroyer, but as a savior and regenerator" (*Menorah Journal*, Feb. 1916).

The extremes to which some of the reformers went can be seen by the action of Dr. Emil G. Hirsch of Chicago, who ordered the *Aron Kodesh* to be removed from the sanctuary on the basis that it was a fetish. But the storm of protest on the part of his own congregation compelled him to restore the ark. He was the first to transfer the traditional Sabbath service from Saturday to Sunday, advancing the argument that the Jewish Sabbath had lost its significance since most Jews no longer refrained from their vocations on the holy day. The Conservative Movement initiated by Morais served as the antidote to neutralize the effect of Reform. If the Conservatives had not stepped into the breach in time, there would have been nothing to save nor to regenerate. As we look back now, we see that the waves of Reform were beaten back, and that Reform today is not what the early fathers intended it to be.

*　　*　　*　　*

Solomon Schechter came to the United States in 1902 to head the Jewish Theological Seminary, and to mold it after the pattern designed by Morais. Schechter brought with him the spiritual materials with which to build Judaism in America, consisting of the wisdom of the ancient sages and seers of Israel, the inspiration of the culture of the day, and the stimulation acquired from the scholars of the modern historic-critical school of Zunz, Frankel, Graetz, Weiss, Krochmal and others. The confused thinking of the new generation of Jews emerging from the darkness of the Middle Ages needed a new "Guide for the Perplexed." Schechter showed how to bring about a harmony and a reconciliation between the Judaism of Isaiah, Hillel and Maimonides and the culture and philosophy of the modern scholar. Schechter could turn without the slightest feeling of conflict from a Midrashic interpretation of the Bible or Talmudic saying to the latest novel. He would often caution his students in class, not to derive their knowledge of Judaism from the editorial pages of the daily newspaper. His condemnation was sharp and caustic against the biblical higher critics, whose ideology he called "Higher Anti-Semitism," not only because their interpretations belittled Jewish contributions of civilization, but because the Jews whom they influenced were falling into the trap, and beginning to lose their self-respect, while echoing the same derogatory statements with respect to Jewish traditions.

Schechter knew German *Kultur* and condemned the leaders who succumbed to its influence. He left his native home even as Abraham, the Patriarch, left Ur of Chaldees. He turned away from the modern idolatry and paganism which had poisoned the hearts of Christian research scholars and distorted the vision of Jews who were hoodwinked into the belief that the sun of righteousness was actually dawning on the horizon of mankind. He called the eighteenth century "the century distinguished both by its ignorance and by the power of ignoring the teachings of history." He was a *Maskil*, but he deplored the extreme to which the school of Enlightenment idealized the intellect, claiming that reason could give the answer to all the problems which confront man here and hereafter. Schechter was forthright in his castigation of the dilettanti who, he declared, "cared to study as little as possible and to write as much as possible. They wrote bad grammars, superficial commentaries on the Bible, and terribly dull poems."

The German commentators of the Bible were taken to task for their attempt to undermine the traditional sanctities of Judaism. Schechter cautioned his students facetiously not to think that the Bible was discovered by Wellhausen and Cheyene. He likewise stressed the fact that without Rashi, Ibn Ezra and Kimchi, the comments of Dillmann, Delitzech and Ewald would have no value. He exerted the full weight of his scholarship in the refutation of the arguments advanced by the Christian scholars that Judaism was outmoded and that a new dispensation had supplemented the ancient faith of Israel.

Liberal in his views to the extent that he appreciated fully the value of any constructive thought regardless of the source, Schechter nevertheless had no use for the pseudo-liberal, who posed as a man of deep learning and great wisdom but who was a fanatic in his own notions. "You may call yourself liberal," Schechter declared, "and be as narrow in your sympathies and as limited in the sphere of your thought as your worst opponent." He guided his students and disciples in the direction of clear thinking in the light of the Torah and Jewish tradition, and warned them not to be led astray by the false, seductive, and disastrous glimmer of rationalism. He saw too many souls bewildered and befuddled by the new thought, prominent men who lost their mental balance by the impact of the intellectual forces arrayed against them. Schechter was a man of strong convictions and his leonine personality, expressed both in his physical features and his spiritual strength, exerted a potent influence on Jews and non-Jews alike. He maintained a close friendship with Professor George Foote Moore of Harvard University, the author of one of the most comprehensive books on Judaism, and with other Christian scholars. Schechter's interpretation of Judaism, which was embodied in his publications, served to counteract the evils which the German school of biblical criticism had unleashed. He channeled Jewish thought in the direction of the hallowed traditions of the Bible and rabbinic literature, and led the way to a renaissance of

Jewish culture. The basis for a live and pulsating Judaism, which would satisfy the spiritual requirements of the most cultured scholar, was laid by Schechter. However, the subsequent development of his philosophy did not follow along the same lines which he had indicated. New winds were blowing in Judaism and his successors were swept away by the current.

Schechter gained his financial support from the lay leaders of Reform Judaism. Jacob H. Schiff, Felix Warburg, Louis Marshall, and many others who were affiliated with Temple Emanuel and Temple Beth El, Reform congregations, were active members of the Board of Directors of the Seminary, and covered the Seminary's deficit each year, at the request of Dr. Schechter. The headquarters of the Seminary on 123rd Street in New York was the gift of Jacob Schiff. It is undeniable that these benefactors did not subscribe to the platform of the Seminary, nor did they seek to impose their ideological preferences upon it. This was a strange phenomenon in the history of Judaism in America!

It is quite possible that if Schechter had come to America before Isaac M. Wise and had organized the Seminary along Conservative lines, there would have been no Reform Judaism in America today. It was Stephen S. Wise who said that if Conservative Judaism had been organized fifty years before Reform would not have come into being. There is no way of explaining the interest which the lay sponsors of the Seminary manifested toward the Seminary. Louis Marshall was especially sympathetic. His closeness to Dr. Schechter is evident by the fact that the latter's book *Some Aspects of Rabbinic Judaism* was dedicated to Louis Marshall, Esq., Jew and American."

The feeling was also strong in the early days of the Seminary, during the administration of Dr. Schechter and continuing for a time under the acting presidency of Dr. Adler, that an alliance with Orthodoxy should be effected. Dr. H. Pereira Mendes, rabbi of the Spanish-Portuguese Congregation, whose Orthodoxy was unimpeachable, was sympathetic to the Seminary and labored zealously, together with the Sephardic Orthodox congregations in Philadelphia and New York, to create a united Judaism, but his efforts were unsuccessful. In 1917, Dr. Adler negotiated with the Union of Orthodox Congregations, in the hope that cooperation would bring the two parties together "in the very necessary work of conserving and advancing Judaism in America." It is unfortunate that the movement of consolidation was frustrated. The undercurrent in the Conservative movement for a revision of Jewish rituals, and the lack of strong leadership to overcome the trend to the left, blasted all hope for a union.

There were no great issues which could not have been reconciled and overcome. In the crucible of time and circumstances, many of the obstacles could have been dissolved. The passing of years and the increase in number of English-speaking, American-born and American-trained rabbis has moved Orthodoxy toward a relative leniency in the observance of Jewish ceremonials. Many Orthodox congregations tolerate mixed pews, hold late services on Friday evenings, and have introduced many innovations to attract Jewish youth, contrary to the wishes of the "Old School."

*　　　*　　　*　　　*

The basic ideological principles of Conservative Judaism have been outlined by Rabbi Moshe Davis as follows:

(a) the centrality of Torah and learning;
(b) the discipline of the *mitzvot;*
(c) the continuity of Jewish Law;
(d) the Hebraic character of Judaism;
(e) the positive influence of the American environment on Jewish group life;
(f) the indissoluble relationship of American Jewry to *Klal Yisrael.*

There can be no quarrel with these basic principles. Perhaps, even the most Orthodox would subscribe to these "dogmas," with the exception of (e) which may be questioned, depending upon its interpretation. If "the positive influence of the American environment on Jewish group life" means that radical changes are to be made in ritual and theological concepts, there would be an emphatic denial on the part of the traditionalists. Even Solomon Schechter made it clear in one of his declarations that it is possible to be a good American and still observe *kashrut*, wear *tefilin*, and observe the *mitzvot*. There is nothing incompatible between Americanism and Judaism.

This list, however, does not include other principles proclaimed by other leaders of the Conservative movement. Rabbi Robert Gordis, for example, has offered Ten Principles as the basis for the organization of an "organic Jewish community," or a "voluntary community dedicated to an organic view of Judaism." Similar in many respects to the principles enunciated by Rabbi Mordecai Kaplan, founder of Reconstructionism, Rabbi Gordis presents the following list:

1. The unity of Israel as a people, the world over, expressing itself in a common religious and cultural tradition.
2. The centrality of the Jewish religion.
3. The role of the land of Israel, to enrich all Jews.
4. The survival of American Jewry, vital to the Jewish people.
5. The survival of American Jewry as an integral element of the American people.
6. The advancement of Messianic ideals—one God, one humanity.
7. The acceptance of non-traditional Jews into a fellowship.
8. The welcoming of groups of non-observant Jews.
9. Cooperative relations with Jews outside the organic community.
10. Jewish education as the basic concern of the organic community.

The first principle expresses the goal toward which we strive, namely, "the unity of Israel as a people, the world over, expressing itself in a common religious and cultural tradition." But, we fail to see how this can be achieved by the acknowledgment of "the right of all Jews, affirmed by Jewish tradition, to fellowship in Israel, however far removed . . . from an acceptance of an affirmative attitude toward Jewish tradition." It is true that we can drive no one away, Jew or non-Jew, who is willing to make some form of contribution to the welfare of our people, either materially or culturally, but that does not mean that we accord his dissenting views equality of status with the traditional doctrines which have been hallowed by *K'lal Yisroel* throughout the ages. We may welcome their participation in Jewish life, but only with respect to the activities which do not conflict with the accepted norms of Judaism.

It is incumbent upon us to express our disapproval of notions which may constitute a menace in the achievement of our goals. Secularism, for example, will ultimately lead to a total repudiation of Jewish religion, if unchecked. In time, the Ethical Culturists and the members of the Community Church will be stricken from the rolls of Jewish membership. Putting a *"hechsher"* on secularism will not strengthen Judaism, but will drive more Jews into the secularist camp.

The secularists have taken over every phase of Jewish communal life. The secular organizations control all Jewish philanthropic, communal, political and defense programs, even education, and *mirabile dictu,* the religious life of our men in the armed services, the chaplaincies, and the religious rehabilitation of the Jews in all parts of the world. One of the most vicious attacks on the part of a secularist against the authority of religion in the realm of education is the declaration that Dr. Berkson, as published in the J.F.C. Bulletin of March, 1950: "The State of Israel . . . will check the doctrinal and congregational trend, and emancipate teaching (Hebrew) from the incubus of clericalism." Furthermore, he states: "The test of its (Jewish education) validity must not be whether it is religious, secular or na-

156

tional, but whether it has meaning or beauty." Can we allow such a challenge to be ignored?

The "Historical School" of Conservative Judaism has based its approach on the "evolving character of Jewish tradition and the acceptance of modernity as a positive factor in its growth." This vague concept of the "evolving character of Jewish tradition" has opened the doors to the confusion which prevails today in the conflict between Orthodoxy and Conservatism. The differing approaches to theology and Jewish law have resulted in the fragmentisation of Jewish life today, which in turn is responsible for the disintegration of Jewish practices among the masses and the break down of the organic interaction between the historic experience of Jewry, and Jewish values.

Conservatism which began as an anti-Reform movement, has fallen into the very trap which is set for the radicals. The unilateral attempt to affect changes in the *halacha* follows the same pattern as the Reform of a generation ago, and if unchecked will ultimately lead to the same destination. In essence the basic doctrine of Conservatism is not unlike the argument advanced by the early fathers of Reform Judaism in America, as expressed in the Pittsburg Platform in 1885!

Within the Conservative movement, a wide variety of opinions have been publicly expressed.

In the Proceedings of the Rabbinical Assembly, 1958 (page 95), Rabbi Jack J. Cohen delivered a paper entitled, "Halacha and the Life of Holiness," in which he declares: "I cannot see what is left of the halachic framework in practice, and I cannot see the value of attempting to restore it. Such restoration is neither feasible nor desirable. Life has irretrievably destroyed *halacha* as law." Other attempts have been made to camouflage *halacha* by the embroidery of "ethnic folkways," or by the more euphemistic term of "standards or forms of action." Of course, there have been strong protests against this method of rationalization. Rabbi Isaac Klein states emphatically: "In our work in the Law Committee (Conservative) we have assumed that *halacha* has the central position in Jewish life, and have subscribed to the belief of *Torah min hashamayim*, the divine source of the Torah." Once the premise has been acknowledged that *halacha* is the foundation of Judaism, there can be further discussion, pro and con, whether "its essential development ended fifteen centuries ago, or still goes on, and how much and what in the law is still binding."

It is clear from the writings of Dr. Schechter and from his personal life and the manner in which he practiced Judaism that he was opposed to sectarianism. He defended Orthodoxy in a statement which was aimed against the Reform movement and its claim to be the originator of an American Judaism:

"You may stigmatize Orthodox Judaism as un-American, and suddenly discover that real Americanism meant reverence for the Bible as the word of God, obedience to the authority of the Scriptures, which lay at the foundation of this country, and that love of institutions and memories of the past is a particular feature with the best American minds."

He deprecated the attitude of mind maintained by the Jewish assimilationists who sought to "out-pope-the-pope," in their effort to convince their neighbors that they were good Americans by being less Jewish, and offered as proof of their loyalty to America by discarding the ancient traditions and customs. Schechter demonstrated that a Jew could wear *talit* and *tefilin*, affix a *mezuzah* to his door post, observe *kashrut* at home and elsewhere, cover his head with a hat at divine services, at meal time and at public banquets, and follow the many distinctive ceremonials of the Jewish code, without violating any of the rules of etiquette, cultured refinement and social amenities often referred to as the American way of life. The hostile attitude of the assimilationists with their derisive jibes against the faith of those who came from *Ost Europe*, who were obsessed by a superiority complex which equated Orthodoxy with boorish, ill-mannered, ill-bred and eccentric behavior, was not a healthy manifestation in Jewish life and steps had to be taken to correct the distorted view. Conservative Judaism aimed to convince American Jews that the ancient faith could be adapted to life in the new world without capitulation of its basic doctrines or surrender to the external pressures upon unfamiliar customs.

The snobbishness and the social climbing of the parvenues constituted a sad chapter in American Jewish history. The movement toward assimilation and the demand for religious change was not prompted by a desire to strengthen the faith, to promote Jewish scholarship and to inspire the youth to perpetuate the high ideals of the Torah and Jewish traditions, but was entirely negative in spirit. The *nouveau riche* saw a deep chasm between themselves and their less fortunate brethren. Unfortunately, the manner in which Orthodoxy conducted services, the lack of decorum, the unschooled worshippers' lack of appreciation and understanding of the prayers, all served to widen the gulf between the segments of the Jewish population.

Conservatism, led by Dr. Schechter, felt the need of bringing the synagogue more in line with the esthetic tastes of the younger generation. Many congregations throughout the country were functioning without guidance, introducing innovations to meet the demands of the membership. They were not Orthodox and not Reform, being unable to adjust themselves to either ideology. They were desirous of maintaining continuity with Israel's past, but they could not subscribe entirely to the manner in which Judaism was practiced by the "old school." There was a vague feeling that something was lacking and that some modification had to be made. What that something was, nobody really knew.

For that reason, Conservatism was in constant flux, without compass, ballast or anchorage. The new school was subject to criticism for its failure to formulate a definite platform. It was called "fifty-fifty Judaism." The status of suspended animation was aptly described by one of the graduates of the Seminary in the words of the prayer which is included in the service on Mondays and Thursdays: "As for our brethren, the whole house of Israel, such

159

of them as are given over to trouble and captivity, who stand between the sea and the dry land; may the All-present have mercy upon them, and bring them forth from trouble to enlargement, from darkness to light." The precarious position of the Conservatives was a source of great concern for the leaders of the movement, and there were no two rabbis who agreed fully as to the nature of the formulation that should be made in order to bring law and order into the practice of Judaism. Many attempts were made to clarify the situation. In each case, the burden of the argument leaned in the direction of defining Conservatism as another sect in Judaism, justifying the changes which were introduced in Jewish law in accordance with the individual interpretations of the *halacha.*

Dr. Solomon Schechter did not pose as a rabbi. Nor did any of the Seminary faculty, with the exception of Mordecai M. Kaplan, exercise rabbinic prerogatives, although each one became a recognized authority in his respective field. Prof. Louis Ginsberg in Talmud, Prof. Alexander Marx in Jewish history and literature, Professor Israel Friedlander in Bible and Jewish philosophy, Professor Israel Davidson in medieval Hebrew literature and Professor Joshua Joffe in Codes, who constituted the original Seminary faculty, have contributed to the enrichment of Jewish scholarship and have left the imprint of their devotion to traditional Judaism upon the minds and hearts of their students. But, it was left entirely to the graduates of the Seminary to chart the course of Jewish life as they struggled with the various religious currents and cross currents which swept across the country. There was no set standard for religious practice. The most that could be done by the Seminary authorities, and there was no disciplinary control, was to establish the basic tenets of Conservative Judaism as embodied in the requirements for admission to the Rabbinical School, to the undergraduate as well as the graduate departments, ". . . must be members of the Jewish faith and loyal adherents of the Sabbath, Holy Days, daily prayers and dietary laws."

Within the scope of this general statement, there were wide divergencies of observance, ranging from strict Orthodoxy to as near Reform as possible without making a complete break. Several graduates did go over to the Reform camp, and many gave their own interpretation of what constitutes "loyal adherents." The conduct of services, the manner of keeping the Sabbath day, and the practice of the rituals deviated to a greater or less degree from the Shulchan Aruch, depending entirely upon the home background of the student or the inclination of his heart.

The faculty made no attempt to interfere with the personal conduct of the student and less with the graduates. The personality of the professors, their home environment, particularly on the Sabbath, which the students enjoyed frequently, the character of the eminent scholars and their consecrated labors in illuminating the pages of Jewish history and opening up the portals of the past to meet the great masters face to face, served to inspire the students and direct their thoughts toward the traditional point of view. But deviations were observed and rituals were ignored. The lack of a definite code of Jewish practice was lamented by the alumni, and every attempt to formulate a new Shulchan Aruch was frustrated, because no one had a clear idea of the extent to which the changes should be made, and no one had the courage to take the initiative to start the movement of revision and reform. There was resistance on the part of the older graduates who were inclined toward Orthodoxy, and who opposed any declaration which would mean a break with the Orthodox. The younger students were more daring and enterprising, and were ready to burn the bridges which connected them with the ancestral faith. The break finally came with the founding of the Reconstructionist movement by Prof. Mordecai M. Kaplan. Sooner or later there had to be an explosion of the pent up feelings which had been allowed to accumulate and which clamored for expression. But more about Reconstructionism later.

The Committee on Jewish Law and Standards of the

Rabbinical Assembly published a report in the Proceedings of the organization (1950), which revealed the magnitude of the task involved in the effort to maintain the equilibrium between loyalty to historic Judaism and the exigencies of the present. No agreement could be reached in the Responsa on the Sabbath, and it was left to the discretion of the individual rabbi to follow the opinion of the minority or the majority report. The issue was left just where it was at the beginning. The rabbis who leaned toward revision of Jewish law continued to interpret the law as they deemed best. It would ease their conscience to know that there were others who held similar radical views. On the other hand, the real Conservative who viewed tampering with Jewish *halacha,* either by the rabbi unilaterally or even by the Conservative rabbis collectively, as a menace to the continuity of Jewish tradition, struggled on, regardless of the action taken by the Rabbinical Assembly.

In course of time, the Committee on Jewish Law and Standards did proclaim a new Shulchan Aruch, which included changes in *halacha* in keeping with the spirit of the age, and the lines were clearly cut to distinguish Conservatism from the other movements within American Jewry. The demand was strong for a rationale of Conservatism, to remove the veil of uncertainty and ambiguity which had obscured the philosophy of the movement.

The attempt on the part of the leaders of the Conservative movement to inaugurate changes in Jewish law and thereby accentuate the differences between one segment of the Jewish population and the other, runs counter to the original intention of Dr. Schechter, whose vision of the future of Judaism in America was indeed prophetic. In addresses published in 1914, he said: "Our policy must remain to minimize the differences between Conservative and Orthodox congregations, not to emphasize them. Only in this way can either Orthodox or Conservative Judaism in this country hope to accomplish its duty to American Israel. It was on this basis that the United Synagogue was created."

It was Schechter's hope that the "United Synagogue"

162

would be broad enough to enlist the cooperation of all synagogues devoted to the cause of traditional Judaism, whether they styled themselves Conservative or Orthodox. He further declared: "Yea, in view of the danger threatening the historic faith dear to Conservative and Orthodox alike, we regard it as a sacred duty, that all such forces unite, irrespective of the differences which otherwise divide them. Such cooperation should not be construed as the organization's approval of all those innovations which some of the constituent bodies may have introduced. The purpose of this union was to conserve all those positive elements which they have in common."

Thus did Schechter lay down the philosophy of the Conservative branch, which his successors did not understand, or if they did, did not accept. There was a clamor for a more positive stand on the matter of Jewish law, a clear cut statement to the effect that Conservative Judaism is different from the other bodies, and that the changes it institutes must be recognized as binding and authoritative for all the constitutent members of the United Synagogue. For many years, there was repeated bickering at the conventions as to the philosophy and definition of Conservatism.

The criticism from the outside which spoke disparagingly of the ambiguous status of the movement, which some declared was neither fish nor fowl, was too severe for the members of the Rabbinical Assembly to bear. The aggressive young rabbis urged a positive break with Orthodoxy. But the more conservative of the Conservatives cautioned against hasty action which would serve no purpose, but bring about greater confusion and greater estrangement among the various segments of American Jewry. The Reconstructionist element endeavored to steer Conservatism in the direction of radical change but did not succeed.

It is indisputably clear from the writings and utterances of Dr. Schechter that he was both strongly opposed to sectarianism and to an unilateral decision to revamp Jewish law. He advocated the principle that "religious usages and practices which have the sanction of the community the world over cannot be set aside or nullified by the fiat of its segments. Otherwise the organic unity of Israel and the synagogue would be dissipated." A cursory glance at the ineffectiveness of the contemporary synagogue and the disorganized state of American Jewry ought to be convincing that the vision of the founder of the United Synagogue of America was prophetic.

In an address delivered before the Rabbinical Assembly in Pittsburgh, February 13, 1923, Dr. Cyrus Adler, then president of the Jewish Theological Seminary, traced the history of seminary from his own personal experience. Dr. Adler stated that he could say "without any hesitation that the Seminary was not the creation of any particular party in Judaism, but its purpose was to establish an institution for the promotion of higher Jewish education in America." In effect, it had rushed to the defense of Orthodox Judaism which was being threatened by the radical upheaval engineered by the Reform rabbis. Dr. Morais, who spearheaded the movement for the establishment of the Seminary had condemned the Pittsburgh Platform on the basis that "it revealed unwarranted antagonism to the five Holy Books, a denunciation of the general character of the Pentateuch, a serious charge against Mosaism as teaching imperfect ideas of the providence and the justice of God."

The Seminary was to be an Orthodox institution, bound by the laws of the Bible, Talmud and rabbinic authorities, having not the slightest intention of entering into a controversy with the Orthodox rabbis with reference to *halacha,* or opposing any legal enactment past or present. The term "Conservative" was used by Dr. Schechter not in terms of a party platform, but as a rejoinder to the Reform movement which aimed to destroy ancient Jewish values. He made his position clear when he championed ". . . the creation of a conservative tendency which was almost entirely absent or lay dormant in this country for a long time. Its aim was to preserve or to sustain traditional Judaism in all its integrity and by means of the spoken and written word, to bring back to the consciousness of Jewry its heroic past, which must serve as a model if we are to have a glorious future at all; but, at the same time, to remain in touch with our present surroundings and modern thought, to adopt what was best in them and, above all, to make use of modern method and system."

The founders of Conservative Judaism were definitely opposed to any alignment which would constitute a segmentation of Israel's forces. The basic philosophy of the work of Schechter and those who founded the Seminary and the United Synagogue was to maintain the historic continuity of Judaism, which should be allowed to develop not by fiat, platforms and resolutions, but by critical study of the original sources of Jewish law and Jewish history, in order to make Judaism alive and pulsating, to create a power for righteousness, and to enable Judaism to make its contribution to human welfare.

Dr. Adler, who succeeded Dr. Schechter as the acting president of the Seminary, endeavored to hold the lines and prevent the establishment of a new party in Israel. When driven to the wall by the clamor for a definite stand on Jewish law which would burn the bridge between Orthodoxy and Reform, he refused to make the declaration because he knew, historically, that any mushroom sect must inevitably perish. Reform, he felt, was a sect in Israel created not by the natural rhythm of growth and development but by revolution, by the impulse of the moment, which is subject to change at any time by similar impulsive action. Dr. Adler, like Dr. Schechter, made it clear that the Seminary "laid down no platform and adopted no creed, for we are of the opinion that religious platforms, like party platforms, are more often made to be disregarded than to be lived by, and that the surest guarantee for the steady maintenance of an enlightened Judaism based upon tradition, was the teaching of the accumulated knowledge and wisdom of the Jewish sages through all the ages."

And Schechter at the very outset tried to channel the activities of all who were to be associated with him in the upbuilding of the Seminary to the goal of unity in Israel.

165

In his inaugural address he stated his position in no uncertain terms: "The Seminary should be all things to all men, reconciling all parties and applying to all sections of the community. This school should never become partisan ground, or a hotbed of polemics, making confusion more confounded . . . formed to anticipate the mission of Elijah, . . . not only of solving the difficulties of the Torah and removing doubt, but also of bringing back the forcibly estranged, arbitrating between conflicting opinions, and giving peace to the world."

In making articulate his earnest desire to maintain the integrity of Judaism, Schechter echoed the prayerful hope of Rabbi Judah Loew of Prague who was especially emphatic in his plea for Jewish unity: "When Jews break up into many fragmentary entities, they magnify the dispersion. On the other hand their unity is a negation of the dispersion, and will in time make possible the full return to their homeland." (Quoted in Bokser's *The Portrait of a Halachist.*)

There may be many methodological interpretations of the meaning of Dr. Schechter's statement that the "Seminary should be all things to all men," but there can be no question of its intent, and that is to prevent a cleavage within the ranks of Jewry in America. Schechter felt that ultimately there would be an amalgamation of all the forces in Judaism, and that the extremes would some day find a point of meeting as the area of their differences would become narrower and narrower.

Only in one point did Schechter take issue with Orthodox Judaism, and that is, with reference to world culture. Orthodox Judaism which was nurtured in the yeshivot of Slobodka, Mir, Volozhin, and similar academies in Russia, Poland and Galicia, developed an antipathy to secular knowledge undoubtedly because of the persecution and the hate which embittered Jewish lives. Foreign books were regarded as *"tref posul";* to read them was a waste of time because it took time away from the study of the Talmud, and that was sinful. There is, perhaps, an ancient tradition which may account for the aversion toward non-Jewish culture. The *seforim hitzoni'im*, the apocryphal books, were kept out of the canon of the Bible because their ideological tendencies did not harmonize with Jewish tradition. The feeling existed that if a foreign book agreed with the Talmud, it had no value, and if there were conflicting views, it should have no place in the Jewish library.

However, in every country, and in every age, up to the last century, beginning with Babylonia during the Talmudic period and throughout the Jews' vicissitudes of fortune in Persia, Egypt, Spain and Italy, the rabbinic scholars were well versed in the cultures of their day. They mastered the literature and the sciences of their respective countries, and found no conflict between secular knowledge and the strict observance of the laws or the cosmic concepts and theological doctrines proclaimed in the Bible and fortified by the transmitted traditions.

It was for that reason that one of the major requirements for admission to the Jewish Theological Seminary was a college degree, besides a knowledge of the Bible and the Talmud. Dr. Schechter had come to America from Cambridge University where he occupied the chair of Reader in Rabbinics at Cambridge University and Professor of Hebrew at University College, London. A new type of yeshiva had developed in Vienna, Berlin, Breslau, Budapest and London, different from the talmudic academies in Poland and Galicia. The chief concern was not with *halacha*, but rather with the literary treasures which had been produced throughout the centuries. Codes was the weakest subject in the curriculum of the Seminary. Talmud was presented to the students not as a book of law, but as a source of historic research. The history of *halacha* and the historic background of the *mitzvot* and rituals was stressed, but the knowledge of substantive law was not emphasized. It may be that this was a serious misjudgment committed at the outset of the Seminary's existence. Nonetheless, *halacha* had a prominent place in the curriculum of the Seminary, and inspired by the penetrating analysis of the late Professor Ginsberg, master of Talmud Bavli and Yerushalmi and the entire field of rabbinic literature, scholarly-minded students and faculty members were stimulated to delve more deeply into the intricacies of Jewish law.

Schechter was interested in deciphering the old manuscripts which had been found in the Genizah in Cairo. The students of the Seminary were encouraged to continue the study of Jewish history and literature after the pattern set by Schechter and the members of the faculty who were associated with him. Inspired by the scholarship of Isaac Hirsch Weiss, Zunz, Steinschneider and the school of *Judische Wissenschaft,* Jewish scholarship was devoted more to the task of digging into Israel's past, blowing the dust off the old manuscripts, and discovering new versions and lost pages of the great masters of old. Dr. Schechter ruined his health by confinement in the library room, musty with the crumbling pages of the old tomes from the Genizah.

The work of deciphering the treasure trove of manuscripts which were brought from the Cairo Genizah is still unfinished; there is enough work for years to come, for many scholars. Like excavations which unearth the relics of the past, delving in lost manuscripts may open up a world which has been veiled in mystery.

But, however rewarding research may be to the scholar and enriching to Jewish science—and its value cannot be belittled—the real criterion of advancement in Jewish scholarship is the clarification of the philosophy of Judaism which will make Judaism more meaningful to the people. The past is the father of the future. Understanding the past is of great value in order to maintain the continuity of tradition and strengthen the foundation upon which Judaism rests. But the past is the foundation, and not the whole building. The superstructure must be erected to house the activities and furnish the living quarters for all the members of the household. Judaism and the Jewish people must live, and in order to give them life and sustenance it is essential to formulate rules of life by which they can live happily *vis a vis* each other. The Jewish way of life is determined by the *halacha,* which is derived from the Hebrew root, *haloch,* which means to walk. *Halacha* is the code of conduct which the rabbis have instituted to guide every act of the Jew, from early morning to the time of retirement at night, and from the cradle to the grave, reaching out into eternity.

The aim of the Seminary was to prepare spiritual leaders for American Jews, by providing maximum knowledge of the accumulated wisdom of the ages, to be transmitted to children and adults through the synagogue. Schechter envisioned the synagogue ". . . as the only true witness to the past, and forming in all ages the sublimest expression of Israel's religious life, [it] must also retain its authority as the sole true guide for the present and the future." For Schechter, the synagogue was the embodiment of all the creative endeavors of our people, including all the saints and seers, the long line of march from the early prophets to the modern rabbis and teachers.

The synagogue should represent the totality of Jewish life, the guide in all educational, social and philanthropic activities. It must be universal in character, the spiritual abode in which all Jews will be at home, a Beth El, a house of God. That is what Schechter meant by the Seminary being "all things to all men." He pleaded, not for uniformity, but for unity. He realized that differences have existed in the past, between Hillel and Shammai, Rav and Shemuel, Abaye and Rabba—and disputes will continue for all time. But, the differences must not be allowed to create iron curtains in the synagogue, separating one group from the other. All members of the family must be able to congregate in the one large auditorium, and pray together to the same God, study together from the same Bible, from the same Talmud, and derive spiritual sustenance from the same sources of wisdom and Jewish scholarship.

The entire concept of "Catholic Israel" has today become a phrase with a very hollow sound. Jewish preachers often refer to the term as the sublime expression of an ideal. Even Reformers have endeavored to claim a share in the

169

glory which the phrase seems to embody. A prospectus of the Hebrew Union College states: "Long before the actual phrase was popularized by Schechter, Wise was a staunch advocate of Catholic Israel. The solidarity of *K'lal Yisrael* was the burning passion of his being." The trouble was that there was too much fire and not enough light, in the "burning passion." What has become of the "solidarity of *K'lal Yisrael?*"

For Schechter, "Catholic Israel" meant a unified Jewry within a traditional synagogue. There was to be no break with the past, no conflict with Orthodoxy, no unilateral changes in Jewish law, but a continuation of study, research, analysis and discussion of the *halacha* and Jewish concepts based on every possible source of information, in which tradition, reason and revelation would all play their respective roles in ascertaining the truth.

Rabbi Simon Greenberg set a lofty goal for the Conservative movement in his plea to maintain the spiritual and historic kinship of all Israel and implement the Schechterian concept of "Catholic Israel" or *K'lal Yisrael.* He said: "We want to match the most ardent Orthodox in the practice of piety, the most ardent Reform in determination to make Judaism esthetically attractive, and the most brilliant secularist in making Judaism contemporaneous and relevant." It is a challenge which, if accomplished, will be a miracle. Judaism cannot mean all things to all men. Judaism is a philosophy, a way of life, which has been handed down to us as an inheritance, *l'tzaref bahem et habriyot,* "to discipline and purify mankind." Even if all these desiderata were accomplished—thorough knowledge of Hebrew, sincere piety, impressive services, and the most advanced cosmic concepts—the duty of the Jews will not be fulfilled. For Judaism is more than a creed and a ritual, it is more than a culture and a civilization. All of these are merely a means to an end, and that is to make all men cultured and all men civilized.

Judaism is a discipline and guide to right conduct. The mission of the Jews is to be the teachers of mankind, to be a priestly people, not only to learn the Torah, but in the words of the daily prayers: "To understand and to discern, to mark, to learn and to teach, to do and to fulfill in love all the words of instruction in Thy Torah." Or in the words of the Pirke Avot: "Not learning but doing is the chief thing" (1:17). Every Jew is expected to know the Torah and abide by its teachings in order to set an example for others to emulate. Every Jew must perfect himself, "to do justly, to love mercy, and walk humbly with God," and become thereby a living Torah.

XXII

RECONSTRUCTIONISM

Reconstructionism was conceived by Professor Mordecai M. Kaplan, and dedicated to the attempt to create order in the chaotic state of Judaism, by bringing together scholars, rabbis, educators, social workers and laymen for a reexamination of the concepts of Judaism. A conference was held in Chicago on February 21 and 22, 1928, as a response to the call issued by Professor Kaplan, Dr. Felix A. Levy, Rabbi Max Kadushin and Dr. Alexander M. Dushkin.

The motivation for this revolutionary movement was expressed in the following terms:

"Many thoughtful Jews in America are ill at ease because of the inconsistencies in their Judaism and the lack of a clear program for their lives as American Jews. They find none of the existing party platforms—Orthodox, Conservative or Reform—either spiritually or intellectually satisfying. . . . Many have felt the need for an authoritative modern program in Judaism. But we cannot wait for the meeting of authoritative synods, representing the whole

Jewish people and vested with binding authority. Such synods may not meet in our lifetime.

"We believe it important, therefore, for those who are dissatisfied with existing party platforms, to meet together periodically for earnest consideration of their problems as Jews, with a view of formulating Judaism in such terms and with such implications as will enable them to unify their lives fruitfully. This does not necessarily mean breaking with existing party organizations. It means rather proceeding in advance of present parties, so that untrammeled by existing organizations and vested interests, they may seek the truth in sincerity and in freedom of thought."

The philosophy at the basis of the Reconstructionist movement is basically no different from previous attempts to organize Jewish religious life in America. During the many years that Reconstructionism has been on the Jewish scene, it has gained a growing number of recruits because of the stimulating influence and dynamic personality of its founder.

The principles which Reconstructionism aims to enunciate, however, have further accentuated the differences between Jew and Jew, and failed to find the common denominator which should unite them. The most serious indictment of the Reconstructionist platform is the declaration that "the survival of Jewish life is by no means dependent upon unity among Jews or uniformity in Judaism." Jewry in our day lives under varying conditions of national and political life. Therefore, the Reconstructionists maintain, "the development of Judaism as a modern religious civilization will vary in different lands." However, realizing that disintegration is bound to take place if disunity is allowed to prevail, Reconstructionism attempts to effect an acrobatic somersault, in the statement: "In order that Judaism may maintain its international character, a central Jewish Homeland in Palestine is most important. . . . The continued interest of international Jewry in such a central homeland, as well as the cultural association and interchange of achievements with it, should prove a unifying bond, very helpful and stimulating to Jewish creativeness everywhere." Why we need a "unifying bond" or a central homeland if unity is not necessary, is a contradiction which has not been explained.

But that is not the only inconsistency in Reconstructionism. In order to allow for the full development of an American Jewish civilization as conceived by Dr. Kaplan, the American Jewish community must include all Jews "who feel physical and spiritual kinship with *Am Yisrael,* no matter what their personal philosophy may be, and even those who are not interested in common worship." Now, if diversity is a virtue and every Jew is entitled "to insist upon determining his cosmic philosophy in accordance with the truth as he understands it, whether he follow any one system, or synthesize the elements of truth as found in several systems, provided these are not inconsistent with his affiliation as a member of the Jewish community," why condemn the Orthodox, Conservative, Reform or secular nationalist as Kaplan does in his books?

In traditional Judaism, non-conformity did not mean rejection of the Jewish status. *Yisrael af al pi shehata yisrael hu,* "An Israelite, although he sinned, is still an Israelite," declares the Talmud. In Tractate Kiddushin 36a, we find the discussion between Rabbi Judah bar Ilai and R. Meir, with reference to the interpretation of the passage in Deuteronomy 14:1: "Beloved are the Israelites, in that they are called sons of God, still more beloved in that it is made known to them that they are called sons of God." R. Judah was of the opinion that the paternal-filial relationship only obtained when Jews behaved like sons. But R. Meir quoted other passages to prove that regardless of their behavior they remain sons. In Deuteronomy 32:30, they are called "untrustworthy sons." Isaiah branded them as "a breed of evil doers, vicious sons" (1:4). "Foolish people" is the descriptive epithet of Jeremiah (4:22), but Hosea is liberal: "Instead of that which was said of them: 'Ye are not my people,' they shall be called children of the Living God" (2:1).

An infraction of Jewish laws was punishable; the commission of a sin required repentance, restoration and retribution. But within the framework of the law, differences of opinion were always existent in the academies in Palestine and Babylonia. However, this is not what Dr. Kaplan had in mind. He believes that by conceiving of Judaism as a "developing civilization," it can retain its individual character, despite latitude in belief and practice. It is difficult to understand how the "individual character" of Judaism can be retained if there are wide divergencies of belief and practice. Dr. Kaplan offers the illustration derived from the teachings of the sociologist, E. W. Burgess, who favors diversification. To quote: "The family does not depend for its survival on a harmonious relation of its members, nor does it necessarily disintegrate as a result of conflict between its members. The family lives as long as interaction is taking place, and only dies when it ceases" (*Family*, March 1926, VII, 4). Dr. Kaplan would have the same situation obtain in Jewish life. The idea may be in keeping with the new trend in sociology, but it is not in harmony with the teachings of Judaism. The Jew believed in *achduth*, unity, and not in conflict. We have seen too many families disintegrate because of sharp clashes in religious ideologies. There is a distinction between dissension and multiformity. All the members of the same family need not follow one profession or occupation. There can be a variety of interests, but there is no conflict. It is hardly conceivable how family integrity can be maintained if the members cannot agree on the form of religion they shall observe, and if their ideas clash in economic, sociological, political, philosophical and religious issues. The right to disagree is undeniable, but, no game is ever won when members of a team do not pull together.

A midrashic legend presents the Jewish point of view regarding family unity. R. Joshua Ben Korcha was drawn into a debate with a heathen with reference to the teachings of Judaism. The heathen quoted the passage in the Bible: "There is a verse in your Torah (Exodus 23:), 'Thou

174

shalt follow the multitude.' Now, we outnumber you, why do you not comply with our form of idolatry?" Instead of endeavoring to explain, as the rabbi would have done in modern times, that minority rights and the freedom of religion grants the right of every individual to worship in his own way, the rabbi asked the heathen: "Have you any children?"

"You remind me of my trouble," was the reply.

"Why?" pressed the rabbi.

"I have many children," the heathen explained in a voice which was plaintive and indicated deep anxiety and vexation of spirit. "When they assemble at the table, one offers grace to his god and the other to another god, and they do not leave until they split each other's heads."

"And do you agree with them?" continued the Jewish sage.

"No," was the sad confession.

"Well then, before you force us to agree with you, bring about a reconciliation among your own children," said the rabbi.

The heathen hastened away in humiliation.

The disciples of R. Joshua who were present while the conversation took place, were puzzled by the rejoinder, and asked their teacher: "Rabbi, you refuted him with a broken reed, but what answer do you give us?"

He replied: "There were six members in Esau's family, and the plural 'souls' is used, as it is written (Genesis 36:6), 'And Esau took his wives and his sons, and his daughters, and all the souls of his house.' Jacob, on the other hand, had seventy members of his family and the singular, 'soul' was used, as it is written (Exodus 1:15), 'and every soul out of the loins of Jacob amounted to seventy souls (*Nefesh*).' Now, Esau, who worshipped many gods is referred to as having many souls, but Jacob who worshipped only one God is referred to as having one soul" (Leviticus Rabba 4, 6).

In a choice between Rabbi Joshua Ben Korcha and E. W. Burgess as the authority for guidance in maintaining family cohesiveness, we prefer the opinion of the former, which is more in keeping with Jewish tradition, and which has been the mainstay of our people throughout the centuries of exile. Had we followed the advice of Burgess, there would probably be no Judaism today. Despite their wanderings and the wide area in which they were scattered which made intercommunication at times entirely impossible, the Jews have maintained a family unity, in which the spirit of Judaism was the common bond which kept them intact. Holiday celebrations were characterized by a singleness of purpose that made the Jewish home the paragon of religious devotion. The biblical mandate was obeyed: "And thou shalt rejoice before the Lord, thy God, thou and thy son and thy daughter and thy man servant and thy maid-servant and the Levite that is within thy gates, and the stranger and the fatherless and the widow that are in the midst of thee." It will be a sad day for Israel when each member of a family will not be able to sit down at table on *Yom Tov* and enjoy the blessings of the festive occasion in a spirit of mutual understanding. If, for example, the father will insist upon the traditional Hagada on *Seder* eve, and the son will be unhappy unless he follows Kaplan's new Hagada, and a third will be dissatisfied unless the Union Hagadah is read, just what kind of a *seder* will there be?

It is a strange phenomenon in Jewish life, that the type of worship in the old-fashioned synagogue, when each worshipper *davened* for himself in a loud voice, from his own Siddur, in his own *nusach*, without regard to his neighbor's devotions, was characterized by individuality. Today, Reformers and Conservatives demand a uniform prayer book, and insist that prayers shall be recited in unison, using the same wording and the same melodies. It is doubtful that Dr. Kaplan who favors non-conformity in religious practice would revert to the old style of *"davening,"* and permit each worshipper to use his own *machzor*, and sing his own tunes.

To advocate disunity in Israel runs counter to every tradition among our people. It strikes at the very foundation of our faith, and frustrates the hope that Israel will ever present a united front to assure its survival in the midst of a hostile world. Professor Louis Ginsberg has brought to our attention the talmudic dictum, that "Israel went into exile only after it became divided into twenty-four sects" (*Students, Saints and Scholars*, p. 88).

Reconstructionism aims to appease the Jews who find Judaism burdensome. It gives them leeway to formulate their own code, or eliminate all codes. The only requirement is to continue nominal affiliation and identification with the Jewish community.

According to the Reconstructionist philosophy, "Religion, if it is to be vital, must be personal and voluntary; it cannot be otherwise in our era of individual freedom of thought." We question the validity of this doctrine. Religion cannot be left entirely to the voluntary inclination of the individual, to accept or reject whatever he pleases. Religion is the composite expression of the highest ideals of a community of individuals. It is concerned with the preservation of the group, the perpetuation of the principles for which it stands, and by which it can best serve its own constituents, as well as humanity. An individual member may choose to dissent from the doctrines which the majority has accepted. To that extent he enjoys freedom of thought. He may even leave the group entirely; but in that case, he is regarded as a deserter. Freedom of thought does not imply that a man can refuse to abide by established rules and still call himself a loyal son. Even justices of the Supreme Court who render minority decisions must abide by majority rule. Disagreement, if backed by cogent reasons and arguments, was never prohibited in Jewish scholastic and academic circles, but in religion as in law, individual opinion cannot be allowed to run riot. An individual cannot take the law into his own hands. Similarly, legislators debate the merits or shortcomings of a new resolution, and endeavor to convince their colleagues to accept their point of view, but when the law has been enacted, observance is no longer voluntary, but compulsory, and a violation is subject to the penalty which is indicated in the statute.

In a pamphlet entitled, "Unity in Diversity in the Conservative Movement," Dr. Kaplan expressed a challenging concept. "Following the advice of our sages that we should emulate the good in our non-Jewish neighbors, we should take a page out of the experience of the Protestant sects. Though they are divided in what they regard as highly important doctrines and religious practices, they nevertheless manage to cooperate within the frame of some of their most influential organizations and institutions." This idea is indeed startling and disconcerting. In the first place, Protestants themselves have acknowledged the weakness of the structure of the Protestant Church. They look with envy upon the strength and solidarity of the Catholic Church, where the virtue of unity has made Catholicism the most powerful influence, not only in religious affairs, but also in local, national and international politics. One may boast of the freedom which each denomination in Protestantism enjoys, and find merit in the feeling that a man is responsible to no one but his Maker, but the challenge of the Catholic Church and its universality of practice should set us to thinking seriously about setting our own religious house in order.

The Protestant Church itself recognizes this challenge. Three hundred delegates to the General Synod of the Evangelical and Reformed Churches voted to merge with the Congregational Christian Churches, proposing the creation of a new body to be known as the United Church. Other Protestant denominations are planning to take similar steps. If, indeed, one is to argue that we should "emulate the good in our non-Jewish neighbors," we should follow their example by removing barriers and building bridges between faction and faction within Judaism.

But it is not necessary to copy others, because there are examples in our own history of movements toward integration and consolidation. We don't have to wait to be shown the way to unity. For centuries we have been trying to teach the world the true meaning of the One God, and its corollary, the oneness of the human race. Why, indeed, should we imitate the example of others in the organization of our religious life! Throughout the ages we have been the Protestants, to the extent that we have protested against idolatry and all the evils which stem from paganism, which have brought strife and suffering to the human race. We should set the example in religious unity and harmony as well. The prophet Isaiah speaks of Israel as "the light of the nations." In his vision of the millenium, Isaiah holds forth great promise for the future of Israel: "And it shall come to pass in the end of days, that the mountain of the Lord's house shall be established as the top of the mountains, and shall be exalted above the hills; and all nations shall flow into it, and many peoples shall go and say: "Come ye, and let us go up to the mountain of the Lord, And He will teach us of His ways, and we shall walk in His paths" (Is. 2, 43). To talk about following the patterns of the other nations and religions of the world seems to be a complete reversal of Jewish tradition. All races and creeds contribute to the totality of world culture, each according to the unique character of its people, in art, in science, in music, in philosophy and literature. It is in the realm of human relations, and in religious thought and cosmic concepts, that Judaism has a unique message for mankind, as embodied in our sacred lore which all the nations must heed. The concept of the One World is derived from the first verse of the Bible: "In the beginning God created heaven and earth." One God, One Universe, One Humanity, One Law, are the four sides of the square which encompasses the whole life of man, giving it solidity and durability.

The idea of One Judaism should be focal in the consciousness of every Jew who understands the divine plan of the universe, as embodied in Jewish tradition. A Jew cannot think in terms of divisiveness and disunity, whether it be with reference to his own religion or in relationship with his fellow man. In these days when the spirit of ecumenicity, spearheaded by the Vatican Ecumenical Council, aims to promote a dialogue among all the diverse religions

179

of the world, when the United Nations is struggling to set the pattern for world federation and world government, and the greatest legal minds of all nations are endeavoring to formulate an international law which shall be respected and obeyed by all people, should disunity, diversity and voluntarism in matters of religious observances and practices be advocated?

If One Law is conceivable on a world-wide basis, it would seem that the establishment of a universal code for world Jewry is an attainable reality. Reconstructionist divisiveness is not helping, but hindering Judaism in promoting the ideals for which our ancestors suffered martyrdom, and which we have pledged to keep sacred.

It is not surprising that complications arise whenever one attempts to take a short-cut or a detour instead of following the main highway, whether traveling in a car, or employing the mental processes of the human brain. Reconstructionism detoured from Jewish tradition, and sought a new road which might bring Judaism to its destined goal. To justify diversity it went to Protestantism for inspiration, and became enamored of the denominationalism which prevails in Protestant circles. Realizing, however, that segmentation is an undeniable menace, the Reconstructionist Magazine writes of the Reconstructionist philosophy: "The present tendency toward viewing Judaism as a civilization will ultimately mitigate, and perhaps eliminate entirely, the denominationalism which has troubled Israel during the past half century. For the idea of Judaism as a civilization encourages diversity, which is vital to growth, but discourages denominationalism which is a deterrent. Denominationalism fragmentises; diversity fructifies. The significant difference lies in the fact that when there is unity in diversity, there is maximum cooperation on those matters which all have in common, with freedom to deviate on those matters where disagreement exists; when there is denominationalism, there is a tendency to carry the differences right down the line, creating factionalism even in those areas where it is both unnecessary and harmful."

Perhaps Reconstructionism would redefine the Protestant in terms of Methodist and Baptist "diversities" instead of denominations. But that is absurd. If by diversity, Kaplan means difference of opinion, the idea is not new in Judaism. Complete unity in the sense that every individual is identical in every respect with his fellow, never existed. The Talmud and rabbinic literature to this day record differences in interpretation of the same biblical texts, leading to diverse decisions in Jewish law.

Every attempt however, was made to curb diversity, because it might lead to dismemberment and disintegration. A diverse point of view in the course of discussion was helpful in clarifying an issue. The truth is the composite of many diverse aspects of the question. But, differences must blend and not conflict.

Society tends to promote conventionality, likeness in conduct and thought. The amalgamation of the polyglot racial and national peoples in the United States is proof that divisiveness cannot last long. Reading the same newspapers, listening to the same radio and television programs, going to the same schools, must lead to sameness in behavior.

"Judaism as a civilization," Dr. Kaplan maintains, "admits of more than one point of view, and deviations have no effect whatsoever on the nature of Judaism if Orthodoxy continues to insist that Jewish civilization is supernaturally revealed, and Reformists cultivate the modernist attitude toward the content of Judaism." It is hard to understand how anyone can state that Judaism has not suffered because Orthodoxy and Reform continue to adhere to their own ideologies which are diametrically opposed in almost every aspect of Jewish life. There is no common meeting ground in systems of education, in observance of the Sabbath and dietary laws, in the entire field of *halacha* and theology. Of course, all Jews cooperate in the United Jewish Appeal, but many Christians also make sizable contributions. All elements within a Jewish community will support the Hospital, the Home for Aged or other local charities, but then charity is a bond which unites all other racial and religious segments in the community. In the present state of Jewish fragmentation—call it diversity, call it denominationalism—one cannot deny that there is rivalry and conflict.

There is, indeed, an aspect of unity in diversity which can be constructive and contributive, and which can serve as the inspiration in organizing Jewish religious life in every community. A chorus or a symphony orchestra is the finest example of the *e-pluribus-unum* concept, where there is no conflict or friction. The diverse musical instruments or voices have their individual parts, and yet play together in a choral group. The soprano, alto, tenor and bass do not sing the same notes; the same is true of the instruments that make up an orchestra. However, all the participants must follow the same leader and keep together in time. Before they begin to play, the instruments must be tuned to one pitch, and the performers must listen to the tone sounded by the leader before they begin to sing or play. To allow diversity in tempo and tune, results in a discord which the audience will not tolerate. The composition in its entirety must follow the rules of harmony, composition and counterpoint.

The structure of the average Jewish community in which Reform, Conservative and Orthodox congregations function cannot be said to follow the orchestral pattern. It is fortunate that the United Jewish Appeal and the vexing problem of anti-Semitism keep the Jews together, and give them a feeling of kinship. *Ach letzoro,* "brother in distress," is perhaps the only bond of union between Jew and Jew. Otherwise, Jews would become entirely estranged from each other, due to their ideological diversities in religion and culture.

There are diversities which cause friction, and diversities which contribute to harmony. We must learn to distinguish between the two. One principle must be firmly established: Judaism must be defined not as a new concept, as if Judaism just appeared on the world scene, but in terms which will have historic continuity. Defining Judaism as a "civilization" is not helpful in integrating the diversities in Jewish life, in spite of the hopes and the claims of its protagonists. We cannot have a flexible Judaism which can be twisted into any shape that may suit one's fancy. Life cannot exist without norms and standards, rules and regulations. Everything in life can be named, measured, weighed and tested. When Adam was told to give names to all the animals in the garden, it was evident that a form of identification must be established in order to be able to distinguish one creature from another. Similarly, who is a Jew and who isn't must be definitely determined. In this respect, diversity must lead to likeness and not to hodgepodge, to homogeneity and not disorder.

Reconstructionism has expressed the hope "that the day may not be distant when all Jews will be spiritually mature enough to recognize that they must cooperate in all enterprises which affect our entire people so that they may be free to express themselves adversely in those areas in which there are legitimate reasons for diversity." We could go along with the prayer if the word "diversity" were omitted. Freedom of expression within legitimate bounds was never prohibited in Judaism. "Come let us reason together" (Isaiah 1:18), is an invitation by the prophet in the name of the Lord, encouraging discussion, debate and argumentation. Even the Divine does not tolerate arbitrary decisions. "The seal of the Holy One blessed be He, is truth." Bring evidence to prove your point, and you will be heard, regardless of who you are. "Though your sins be as scarlet, they shall be as white as snow." There can be no fairer or more liberal doctrine conceivable. Perhaps one of the distinguishing characteristics of the Jew is the urge to argue. *Ipcha mistavre,* "perhaps the reverse is true," is a well known Jewish cliche. Talmudic study aimed to clarify thought. And today, public forums, debates, symposia, and general discussions which take place daily and which occupy a great deal of time on the radio and television are instituted not for the purpose of fomenting schisms and factions, and creating diverse parties, but to

183

allow deviations from the traditional restrictions. There is an old saying: "If you give the Jew a finger, he wants the whole hand." Concessions will be gladly accepted by many Jews, but there is no guarantee that satisfaction will be achieved. One concession will create a hunger for more. *Avera goreres avera*, "one sin brings another in its wake."

How much more effective the project of the "revitalization of the Sabbath" would be if the other sectarians in Judaism would join in the movement. While the Conservatives are urging their congregants to keep the Sabbath holy, others stand by idly and watch. The early reformers were quite ready to scrap the entire institution of the Jewish Sabbath on Saturday and substitute Sunday as the day of rest. Today many Reform congregations do not hold Sabbath morning services for lack of a *minyan*. Celebration in the home may, in time, be completely forgotten, because in Reform congregations the lighting of the Sabbath candles and the Kiddush is performed in the temple, and the entire community is *yotze*, that is, it is "absolved" from individual responsibility.

Conservative Jews still maintain the sanctity of the Sabbath in the home and synagogue, and endeavor to enforce the Sabbath laws, each rabbi in his own way, depending upon the extent of "piety" he harbors as a result of his own home environment and the surroundings in which he was nurtured. But there have been rumblings within the ranks, and a demand for a revision of the Sabbath laws. Yet when the Committee on Law and Standards endeavored to crystallize the opinion of the Conservative rabbinate in order to establish an authoritative code for the entire body, the futility became at once apparent. The more conservative of the congregations would not sanction a change in the law to permit traveling on Shabbos and the use of electricity. All that could be done was to leave the matter to the discretion of each rabbi, to follow the majority or the minority report.

Reform Judaism's laissez-faire attitude in the matter of religious observance militates against any hope for unity in that movement. The rabbis in the neo-Orthodox camp likewise permit liberties which the Agudas Harabonim would surely condemn. From time to time a voice of vigorous protest is sounded against the leniency which closes an eye to the concessions made by the younger Orthodox rabbis.

All of this may be summed up in the conclusion that "religion" has come to be a flexible term which does not have the same meaning to any sizeable group of Jews. The "expression of the collective Jewish life" will never be achieved by advocating "'the primacy of religion," if religion is diversified in concept and practice. We must speak in terms of the "primacy of Judaism," and Judaism must mean the same to every Jew, otherwise religion is far from an area of agreement. It becomes an area of conflict and hostility, as we see it today.

The third area of agreement which Dr. Kaplan proposes is "The maximum possible plenitude of Jewish content, including the use of Hebrew." The word "possible," should be omitted. Attempts should be made to render Jewish life content-ful to the *maximum* degree. The implication which is contained in the concession "possible" is conducive to a looseness of conduct and a laxity of effort which ultimately results in complete abandonment of the law or custom in question. Human nature in general, with the few exceptions of the hardy and ultra-serious, is fickle, and seeks the line of least resistance. Obedience to law cannot be left to the discretion of the individual. It is expected that everybody obey the laws of the state, not only when it is convenient and possible, but under all circumstances. If there are urgent extenuating conditions which render the enforcement of the law impossible, consideration is given by the court; but the justification for the deviation must be indisputable. The laws of the Sabbath are not enforced in extreme cases where the life of a person is at stake. And there is provision within the framework of Jewish law for leniency under extraordinary circumstances. However, while the law has due regard for the welfare of the people, it is not implied that the individual has the right to decide for himself to what extent he will observe the law. Today, it would seem that insubordination governs the attitude of the average *baal habayis* toward Jewish observance, which is limited to the minimum Jewish content, which in most Jewish homes is a *reductio ad absurdum*.

There can be no area of agreement if every Jew merely promises to do as much as *possible*. The term "possible" is indeterminate and unpredictable. How can we expect agreement when each one can "make Shabbos for himself?" People do not need encouragement to find ways of evading the law. It is not difficult to find an apparently valid reason for breaking a rule. New laws are often instituted not because new conditions have arisen, but because an old law was unclear and equivocal, and a clever lawyer took advantage of a loophole. The demoralization evident in political scandals and in the increase in crime can be traced to a lackadaisical regard for law enforcement. No society, no democracy, can be stable and long endure if people obey the laws "as much as possible."

The concept of "voluntarism" seems to be tantamount to sanctioning chaos in Jewish life. How can one expect to maintain unity and homogeneity, if every Jew can do what he pleases? The Bill of Rights guarantees to every individual, the right to live in accordance with the dictates of his conscience. A man has the right to accept or to reject Judaism. But if he accepts Judaism as his way of life, he must conform to the norms of conduct by which we identify a Jew. Suppose the Supreme Court of the United States would issue a proclamation (which is implied in the principle of "voluntarism") to every citizen: "You don't have to obey the rules and regulations laid down by the states and municipalities. It is voluntary."

It is apparent, therefore, that "the maximum possible plenitude of Jewish content" is not an area of agreement, but an area of disagreement.

With regard to the "use of Hebrew" there can be no debate. The Hebrew language is the universal language of the Jewish people, and should be cultivated by every Jew, regardless of ideological differences. But here again, a word of caution must be sounded. The ability to speak Hebrew cannot become a substitute for prayer, which unfortunately is the belief of our secularists and nationalists. Hebrew must not lose its character as the *lashon kodesh,* the "holy language." When Hebrew was the language of prayer, world Jewry was united. A Jew felt at home and among kinsmen when he visited any synagogue in any part of the world. Praying together in the same language brought their hearts closer together. But the same cannot be said, when Hebrew is only a conversational language. Language in itself is not a medium of creating unity. It is a help undoubtedly, but it must be stressed that an international language will not create international unity. On the other hand, unity will create a common language. When the nations of the world will come to an agreement on the major issues which now divide them, and cooperation will be achieved in the promotion of the welfare of all people regardless of race or creed, there will be no difficulty in formulating a language which all will understand. Before people can talk together, they must have something in common to talk about.

Hebrew, therefore, can become an area of agreement—when Jews agree to talk to each other and discuss issues in which they are mutually interested.

The "scientific approach" to Jewish higher learning is urged by the Reconstructionists as the fourth "area of agreement." Here again the ambiguity of the term "scientific" may lead to greater divisiveness and misunderstanding than to harmony. The term "scientific" has been offered as an excuse for every scholar and would-be scholar to interpret the concepts of Judaism, Jewish history and Jewish law to suit his own fancy. The term "scientific" has become sacrosanct to the extent that any criticism of a "scientific truth" is tantamount to heresy and blasphemy. "Scientism" had become a cult, a new religion, and its extreme deification has led to excesses, which have been manifest in the debasement of humanity. Scientism has scoffed at revelation, faith, humanitarianism, spirit, and the intangibles in

189

life which cannot be measured, tested and weighed, but which are real, nevertheless. Yet the greatest scientists admit that there is no answer to life's mysteries except the "Will of God."

The "scientific" approach by itself cannot become an area of agreement, unless we agree on the goal which we strive to reach. "Scientific truths" are not absolutes. Many of the so-called "scientific proofs" of the Graf-Wellhausen school of German Higher-Anti-Semitism which aimed to rob the Jews of all originality in their contribution to religion and civilization have become myths today. Yechezkel Kaufman has exploded the Wellhausen theories in his *Toldot HaEmuna HaYisraelit.*

The scientific approach is acceptable and valid only when utilized by men who are competent and open-minded, and who are imbued with reverence and respect for tradition and the promptings of the heart and soul, as well as with powers of observation and analysis. The truth cannot be ascertained unless every possible aspect and every source of information has been explored. The Gaon of Vilna, according to a statement by his pupil, R. Baruch Shklaver, expressed a view which leaves no doubt that true science was welcomed by Orthodoxy: "When a man lacks the knowledge of the various sciences, he lacks a hundred times more the understanding of the Torah, because the Torah and science are united."

Jewish higher learning can become an area of agreement, provided it is undertaken in the spirit of constructive endeavor, with the understanding that all aspects of a problem will be studied and, before conclusions are reached, all data will be checked and rechecked. Every individual has the right to present new concepts and new ideas, as a result of his researches in the original sources, but he must be prepared to meet the challenge of other scholars who have additional data which he failed to include. *Kinas soferim tarbe chochma,* "the rivalry of the scribes increaseth wisdom," is a rabbinic saying. The rabbis encourage research and study as the only means of increasing the sum total of human culture. In commenting on the verse, "Iron sharpeneth iron, so a man sharpeneth the countenance of his friend" (Proverbs 27:17), R. Hama, in the name of R. Hanina, explained that just as iron helps to sharpen another piece of iron, so do two scholars sharpen each other's minds in discussion of *Halacha*. The rabbis are opposed to unilateral conclusions and decisions, and support the principle of exchange of views by quoting Jeremiah 23:29, "Is not My word like as fire?" which is interpreted to mean that just as fire does not burn alone, so words of the Torah cannot be confined to an individual (Taanith 7a). The Talmud also indicates that rabbinical statements were made merely for the purpose of stimulating queries on the part of the students (Nazir 59b). The same spirit of "asking questions" and offering new interpretations (*chidush*) has been carried over to the Yeshivot in our day. The voluminous literature of *She'eloth Uteshuvoth*, "Questions and Answers," is an indication that the minds of the scholars were not closed.

The movement to find the "areas of agreement," is a healthy sign which is symptomatic of an attempt to effect a spiritual recovery from the ailments which Judaism has suffered during the past decades. *Yagata matzasa*, is a familiar Talmudic saying which means that sincere search is rewarded by discovery. If all the sectarians in Israel will approach each other and endeavor to find an agenda upon which they may all act for mutual benefit, the common denominator can be found, regardless how small it may be at the start. More can be added later. It cannot be expected that all the leaders of the various trends in Jewish theology will immediately come together in complete harmony. The lines have been hardened for too long and the sects function independently today, each one anxious to convince the American people that it holds the key to the Jewish future. Our only hope for some measure of success in breaking down the barriers is for the cooler minds in each group to meet in a round table discussion and agree on a program of action which will embody the virtues of all the segments, and table

191

for the time being those diversities which have caused conflict and vexation of spirit, and which in reality have done irreparable damage to the cause of Universal Judaism.

One must welcome and encourage every suggestion for the establishment of a *modus operandi* by which all community-minded Jews who share a common outlook will be able to talk to each other in terms of kinship and in a language which all will understand.

But there is little hope that Reconstructionism will create an organic Jewish community which will function harmoniously and effectively, because of the drastic changes which it has made unilaterally and which have created resentment on the part of the Orthodox and a great deal of criticism on the part of both Reform and Conservative groups.

The radical changes which Reconstructionism has catapulted into the lap of American Jewry, should have been avoided. The zeal and the enthusiasm of a new movement unquestionably was a source of inspiration to its founders and to their followers. The dynamism of the leaders of the Reconstructionism is inspiring. But, in spite of the apparent glamor on the surface, Reconstructionism can never hope to reach the masses of the people for whom the terms "religious civilization" as distinguished from religion *per se,* the repudiation of the concept "chosen people," and the other philosophical gyrations have little meaning or significance. Even among scholastic circles, the issues raised by the Reconstructionists are debatable and many have been rejected. There is nothing wrong in advancing new concepts and revamping old ones, but it is wrong to build a separatist movement and insist that there can be no hope for Judaism unless the program adopted by Reconstructionism becomes the law of the land.

A Program for Jewish Life Today was issued in 1950 by Professor Kaplan, and circulated among the spiritual leaders of the country for their comment and criticism. The objectives outlined were exemplary beyond question. The functions of the local Jewish community should receive full endorsement! The program of Jewish education on every level, the promotion of Jewish culture and art, and the principles of social justice are entirely acceptable, because they are in accord with basic Judaism! It is inconceivable that any Jew, excluding a few fanatics, would be opposed to the goals which have been set.

If the statement had presented a positive program for action, sponsored by the rabbis under the auspices of the synagogue, it is certain that it would have been warmly received. However, one cannot hurl a challenge and invite a battle, and with the same breath ask for peace and unity. The preface to the program stated: "Our times call for a new emphasis on Jewish unity." Spendid, and we say, Amen! But how can you achieve unity if a controversial issue is injected which arouses resentment? We are united by the things with which we agree. That seems to be axiomatic. Arithmetic teaches us that fractions must be reduced to a common denominator, if they are to be added together. Likewise in a heterogeneous society, diverse elements can be added or joined together only in matters which all accept.

The view that traditional Jewish concepts must be changed in order to restore "the confidence of many Jews in the validity of their religious tradition which has been shaken by the impact of modern thought," is debatable. Are the philosophies of John Dewey, Santayana and Kierkegaard superior to the teachings of Isaiah, Rabbi Akiva or Maimonides? There is nothing wrong with Judaism that education will not cure!

Unfortunately, the ignorance among our youth of the basic teachings of our faith is shocking. The demand for change in ritual and the removal of the many annoying restrictions is not prompted by a sincere wish to preserve and perpetuate the religion of our forefathers, but by the failure to appreciate the rich spiritual content which they embody. The spiritual leaders have succumbed to the clamor of the populace in the same manner as the Israelites in the desert appealed to Aaron for a tangible and visible deity.

The worship of the Golden Calf was the outcome of the popular demand for a god, "like all the other nations of the world." Today, too, it would seem that religion must be dressed up with glittering decorations in order to make an appeal to the unthinking masses.

The great novelty of the Reconstructionist movement is that it has rejected the concept of supernaturalism, and declares categorically that if religion is to be saved, it must be wedded to scientific naturalism. A new term, "trans-naturalism" has been coined to indicate that a union must be established.

It is, however, not true that Judaism has rejected science and reason. There has always been a close relationship between natural science and the study of *Halacha,* as revealed in the lengthy discussions in the Talmud and rabbinic literature, by which effort has been made to determine how God's laws function in nature and can be applied to the observances and rituals which constitute the daily life of the Jew. Scientists are impressed by the knowledge which the ancient scholars revealed in many areas of science. The Yeshivah University of our day, with its departments in every aspect of modern science, may be regarded in terms of the continuation of the time-honored tradition, in keeping with the rabbinic dictum: *"Chosamo shel hakadosh baruch hu emes,* The seal of the Holy One Blessed be He, is truth."

But the rabbis recognize that there are areas of cosmic phenomena which cannot be explained by natural causation, and that we must rely upon intuition and revelation to understand the intricacies and the mysticism which are manifest in the world in which we live. That realm of the unknown must have a name. It is supernaturalism. Scientists admit that they have no explanation for the simplest processes in nature. Every child knows that a blade of grass grows from a seed. We know how it grows, but why it grows uniquely the way it does, is a secret which goes beyond the realm of logic and human understanding. The number of similarly unknown miracles of nature is untold.

Sir James Jeans, an outstanding astronomer and cosmologist, stated that "happenings in the natural world are not determined by causal laws, but by some substratum in the world which lies beyond the world of phenomena and so also beyond our access." What is that "substratum," the term which the scientist employs to describe the unobservable? The theologian speaks of it in terms of supernaturalism, a concept without which there is no foundation for religion.

Reconstructionism would shift the center of gravity embodied in the concept of the One God, to man. By wedding religion to scientific naturalism, God is no longer the center of all creation. He is no longer the transcendental, omnipotent, and omniscient Supreme Being, the Creator of all things, who has been, who is and who will be. Reconstructionism defines God as a cosmic power that has formed and sustained us, the totality of all the forces in life which render human life worthwhile. What contribution does Reconstructionism make to an understanding of that power which is more illuminating than the teachings of our prophets and sages? Eliezer Berkovitz, in his *Critical Evaluation of the Reconstructionist Theology,* declares that it is a form of pantheism.

We must no longer identify the sovereignty of God, Kaplan declares, with the expression of the will of a superhuman, immortal or infallible individual personality, but with that "power on which we rely for the regeneration of society and which operates through individual human beings and social institutions." The entire concept of the unity of God is destroyed if we rely upon the power of God which operates through the agency of the human being. Instead of man being created in the image of God, God is created in the image of man. Emphasising naturalism and human experience instead of faith and mystic contemplation is a rejection of the basic concept of monotheism.

It is indeed a strange phenomenon that as scientists are turning more to the world of the spirit, a theologian attempts to interpret religion in terms of physical research and experimentation. It is far from the truth that modern science has invalidated the distinction between natural and supernatural. Einstein declared that "for such parts as do not exist physically, we must provide spiritual substitutes." Scientists are becoming more and more aware of the spirit of energy that was present in the beginning of creation.

Developments in science during the last decade have made all the text books obsolete, and modified all the theories that were sanctified with mathematical exactness as the absolute truth. The laws of causation have been challenged; even the universality of natural law. No one can be dogmatic in any concept, whether it be that of religion or science! Therefore, to base our theological views on ephemeral scientific hypotheses which, like Jonah's gourd, came up in the night and perished in the night, seems foolhardy.

It is hard to understand why Reconstructionism declares that modern man is incapable of entering into a relationship with the supernatural. Of course, there are many people who, in times of crisis, regard God as a miracle worker or a reservoir of magical power. There are many devout Jews who entertain notions that border on superstition. But that is entirely a different subject, which has nothing to do with the validity of our traditional spiritual heritage. The advancement of science does not warrant the condemnation of the customs, the ceremonies, the rituals and the basic laws which *K'lal Yisrael* has maintained inviolate throughout the ages. Without attempting to hold a brief for Orthodoxy, it seems wrong to disparage any Jewish system which has withstood the acid test of time.

The Reconstructionist statement that "Judaism is more than a religion" would seem to imply that the Jewish people throughout the ages have neglected or ignored the other manifestations of civilization, such as art, music, drama, belles lettres, etc. But even a cursory glance at the pages of Jewish history will indicate that the Jewish people have richly contributed to all fields of intellectual endeavor and every phase of craftsmanship. Our scientists and students have excelled in every branch of learning, as manifest in the Nobel Prize winners, among whom Jews have been represented in numbers far in excess of the ratio of their numbers within the world's population. There is even danger of an overemphasis on the *parpara'os l'chachma,* "the aftercourses of wisdom," which the rabbis in Pirke Avot relegate to an inferior status in the face of the *guf halachot,* "the main ordinances," which are breached. It would seem that Reconstructionism has reversed the order of importance and has granted priority to art and science, judging religious practices and spiritual concepts to be secondary, and even expendable.

With regard to religious observances, Reconstructionism has gone even further than Reform Judaism by repudiating the *halacha* entirely, as evidenced by the statement: "The Sabbath, the Festivals, the liturgical prayers, and the dietary laws have grown in complexity and hamper the Jew in the pursuit of his practical affairs to a degree altogether out of proportion to the good to be derived from the punctilious observance of them." It is further declared that "our problem is not how to maintain beliefs or uphold laws, but how to enable the Jewish people to function as a highly developed social organism."

Judaism must be reconstructed because, according to Dr. Kaplan, "it is inevitable that we should inwardly rebel against many of the observances that habit and general expectations lead us to conform with."

The Jews have been a rebellious people from the beginning of time. They rebelled in the wilderness when Moses ascended Mount Sinai and demanded a God whom they could see with their eyes, and not an imaginary God conceived only by intuition and an act of faith. Korah rebelled against Moses and refused to bow to his authority. The sons of Aaron rebelled and brought strange fire upon the altar which led to their doom. And so down the ages, in every generation, there were dissident elements who refused to bear the "yoke of the Torah." There will always be dissatisfied Jews in the future, as in the past, who will find fault with the rituals and the restrictive laws of the Shulchan Aruch. But the rabbis have cautioned those who would refuse to be bound by the traditional customs and habits hallowed by our people throughout the centuries and for which our forefathers willingly made extreme sacrifices. It is a warning that still holds meaning: "Who so receives upon himself the yoke of the Torah, from him the yoke of the kingdom and the yoke of worldly care will be removed; but who so breaks off from him the yoke of the Torah, upon him will be laid the yoke of the kingdom and the yoke of worldly care" (Perek 3:5).

XXIII

A JEWISH ECUMENICAL COUNCIL

Since the Ecumenical Council was convened in Rome, the spirit of ecumenicity seems to exert a profound effect upon all mankind. It is time that we think in terms of One World, a united family of diverse peoples, whose hearts beat in unison. When we listen intently, even amidst the din and clatter of raucous voices, we can hear the still small voice of the human conscience, proclaiming the eternal truth of "the Fatherhood of God and the brotherhood of man." An inspiring enunciation of the doctrine of ecumenicity was voiced by our American philosopher, Ralph Waldo Emerson, in *The Over Soul*: "The heart in thee is the heart of all, not a valve, not a wall, not an intersection is there anywhere in nature; but one blood rolls uninterruptedly, an endless circulation through all men, as the waters of the globe is one sea, and truly seen, its tide is one." The Emersonian dictum may be regarded as an echo of the prophetic utterance: "Have we not all one Father? Hath not One God created us? Why do we deal treacherously every man

against his brother, profaning the covenant our fathers?"
(Malachi 3:10).

It was a pertinent question which the prophet Malachi
asked centuries ago, and its relevancy is even more apparent in our day, as we contemplate the conflicts between
nations, peoples and religions. Within Judaism too, the
spirit of argumentation and debate has characterized our
people throughout the ages, but the solidarity of the Jewish
people was not disturbed.

Fragmentation in Jewish life is by no means a new
phenomenon. It was rampant in the beginning of Jewish
history. Moses in the wilderness was deeply conscious of
the diversity among the tribes he was leading from Egyptian bondage to the freedom which they hoped to enjoy in
the Promised Land. How pathetic was his plea to the Lord
when he began to realize that he would have to relinquish
the shepherd's staff and hand it to his successor. We can
appreciate his anxiety when we read his words (Numbers
26:16, 17): "Let the Lord, the God of the spirits of all
flesh, set a man over the congregation, who may go out
before them and who may come in before them, and who
may lead them out and who may bring them in; that the
congregation of the Lord be not as sheep which have no
shepherd." And our sages have noted the expression: "The
God of the spirits of all flesh," "spirits" in the plural and
not singular. They explain that men do differ. Just as their
faces are not alike, so are their opinions varied. Each man
has his own decisions to make in his own spirit because of
his background and experiences. Man's natural tendency
is to live his own life as he understands it. And yet, Moses
was convinced, and that same conviction has continued
throughout all our history, that every effort should be made
to establish a *modus vivendi* whereby we can live together,
bound by a common denominator and yearning for a common destiny. It is for that reason that the *Shma Yisrael*,
"Hear, O Israel, the Lord our God the Lord is One," has
become the foundation of Jewish belief.

We are living in a pluralistic society, consisting of every

199

variety of ideology, religion, political theory, social relationship and personal mores. Every human being in a free society is legitimately entitled to be different. It would be a drab and dreary world if sameness prevailed. The rich coloration of life is derived from the diversity in tastes characteristic of human beings who observe life from different angles, and reach conclusions and make decisions which are peculiarly their own. In a speech entitled "Unity in Diversity," Professor Robert MacIver said that "the coherence of every social unity depends on the functional diversity of its components. You can't build anything out of units that are exactly alike. They could only make a heap, an amorphous mass, or a mob. In a society there can be no important interchange, no reciprocity, no effective give and take."

There can be no dispute with this view, which champions the understanding and appreciation of the other fellow's point of view. The Jewish people have been the greatest victims of intolerance and bigotry, and for that reason they have been in the forefront of every liberal movement, and have strongly advocated the doctrine of human brotherhood and the Fatherhood of One God. But children of the same parents adopt different patterns of life. Each serves mankind in his own way, and it would be a tragedy to force any one of them to pursue a vocation for which he was not suited. One cannot, according to the proverbial saying, "put a square peg in a round hole."

All of this is axiomatic, although in practice the average person who is poisoned by prejudices cannot see the application of the principle to human relations. We are remote from the ideals presaged by our prophets, the cardinal doctrines of the Jewish faith, "Thou shalt love thy neighbor as thyself," even though he differs from you in race and religion, and "Thou shalt love the stranger, for ye were strangers in the land of Egypt." This implies that we must not despise the stranger because he has different views, or observes different customs or practices than you do.

However, we must recognize the other side of the coin, lest by making a fetish of differences, human existence become a crazy quilt, as it were, a conglomeration of disjointed units which conflict with each other and lead to a morass of trouble. With all Dr. MacIver's impressive pleas for recognition of differences, he did deplore the fact that "difference is magnified out of all proportion, and the embracing good is minimized and rejected." We cannot allow differences to run riot. The evil of fragmentation is no less frustrating than the evil of regimentation. Differences are not sacred *per se*. Society cannot possibly exist unless we find the common heritage, the common denominator which instills in all men the "consciousness of kind," the feeling that there is a common bond that unites them, which transcends the divergencies which separate them. That is the burden of the Vatican Ecumenical Council which attempts to find the common platform upon which all Christian denominations, Catholic and non-Catholic, can stand. That is also the motive behind the establishment of the Institute of Religious and Social Studies of the Jewish Theological Seminary, which brings together Catholic, Protestant and Jewish leaders in an effort to discover the tenets which each holds inviolate and by which contributions are made toward the enrichment of our social life.

The basic precept of Judaism is unity. Stressing belief in the One God, led to the mandate: "One law and one ordinance shall be both for you, and for the stranger that sojourneth with you" (Numbers 15:16). Throughout the Bible the plea for unity has been sounded again and again. Besides the direct exhortations in the Pentateuch and the Prophets, by midrashic interpretation our sages have found affirmations of the cardinal precept. For example, when Jacob fled from his brother Esau, and lay down to rest from his weary travels, the text reads: "And he took of the stones of the place and put them under his head." The implication is that he took many stones. Further on we read: "And he took the stone that he had put under his head," indicating that he had only one stone. The Midrash amplifies the story, and states: "He took twelve stones, saying, 'The Holy One blessed be He, has decreed that twelve tribes should spring forth. Now neither Abraham nor Isaac has produced them. If these twelve stones cleave to another, then I know that I shall produce the twelve tribes.' " When, therefore, the twelve stones united, he knew that he would produce the twelve tribes. The Rashi commentary adds: "He placed them like a roof gutter around his head because he was afraid of the wild beasts." The stones began to quarrel among themselves. One said, "Let the righteous man rest his head upon me," and the other said, "Let him place his head on me." Immediately the Lord turned them all into one stone, and therefore it is said: "And he took the stone" (Genesis 28:18).

We may apply this legend to the present state of religious conflict in Judaism. Each denomination claims to be the foundation stone upon which Judaism rests. In advocating the principle of One Judaism, it is hoped that all the sects will unite in building a Judaism which will be an amalgam of all the doctrines embodied in the ancient traditions of our faith.

Ezekiel urged the establishment of unity within the ranks of our people. In chapter 37:15 we read: "And the word of the Lord came unto me, saying: 'And thou, son of man, take thee one stick, and write upon it: For Judah and for the children of Israel, his companions; then take another stick, and write upon it: For Joseph, the stick of Ephraim, and all the house of Israel, his companions; and join them for thee one to another into one stick, that they may become one in thine hand." And the prophet concludes: "and I will make them one nation in the land upon the mountains of Israel, and one king shall be king to them all, and they shall be no more two nations." The division of the kingdom into two dynasties after the passing of King Solomon was the beginning of the end of Israel's solidarity, an evil from which our people have never recovered, which has left us weak and helpless in the face of the titanic forces which have been arrayed against us in every generation.

Our sages have admonished us that our people's exile and afflictions were due to the fact that our ranks were splintered into 24 sects. Lack of unity is the downfall of many a nation. Within Judaism there has never been complete uniformity and rigid regimentation in the practice of ritual. In the Talmud, recognition is given to the fact that there were many differing customs in the various localities where the Jewish people lived. There was an understanding, however, that when a visitor came to a city in which the customs were different from his own, either stricter or more lenient, a definite rule had to be adopted. He had to follow those customs which were more strict in his own place of residence, and those customs which were more strict in the place he visited. The purpose was to avoid any disturbance of the local practices.

A contemporary illustration indicates that this guideline still holds. Because Jews in the Diaspora celebrate two days of each Festival, while Jews in Israel celebrate only one, the holiday of Passover lasts only 7 days in Israel, but 8 in the countries outside Israel. Thus, on the eighth day of what is still Passover to diaspora Jewry, the Jews in Israel eat *chometz*. Jews from other lands who are visiting in Israel, however, must continue to eat matza, unless it is their intention to become citizens of Israel.

In Israel today, there are 57 varieties of Jewish customs followed by the Jews who have come from every corner of the world. Nevertheless, the Bukhari, Yemenite, Persian, Ashkenazi, Hasidic and other synagogues, located in close proximity to each other, exist peacefully together. Each Jew goes to his synagogue, *davens* in his own *nusach*, follows his unique rituals; but the underlying feeling is that they all belong to *Am Yisrael*.

Would that this were the feeling today among the three major denominations in Judaism. On a religious basis, there is no feeling of kinship among the Orthodox, Conservative and Reform Jews. Of course, there is complete cooperation in areas of philanthropy and combatting anti-Semitism, despite a good deal of deplorable duplication. But the religious rivalry which splits these groups is working havoc among our younger people, driving them away from their faith; and the tide of assimilation is gathering strength.

A Jewish ecumenical effort is urgently needed to stem this tide which threatens to engulf our people. Strengthening our ranks would be beneficial not only to the Jews, but to the entire world. We have the message which mankind needs today, the message of the prophets, which will give mankind a faith to live by in this nuclear and space age. With the acknowledgment of the Catholic Church that they are "spiritually Semites," and that Judaism is the basis of their religion, Judaism is today in a position to become a universal religion. Better than any other faith or creed, it can bring the message of universalism or ecumenism, to a fragmentised world.

The prophet Isaiah (42:6) proclaimed: "I the Lord have called thee in righteousness, and have taken hold of thy hand, and kept thee and set thee for a covenant of the people, for a light of the nations." The role of the "Chosen People," which rightly understood means that we should be the teachers of mankind in the lessons of the Bible, cannot be fulfilled if we are a splintered people. Bolstered by the conviction that we speak with the authority of God's Revelation at Sinai, we must strengthen K'lal Yisrael by stretching out the hand of brotherhood to all our fellow Jews regardless of their unique way of life and practices. Before we can expect to enjoy brotherhood on the global level, we must learn to practice genuine brotherhood on the Jewish level. Genuine brotherhood is not lip service, but the sincere feeling that we have spiritual components in which our souls are linked together in a common bond. This, unfortunately, is sorely lacking among Jews today.

Jewish ecumenicity challenges all segments of Judaism to cooperate in a movement to bring about unity and harmony within our ranks and to eschew every step which will cause a "Kultur-kampf," especially in Israel. Recently, the President of the Union of American Hebrew Congregations declared: "Reform Jews are called upon to break the silence and face up to the problem of breaking the Orthodox stranglehold in the state of Israel, especially pertaining to church-state relations. We have been far too hesitant and silent in confronting this very real menace to our struggling Progressive movement and to the welfare even of the very survival of Israel itself. The very emboldened audacity of entrenched political orthodoxy must be vigorously and courageously countered."

The word "audacity" makes us think. Who has the *chutzpa*, Eisendrath or the religious leaders of Israel? Charged words of this nature can cause a religious war in Israel. Injecting oneself gratuitously into the religious affairs of Israel, presuming to dictate to the religious authorities how they should administer religious institutions, threatening to combat the Orthodox "stranglehold" over Israel runs counter to all plans to bring about a reconciliation of the divisive groups in this country, and constitutes a threat to the integrity of Judaism here and in Israel.

In the first place, any movement foisted upon the Israelis by outside interests and not arising from within the state of Israel itself, is suspect. Moreover, any suggested religious reform must be of a responsible nature and not couched in the extreme language of instigation for rebellion and civil war.

We have seen the havoc wreaked in Israel by the belligerent Neture Karta who have rebelled against the government, and played into the hands of the Arabs, because these extremists believe that the time has not arrived for the establishment of a Jewish state until Messiah will come. A revolution launched by a movement outside Israel will leave scars and wounds within Israel and perhaps lead to irreparable damage.

The rebellion of Reform against the laws established by the Israeli government is not unlike the upheaval aroused by the decision of the Supreme Court in the United States with reference to the recitation of prayers and the reading of the Bible in the public schools. The Supreme Court was viciously attacked on the same basis, in effect, that it has a "stranglehold" on the religious life of the people. The Secretary of Education in the Roman Catholic Archdiocese in New York has called the United States Supreme Court "the greatest evil in the country today." "The thinking of the Supreme Court is all off-center," he declared. Such extreme declarations are a menace to the country in that they instill lack of respect not only for the highest legal tribunal in the land but for all law and order. It is one thing to express dissenting opinion, which every citizen has the right and the duty to exercise, but it is quite another to condemn others, especially those in authority who are vested with the power to interpret the laws in the light of the wisdom, the knowledge and the experience which they possess.

Incitement of religious rebellion in Israel savors of the confusion of biblical times, when the authority of Moses was questioned by Korah and his company. "Ye take too much upon yourself, seeing all the congregation are holy, every one of them, and the Lord is among them; wherefore then lift ye up yourselves above the assembly of the Lord?" (Numbers 16:3). It is in this same tenor that the reformers today are hurling defiance against the rabbinic authorities in Israel. The fate that befell the rebels in Korach's time was catastrophic. It must not happen today.

Not all of American Reform speaks the language of extremism. In an address delivered at an annual religious awards dinner of the Synagogue Council of America, Dr. Solomon B. Freehof, as President of the World Union for Progressive Judaism, characterized the unique features of the major American Jewish groups and regarded them as the "three-fold cord" which the rabbis declare cannot quickly be broken. What a boon it would be if the Jews of each group would approach each other in the same spirit! That is what we call Jewish ecumenicity, and that is the goal toward which we strive in our championship of One Judaism.

As evidence of the possibility of the three religious groups to come together, Dr. Freehof cited the agreement which was reached in the chaplaincy service. About one hundred and fifty legal responsa were accepted by the Orthodox, Conservative and Reform rabbis and became operative in the army during the war. Of course, this is not exactly a criterion for the administration of religious affairs in peace time and under normal circumstances. The laws of *hora'as sha'ah*, temporary expediency under abnormal circumstances, are an integral part of the *halacha* in Orthodox practice. Nevertheless, the point is that when the spirit of good will prevails, and the dispute is *leshem shamayim*, for the glorification of God's name, and not for self-glorification, it is possible to arrive at a *modus vivendi*, whereby even groups of diverse ideologies can live together. Dr. Freehof does not talk in terms of "stranglehold," accusing one or another group of seeking a dominant role. Dr. Freehof finds a place for all the denominations. He is sympathetic toward the Orthodox, and declares that "only Jewish Orthodoxy can keep it (learning) up in its unique suffusion among the masses of the people. Only Orthodoxy will build yeshivas and man them with their sons. Only Orthodoxy will have average business men (*ba'ale-batim*) studying Talmud, and will maintain the deep, learned studies among the simple, plain, unpretentious Jews." He finds a place for Conservatism, to whom the "oneness of the Jewish people is central," who maintain that those observances which still have meaning and awaken response in the Jewish people must not be touched. However, when in doubt, Conservatism suggests that we follow the rabbinic dictum: "Go forth and see what the people say, see what they do." Reformers, Dr. Freehof maintained, had to rebel, because there was no compromise when they tried to do new things. They did not believe that every new idea derived by the latest scholar had already been said on Mt. Sinai, and that everything in Judaism is eternal and was there from the beginning. Judaism, he argued, would never have continued unless it had the constant ability to change. He noted some changes that have gone into effect, such as the Sabbatical Year and the Tithes and Heave Offerings, which became inoperative in the Galut.

Dr. Freehof concluded his thesis urging the cooperative endeavor of the three divisions in Judaism, by declaring that "it is a blessing that we have three religious forces, because each one does something unique. Orthodox Judaism insists: *"Kol bonaich,"* All thy children must be absorbed in God's law. Conservative insists: *"Es achai,"* I seek my brethren. And Reform insists: *"Shiru shir chadash,"* Sing a new song unto the Lord.

Achdut, unity, has been the cry of our people from time immemorial. In every generation our scattered remnants were united by the cry: *"Shma Yisrael,* Hear, O Israel, the Lord our God, the Lord is One." We cry *Shma Yisrael* in our prayers. We invoke the Oneness of God, and subconsciously, we have in mind the Oneness of Israel, the Oneness of the Jewish People. We offer prayer on the occasion of the blessing of the new month, and we declare: *"Chaverim kol Yisrael,* All Israel united in fellowship." We repeat the dicta, *"Yisrael arevim zeh bazeh,* Israelites are responsible for each other," (Shevuot, 39a) and *"Kol Yisrael achim,* All Israelites are brothers" (Tanchuma, Naso 3). The bond of unity is very strong among our people, despite the marked differences which characterize their religious views, as well as the divergent habits and ways of life which have been developed by living in different environments. When a Jew is persecuted anywhere in the world, all Jews feel the pain. When our brethren suffer want and are driven from pillar to post, all Jews band themselves together in the United Jewish Appeal and other philanthropic endeavors, and money gushes forth like a mighty stream.

A United Jewish Appeal should become operative not only in the field of charity, but also in the field of religious and cultural endeavor! If we are ready to give our money to any Jew who is in need, in the spirit of brotherhood, we should be ready to give our hearts and our minds in the same spirit. This is the keynote of our plea for One Judaism, which in essence is no more and no less than the implementation of the ideal which we have harbored in our hearts throughout the ages. It has been proven time and again that failure has been the outcome of the conflicts caused by Judaism's splintering into sects and schisms. Our leaders in every generation have sought to hold back the flood waters of discord and disunity. From Moses down to the present, our leaders have decried fragmentation. The prophets of old deprecated the internecine strife which dissidents were wont to stir up, and warned the people to beware of the trouble makers. "The destroyers and they that made thee waste shall go forth from thee" (Isaiah 47:17). While we lament our tragic plight caused by our enemies outside, we must realize that a great deal could have been prevented by more internal unity.

The Talmud is a compilation of treatises which contain the debates covering all the problems of Jewish jurisprudence in the fields of theology, ritual, civic and criminal law and procedures. Within the limits of the hermeneutical rules, following the standards of rabbinic logic by which decisions are reached, there is complete latitude in rendering opinions in all legal matters. The redactors of the Talmud did not hesitate to record the divergent opinions, on the basis that there can be no complete understanding of the issues without a knowledge of all the factors involved in the dispute. For example, the Shammaites argued that two applications were required for atonement by sprinkling on the outer altar; the Hillelites held that in the case of a sin offering a single sprinkling was enough. The representatives of an anonymous opinion, called the Rabbis, declared that a Succah needs at least two walls of the prescribed dimensions, while R. Simeon disagreed and held that there must be three complete walls (See Sanhedrin 4a).

Nevertheless, our sages sensed the danger of extreme divergence which might result from unbridled and uncontrolled legal casuistry. In Tractate Sota 47b, the rabbis deplored the excesses which led to dissension and to the "miscarriage of justice and happiness ceased." To quote from the Tractate: "When the haughty of heart multiplied, dissensions increased in Israel. When the disciples of Shammai and Hillel multiplied who had not served (their teachers) sufficiently, dissensions increased in Israel and the Torah became like two Torahs." This talmudic passage recorded conditions existing about two thousand years ago which are not unlike the present confused status in Judaism. Then there were two Torot; today the Torah is split in more than two. There is a multiplicity of Torot, reflecting the number of schisms into which Jewry is divided in modern times. To restore the Torah to its pristine state of Oneness, should be each Jew's aim and goal, in fulfillment of the prophetic utterance of Ezekiel: "And I will make them one nation in the land, and they shall be no more two nations" (37:22). To maintain the integrity of Israel should be the sacred ambition of every loyal Jew.

The term "union" has been employed universally by our people as an indication that the greatest desire in our communal life is to bring about an integration of forces giving articulation to the oft repeated cliche, that "in unity there is strength," and "united we stand, divided we fall." There is no one who will dispute the doctrine of unity, except that the extremists on all sides among us can see unity only in terms of their own ideology, and condemn the dissenters from their point of view. Jewish life in the United States was founded on the principle of a unification of congregations, not on dismemberment into factions and denominations.

We have seen how Sabato Morais, sensing the danger of fragmentation and disintegration, issued a call inviting the cooperation of "all Israelites for the perpetuation of historical Judaism in America." He was followed by Solomon Schechter, who came to this country in 1902, and dedicated his heart and soul toward the organization of the new Jewish Theological Seminary of America, which merged with the institution founded by Morais. Schechter spoke in terms of "Catholic Israel," which was a translation of the term *Klal Yisrael,* so often repeated in general conversation among our people. The Seminary, and later the United Synagogue of America which was organized by Schechter, was not to be identified with one sect or party in Israel, but with the whole of the Jewish people. The Seminary was to be a force for reconciliation of all segments of the population. It was to be a bridge, arching over the extremes in Judaism, in an effort to bring about a two-way traffic on the part of the Reform and the Orthodox. The Conservative movement as envisioned by Solomon Schechter was to conserve all the Jewish values regardless of the source from which they emanated. Ecumenism was the ideal toward which it strived, but after Schechter was gone, new winds began to blow and new forces came into action. Instead of building a bridge, barriers were set up, and Jews became strangers to each other in the realm of religion, at times indulging in recriminations and bitter attacks against each other. Professor Louis Ginsberg was most emphatic in his denunciation of denominationalism in Judaism, as indicated in the statement which has become classic: "We are opposed to all separatist movements in Israel, and are prepared to fight sects, and still more, sectarians without sects. It would be a comparatively simple process to affix a label of theology to our organization. But labels are devices for saving talkative persons the trouble of thinking." This is characteristically a Ginsberg effort to emphasize "quite clearly" (a term he often employed) his convictions and his admonitions to his students and to the many audiences which he addressed.

Backing the appeal made by Isaac Mayer Wise for Jewish unity, Stephen Wise likewise heralded the call for ecumenicity at the time of the merger of the Hebrew Union College and the Jewish Institute of Religion. The legacy which he left in this respect should have equal emphasis together with all the other contributions which he made to the enrichment of our social and religious life. He declared: "We urge the inclusion of *Klal Yisrael* in our 'Common Statement of Purpose.' Such an inclusion was and is felt to be another way of reaffirming the Institute's resistance to that embittered and un-Jewish sectarianism which has become the by-product of the conflict between Orthodoxy and Reform in American Jewry." Stephen Wise was sincere in his attempt to bridge the chasm between Orthodoxy and Reform, but he did not succeed, because of the many vested interests which would not allow the liquidation of their respective pet and petty notions regarding the essence of the Jewish faith. It was Stephen Wise's ambition to organize the Institute to be a training school for rabbis regardless of their ideological inclination. He had as members of the faculty men who were strictly Orthodox, like Rav Tza'ir and Chaim Tchernowitz, as well as men with radical views. When the merger was effected, the Wise ideal was discarded and the sectarianism which he opposed prevailed. The policy of the Hebrew Union College in practice runs counter to the declaration made by President Nelson Glueck, in his acceptance of the presidency of the two institutions: "The confusion and the controversies and lines of demarcation which have fragmented our forces are giving way to an encompassing circle of related purposes and common goals. It is high time. Let us not linger on labels."

The labels, Orthodox, Conservative and Reform, were coined in the Diaspora, and to introduce these schisms into Israel would be catastrophic. Whatever value or merit these distinctions may hold for lands outside of Israel, is debatable. They may have served their purpose for some Jews who sought to interpret Judaism for reasons peculiar to their own mental, intellectual, emotional, and other less meritorious idiosyncrasies. But all this baggage which the Jew has taken with him in his wanderings must be sloughed off and left behind when he enters the Holy Land. There he must start with a *tabula rasa*. There he must work unencumbered by foreignisms, unhampered by discordant bickerings and uncontaminated by the virus of ambivalent emotions.

Sectarianism should be avoided in Israel. Now is the time to put Judaism on a firm foundation, not merely in behalf of the Jews in Israel but in behalf of world Jewry as well. It would seem to be presumptuous for any Jew in the Diaspora to venture any interference with the course of religious development and progress in the Holy Land. While it is axiomatic that the political life of Israel must be unmolested by external influences, the same principle must apply with even greater relevancy to the religious life of its people. No one knows what form Judaism in Israel will take in the course of the years. It is not within the jurisdiction of so-called Orthodox, Conservative or Reform Jews to demand recognition of their respective points of view, because it is not impossible to conjecture that the normal development of Jewish law in Israel will be different in many vital respects from the concepts championed by the diverse sects in Jewry, concepts spawned by the alien influences of the exile.

No Jewish group can demand the right to violate a rule or law which is contrary to the established religious authority in Israel, or they will erect an Iron Curtain between themselves and the rest of the Jews in Israel. It will mean the creation of new sects, like the Karaites or the Samaritans. If the laws of marriage and divorce laid down by the Israeli Rabbinate will not be followed by the Reform Jews, one result will follow inevitably: the prohibition, *"lo tit'haten bam,* thou shalt not make marriages with them"* (Deuteronomy, 7:3), will be applied to the Reform Jews as it is applied to the Christians and Moslems. Judaism will begin to disintegrate along the same lines which have played havoc with the Protestant Church. We can see "Catholic Israel," as Dr. Schechter conceived the term, splintered into a multitude of petty sects, vying with each other for control, not on the basis of scholarship and the advancement of Judaism, but for their own personal aggrandizement. Israel must not become the arena for staging a gladiatorial combat between rival religious factions. The recorded history of our people reveals the tragedies which resulted from the internecine strife between the Sadducees, the Pharisees and the Essenes, the Karaites and Rabbinites. The sad

213

state of Judaism in America is a result of the confusion
caused by theological dissidence, which has been climaxed
more than once by a volcanic eruption, leaving scars, wounds
and lacerated feelings.

We have been warned not to follow *b'hukath hagoyim*,
the way of the Gentiles. The motivation behind the prohibition was not prompted by the spirit of discrimination,
nor evoked by the feeling of prejudice, nor stimulated by
the desire to be segregated from the nations of the world.
There never was a prohibition against assimilating the
virtues, the righteous practices and teachings of the philosophers and scholars of other faiths and peoples. Rather,
the biblical warning aims to protect Israel from making
the same mistakes committed by the nations and from being
contaminated by their pagan philosophies. Let us rather
observe other groups, and learn from their blunders.

Years ago, the Protestant Church began to realize the
danger which it faced from the multiplicity of separatist
movements within its ranks. A movement has been afoot
to unite the Protestant groups, to eliminate the petty differences in theological ideology which divided them, and
which made them an easy prey either to the forces of
atheism or to the tremendous pull of new religions spring-
ing up on all sides. More recently, the Catholic Church
has been sponsoring a philosophy of ecumenicity, and
cooperation with the Protestants now exists where aloof-
ness and total estrangement prevailed before. "In unity
there is strength" may be an aphorism which has lost its
charm because of its commonplaceness, but never in the
history of civilization has its relevancy and its significance
been more poignant and vital than in modern society.

The time has come for us to put our religious house in
order. The State of Israel has been able to bring about
a coalition of all the conflicting parties under one constitution, one Knesset, one flag, one government, and one law.
Is there any reason why the same achievement should not
be enjoyed in the realm of religion? What problem of transcendent import warrants the setting up of Iron Curtains

and the fragmentation of Judaism into rival factions? There is no problem in Judaism, ritualistic or legalistic, that cannot be argued and debated in a duly constituted Jewish legislative body representative of all shades of opinion, or in a Supreme Court or *Sanhedrin*, as such institutions function in all civilized states of the world.

The multiplicity of denominations has given Judaism no rest. Our sages declare that, in addition to Israel being in *Galut*, the *Shechina* is also in *Galut*. We may point with pride to million dollar temples which have been erected in every part of the United States, to magnificent structures, to tens of thousands of members on the congregational rosters, and to heavy budgets which finance the bee-hives of synagogue activities. But the *Shechina* is still in *Galut*. God's spirit is conspicuous by its absence. Who is blind and is hoodwinked into the belief that all of this is a criterion of genuine religious fervor? Every rabbi is taxed to the limit of showmanship and ingenuity to find new schemes and new devices in a desperate effort to "attract a congregation." Very few come to pour forth their hearts in prayer, as did our ancestors. The synagogue with the "biggest show" is the one that is most successful. Some of the questionable gadgets would shock Isaiah today, even as he was embittered against his people in his day, declaring, "When ye come to appear before Me, who hath required this at your hand to trample My courts? Bring no more a vain oblation. It is an offering of abomination unto Me. New Moon and Sabbath, the holy convocations—I cannot endure iniquity along with solemn assembly."

Jeremiads are heard on all sides, bewailing the vacuity of Jewish life, the decline of interest in ritual practices, the synagogues empty except on the High Holidays, the desecration of the Sabbath and Jewish sanctities, the homelessness of the Jewish spirit, the appalling illiteracy among the Jewish masses. There are many factors which may account for the tragic decadence of the Jewish religious spirit; but there is one factor which has caused incalculable harm, and that is, the sectarianization of Judaism.

The time has come for the cool heads among all the parties in Judaism to get together and take an inventory of their spiritual assets and liabilities. There must be a re-evaluation of the common cliches, the terms which have become so stereotyped in the minds of the average American Jew and accepted at face value, but whose market value is far below par. We speak of Orthodox, Conservative and Reform Judaism as if they were divinely ordained from Sinai, *"halacha l'Moshe mi-Sinai."* There is nothing very sacred about these labels. It is questionable whether the average Jew could clearly define their essential differences in positive terms. There are many Jews who show their entire indifference to all the theological casuistry and belong to all three congregations in their community! They maintain their affiliation with the old Orthodox *shul* in deference to their aged parents, and attend services on Yom Kippur either to sit near their parents or to participate in the Yizkor services. They join the Reform temple because their wives and daughters have social contacts with some of the members. They also belong to the Conservative synagogue because of business associations with some of the active workers in the congregation, or for other reasons which have absolutely nothing to do with religion or theology. In the eyes of the average Jewish layman, Orthodoxy is identified with long beards, ramshackle synagogues, undecorous services, and unesthetic and burdensome customs which are unintelligible and primitive. Reform Judaism is defined in terms of smoking on the Sabbath, ham sandwiches, organ accompaniment, and hatless attendance at services. Conservatism is called 50-50 Judaism, a sort of local stop in the onward progress of the Orthodox Jew headed toward Reform. No wonder the average Jew is inclined to cry out in desperation, "a plague on all their houses."

Talmudic students are familiar with a traditionally just manner of adjudicating a dispute. In the opening chapter of the Tractate Baba Metzia, we read, "Two (persons in dispute before a judge) hold a garment (*talith*) ; one of

them says, 'I found it,' and the other says, 'I found it'; one
of them says, 'it is all mine,' and the other says, 'it is all
mine'; then one shall swear that his share in it is not less
than a half, and the other shall swear that his share in
it is not less than a half, and (the value of the garment)
shall then be divided between them."

In the same spirit we may attempt adjudication of the
dispute concerning the ownership of the garment (*talith*)
called Judaism. Each denomination claims to possess the
only genuine interpretation of our faith. It is indeed most
significant that the Talmud refers to a *talith*, a prayer
shawl, in describing the garment in dispute. The *talith*
is symbolic of the faith of our fathers, of which each one
claims to be the sole possessor. The litigants stand before
the bar of public opinion for judgment and settlement. There
can be but one solution. They must all share in the *talith*,
share and share alike. The *talith* belongs to all Jews. It
must embrace *all* our people, of every belief and opinion.
The spirit of sanctity envelops all who claim a share not
less than half of its spiritual value. It is also significant
to note that the Talmudic term, "They shall divide between
them," is "*yahaleku*," which may also be interpreted to
mean, "they shall smoothen, tranquilize and compose their
difficulties." It is in the light of this Talmudic mandate that
every effort should be made to disentangle the skein of sectarian confusion which harasses Jewish life in America and
which threatens to do the same in Israel, if unchecked.

The founders of Conservative Judaism in America were
on the right track in trying to build the bridge which would
have united all factions in Judaism, and which would have
rendered real service in strengthening Jewish life in America and paving the way to the establishment of the Universal Synagogue, with headquarters in Jerusalem. It is
an inspiration to recall the declarations made by Jewish
leaders in the past, and profit by their words of wisdom
and sound judgment.

We may infer that a similar thought was in Dr. Schechter's mind when he spoke of the "collective conscience of

Catholic Israel as embodied in the Universal Synagogue."
It was his ambition that the Jewish Theological Seminary
and its students "should in some way participate in, and,
as it were, anticipate the mission of Elijah, that was to
consist not only in solving the difficulties of the Torah and
removing doubt, but also in bringing back the forcibly
estranged, arbitrating between conflicting opinions and
giving peace to the world." The Seminary was to be dedicated to the task of reconciliation, a sort of clearing house
where all the conflicting views in Jewish theology should
be carefully analyzed, evaluated and disseminated, to the
end that the Jews in America might derive spiritual enrichment therefrom, and maintain a high standard of Jewish living. The spirit of reconciliation, as enunciated in the
words of the prophet, "And he shall turn the heart of
the fathers to the children and the heart of the children to
their fathers," was the motive power which permeated the
souls of the founders of the Jewish Theological Seminary.

The objectives of the Seminary and the United Synagogue were expressed by Dr. Louis Ginzberg in clear and
unmistakable terms when he declared: "We are opposed
to all separatist movements in Israel, and are prepared to
fight sects and, still more, sectarians without sects. It would
be a comparatively simple process to affix a regulation label
of theology to our organization. But labels are devices for
saving talkative persons the trouble of thinking. Nothing
is easier and nothing more dangerous than definitions." It
was far removed from the thought of the builders of Conservative Judaism that it should constitute a new party
in Israel.

Every past attempt to establish an agency which could
coordinate Jewish activities has failed. All the conferences
which have been called have endeavored to build a shadowy
structure upon a foundationless bottom. It could not be expected that anything constructive would come into being.
Only God can create a *yesh me'ayin*, "*creatio ex nihilio*."
Material man must have something tangible to build with,

and the materials must be cemented; otherwise they will fall apart.

Attempts have even been made by lay leaders to consolidate the dismembered elements of contemporary Judaism. In an article in the *Menorah Journal*, Autumn 1948, Henry Hurwitz called for a conference, to be known as the JARA, Jewish Assembly of Representatives in America. The JARA would not presume to be the authoritative agency for all the Jews in America. The purpose would be exploratory, to gather all the available information, and in time win over the majority of American Jews to think in terms of Jewish unity. There have been many others, both lay and rabbinic, who have sent out a call to Jewish leaders in America to consider the future of Judaism and the Jews in America, in Israel and the world over. Nothing has emerged from any proposal thus far, because the purpose was not to bring about a harmonization and a consolidation of Jewish groups, but rather the promotion of the particular ideology which the prime mover might harbor. Every rabbi is "sold" on his own concept of Judaism, and he will not be satisfied until he has convinced his colleagues that the salvation of Judaism and of the Jewish people lies in the acknowledgment of his formulation and interpretation of the Jewish religion and Jewish law.

Until Jewish leaders can convene as Jews, and not as representatives of Reform, Conservative, Orthodox, or secularists, there is no prospect that Judaism will ever thrive, regardless of the outer manifestations of progress which only blind the eye and have no substance. In an article in *World Unity*, "Shall We Give Up Proselytizing?" Arthur E. Holt has this to say: "There are three ways of treating one who disagrees with you. You can fight him, you can agree with him, or you can take your place beside him until there is evolved something new and creative which is better than that which both held." Here are words of wisdom coming from a man who is not of our faith, but whose concept of "world unity," is thoroughly Jewish. It makes common sense, and is indicative of a maturity of mind and heart which must lead to understanding and mutual benefit. Thus far Jewish sectarians, as well as the secular Jewish leaders who seek to dominate the Jewish scene, have been fighting each other in an effort to make everybody agree with their respective brands of Jewish ideology. The Jewish community leaders have not yet become mature enough to stand side by side as brothers in flesh and in spirit, and admit that the final form of Judaism in the future is yet to be molded; that no one has the formula which will meet all the requirements, but that each has something to contribute toward the totality of Judaism; that whatever is seemingly new must not conflict with, but complement and further enrich, the ideals of our faith.

The present civil war in Judaism must cease, and the brothers who have been estranged must learn to become reconciled, to emulate the example of Jacob and Esau. We learn from the Midrash that when Jacob sought to pacify his brother after many years of forced exile because of the enmity which had been aroused, he was prepared to meet Esau in three ways: 1) with gifts, 2) with supplication, and 3) with physical combat. Fighting was to be a last resort if all else failed. The gifts which Jacob sent to his brother and the appeal which he made seemed to have produced the desired result. The bitter feeling of hatred seemed to have dissolved.

Likewise, it seems to us that reconciliation with our brethren can be attained only by the exchange of gifts in the form of constructive ideas for the improvement of the methods of Jewish education, the promotion of Jewish scholarship, the encouragement of literary endeavor, the invention of new techniques to attract the youth of our people to the synagogue, and the revitalization of Jewish life in every aspect. There has been too much scrapping among the sects, too many acts of provocation; and now the only form of scrapping which would be helpful would be to scrap all the labels and approach each other sympathetically.

There is a biblical precedent to guide us toward the

revitalization of Judaism in Israel and throughout the world. Upon the return of the exiles from the Babylonian captivity in 536 B.C.E., Ezra brought into being the *"Kneseth Hagedolah,"* the "Great Synagogue," composed of the elders and the prophets. They proceeded to regulate Jewish living in accordance with the teachings of the Torah, which had well nigh been forgotten during the exile. Many of the customs and the practices which are in vogue to this day have been ascribed to the legislative enactments of the *"Anshe Kneseth Hagedolah,"* the "Men of the Great Assembly." The Great Assembly was the connecting link between the prophets Haggai, Zechariah and Malachi, and the rabbis of the Talmud.

The Chief Rabbi of Israel can most worthily become the modern Ezra. He can and should proceed at once to call together the elders of Israel, the scholars throughout the entire world, and revive the *Kneseth Hagedolah.* The heads of all the institutions of learning, the yeshivoth and the seminaries, should be invited to join the *Kneseth,* and continue the development of Jewish law, which was arrested in the diaspora. The enactments of the *Kneseth Hagedolah* served as the basis for the Mishna and the Gemara. The entire structure of the Talmud, the treasure house of Jewish wisdom, the academies in Babylonia and Palestine, where the problems of Jewish law were debated in full academic freedom, were the fruition of Ezra and Nehemiah's consecrated labors.

Scholars of every segment of Judaism should willingly join the *Kneseth Hagedolah* with open minds and open hearts, to make their contribution to the advancement of Jewish jurisprudence, in the same spirit as did the *Tannaim* and *Amoraim* of talmudic times. They must come to the *Kneseth,* not as Orthodox, Conservative or Reform Jews. These terms must be scrapped completely. They must come as Jews! They may argue their respective points of view, as legislators present their arguments, pro and con, with respect to the vital issues of the day. It is to be expected that there will always be differences of opinion. In the days of Shammai and Hillel, there were two separate schools which clashed sharply on essential issues of law. Students of the Talmud are familiar with the *"zugoth,"* or pairs of rabbis, who were diametrically opposite in their interpretation of Jewish law. And yet, this diversity did not result in the formation of rival sects and the fragmentation of the Jewish community. Each had his followers, although in time the decisions of one held greater sway.

Conservative rabbis do not follow in the footsteps of their preceptors. They are still groping in the dark in an effort to find a "philosophy of Conservative Judaism." Is it a religion or a civilization? Is it a "civilizational religion," or a "religious civilization?" Nobody to this day knows exactly what it is. That in itself is an abnormal condition. A movement looking for a philosophy is like the man in the proverbial story, who ran into the Beth Hamidrash, exclaiming, "I have a wonderful answer, who has a question?" A movement looking for a philosophy is like a foundling looking for its parents, or one in doubt of his paternity. It is the philosophy that gives birth to a live movement.

This confusion is attributable to the fact that there has been a deviation from the original philosophy of the founders of Conservative Judaism. And *"teshuva,"* recantation and return, are in order. A re-orientation of Jewish life is imperative. The dictionary definition of "orientation" reads: "the finding of the East point so as to get one's bearings," Also, "the setting up of a crystal so as to show the relation of the planes symmetrical to the other elements." "Symmetry" involves "distribution, proportion, congruity, harmony, and free balancing of parts in relation to a totality or a whole." Herein we can find a philosophy not only for Conservative Judaism, but also one to which all segments of Jewry can be dedicated, with an assurance that Judaism as a totality will benefit by the spirit of sincere cooperation as expressed in the old saying, "all for one and one for all." Judaism can find its bearings by turning to the East, and setting up a symmetrical relationship among all the elements of our people.

It seems almost fantastic to suggest that the leaders of Orthodoxy, Conservatism and Reform, like the Big Four on the international level, should get together in conference. One can sense the snicker of scepticism at the utter impossibility of even "reaching first base" in the endeavor. If Jewish religious leaders who profess belief in the unity of God and in the unity of the human race, cannot meet, what can we expect of the nations of the world? However, on closer scrutiny, the obstacles are not insuperable. While it may not be possible to remove the denominational barriers in the Diaspora, at least in Israel a pattern of Jewish living should be formulated which will be true to Jewish tradition and at the same time meet the spiritual requirements of modern times, entirely acceptable to men of culture and scientific advancement.

It is the duty of the liberal rabbis in every camp to join the movement of reorientation and integration. By "liberal," we mean those who have no vested interests and no "axe to grind," but who are interested solely in the advancement and the strengthening of Judaism in America and in Israel. The call of the *Kneseth Hagedolah* should receive a favorable response among all the rabbis and laymen of the world. The Chief Rabbi of Israel should be urged to convene the *Kneseth Hagedolah* at the earliest possible moment. It is a herculean task, but we can and must encourage its undertaking.

Jewish ecumenicity must be considered not only in the light of the present status of Judaism, but in terms of the future. Our modern day "prophets" who have studied current trends on the Jewish scene decry the short-sighted view of the religious boom which blinds the eye to the reality of the erosion and disintegration of Jewish loyalty and identification. In the words of Jacob who called unto his sons before he went to his reward, our prognosticators appeal to us: "Gather yourselves together, that I may tell you that which will befall you in the end of days" (Genesis 49:1).

Surveys have been conducted to determine the attitude of our college students toward the religion of their fathers,

223

and interesting and enlightening facts have been revealed. With open eyes we must face the facts, because our college youth, our future leaders, are the barometer of the climate in which they live. The survey shows that there is confusion among the Jewish students on the college campuses, due to the spread of sectarianism and fragmentation.

One of the prime problems for all Jewish leaders today is the recapturing of our college youth for Judaism. These young people will be leaders of our society, and if we lose them to Judaism, there can be no future for our people, and all the effort that is being expended to build institutions, to solve the problem of anti-Semitism, to rescue our people, even our support of the State of Israel, will be in vain. It is a hard challenge to face; but face we must with open minds and open hearts. We can no longer talk in terms of Orthodoxy, Conservatism and Reform, or any other schism, but we must close ranks today, if we will have any form of Judaism in the future.

Unless our religious leaders find a method of strengthening American Jewish feelings of attachment and identification to the Jewish community, the organized Jewish community in the United States will wither. There are many factors that reduce the cohesive nature of the Jewish group, but one of the major factors, we contend, is the separatism which prevails in the Jewish community and which spills over into the college campus. The place to cure this plague of separatism is at home, because when it afflicts the college campus it is too late to do anything effective. We must begin at home to bring about an integration of all the religious sects, and fortify the Jewish college student with a maximum Jewish, but not sectarian, education, so that when he comes into contact with scientific and philosophical teachings in the classroom, he will be able to face the challenge to his faith with knowledge.

Prognostication is an idle pursuit. No one knows what the future will bring. It is true that according to our sages we are forbidden to speculate "what is above and what is below," and we may add, "and what is beyond." Nevertheless, we can and should determine in our own minds what we would like the future to be, and we should strive courageously to achieve the goal of our ambitions. That ambition must be untainted by any desire for personal aggrandizement, uninfluenced by any momentary disturbance or ephemeral circumstances. The only motivation for all human endeavor should be the promotion of just and righteous causes. This affirmation is indicated in the divine mandate, "I call heaven and earth to witness against you this day, that I have set before thee life and death, the blessing and the curse, therefore choose life, that thou mayest live, thou and thy seed" (Deuteronomy 30:19). Freedom of the will is one of the cardinal doctrines of Judaism, which all the medieval Jewish philosophers from Saadia to Joseph Albo expounded in great detail. The survival of the Jewish people and the rebirth of the Jewish state of Israel is an indisputable substantiation of the truth that "nothing can withstand the power of the will." The rabbinic authorities in the Talmud find support in the Torah, the Prophets and the Hagiographa that "in the way that man wishes to go, they (the heavenly powers) will lead him" (Macoth 10a).

It is for that reason that we must think only in terms of the eternal truths when we discuss every phase of Judaism and the Jewish people. That does not mean that we must lose sight of the exigencies of the moment, the dangers that are imminent and require extraordinary precaution and exceptional treatment or attack. At times a *hora'at sha'a*, legislation to meet an emergency, is necessary; but the emergency measure must not be permitted to dethrone the substantive law which must forever remain the norm and the standard to guide human conduct. It is a defeatist attitude to feel that we must capitulate completely to the forces which temporarily prevent our onward progress. Of all the doctrines which Judaism has contributed to the enrichment of faith, one of the outstanding may be termed "freedom from fear," as proclaimed in the divine message of Joshua, "Have I not commanded thee? Be strong and of good courage; be not affrighted, neither be thou dismayed;

for the Lord thy God is with thee withersoever thou goest" (Joshua 1:9). Let us not give in to the cry that Judaism must bend the knee to the idol Modernity, and surrender to the demands of modern sophisticates for "streamlined" religion. The willingness of leaders to follow the crowd is indicative of timidity and weakness, unworthy of the consecrated calling to which they have sworn allegiance.

If Judaism is to have any future at all, it must face human life with the same fearlessness that the Haganah and the heroes of Israel's struggle for national independence evinced in our day, which culminated in a triumph unprecedented in human history. However, to be satisfied merely with a political state in Israel, a mere refuge for the survivors of the Hitler purgatory, would be a mockery and a travesty of the monstrous sacrifice which our people have made. A strong Judaism must now take up the struggle and defeat the enemies of society, not on the battlefield, not with military weapons, but with the spiritual armaments of our biblical and rabbinic tradition.

The prophets characterized Israel as the Messiah of the nations. The Messianic Age will become a reality, according to our sages, when all the nations of the world will accept the commandments of God in the spirit in which they were received by Moses on Mt. Sinai and promulgated by the teachers of Israel throughout the ages, freed from all the encumbrances and the alloys, the accumulation of ages of sophistry, casuistry and factional rivalries for power and glory.

In order that Judaism may play its role in society, and become the "light of the nations," in accordance with the divine mandate, all sectarianism within our own ranks must be abolished. The same discipline which united the fighting forces of Israel, must also govern the religious forces in Israel. It is in that spirit that we advocate the establishment of the Universal Synagogue. All the Jewish sectarians must rally about the standard of Israel's Torah, and help create the pattern of Judaism as the Universal

Religion, inspired by the eternal truths which will bring redemption not only to Israel but to all humanity.

No matter how powerful the Jewish State may become in the military, industrial and political sense, the absence of religious unity and harmony will inevitably prove to be disastrous. It is only by creating a strong religious bond that the political state will be assured permanence and stability. The Universal Synagogue can serve as the strongest buttress for the State of Israel, giving assurance of its continued existence, warding off another cataclysmic upheaval, a recrudescence of another Diaspora with all its horrors.

There will undoubtedly be opposition from all the vested interests in the diverse denominational groups in Israel. We cannot expect cooperation on the part of the leaders of the organized religious bodies, who are committed to their respective programs. But we can and should have support from the masses of the Jewish people, particularly from those who stand on the periphery of Jewish religious life, the unaffiliated and the un-synagogued, and their number is legion. The Universal Synagogue aims to reach the Jewish religious declassed and give them status, to the end that they may be able to find themselves spiritually, to help revitalize Judaism and contribute to the revitalization of the concept of religion for all mankind.

It must be made absolutely clear that opposition to sectarianism in the Jewish religion does not mean curbing varying schools of thought nor the free exchange of ideas, discussion and argumentation of the pros and cons of the legal and theological doctrines of Judaism. There is a vast difference between a sect and a school, and the line of demarcation must be kept scrupulously in mind. A sect is an organized body of dissenters from an established form of faith. It involves a complete cleavage, the setting up of a wall or barrier, between two opposing camps. Usually there is open hostility, refusal to compose the differences, keen rivalry and a competitive race for gaining adherents, resulting in bitterness and often leading to excesses hardly in keeping with the spirit of religion. A sect has burnt down all the bridges which maintained a close connection with the original body, and like the proverbial East and West, "never the twain shall meet."

The condition obtains today among the religious sects in Judaism. The bridges which might unite the Orthodox, the Reform and the Conservative have been destroyed. It is impossible to conceive a conference today, in which the various denominations will sit down and discuss religious doctrines academically, in a deliberate and unimpassioned spirit of give and take. More than once the *herem*, the ban of excommunication, has been issued, ruling dissenters out of Judaism for proclaiming alleged heretical opinions. There is no justification for the use of the ban in these days. It is also reprehensible for religious leaders to stir up feelings of resentment against other groups in an attempt to advocate a new idea, regardless of its merits. There must be a change in tactics and an entirely new approach to the solution of Jewish legal and doctrinal problems.

If religion has any significance at all, it means that man is his own master, responsible only to God for his thoughts and his acts, in matters relating to his conscience. Every form of totalitarianism is repugnant to genuine religion. The one party system which has dethroned the democratic form of government in many countries of the world today, is not in harmony with Jewish religious doctrine. Judaism does not demand that all people adhere to the same system of theology. The prophet Micah has enunciated the cardinal precept as recorded in holy script: "For let all the peoples walk each one in the name of its god, but we will walk in the name of the Lord, our God, forever and ever" (4:5).

Judaism encourages differences of opinion, holding that only by argumentation can a true understanding of a problem be reached. There are legitimate disagreements which are understandable, and which must be respected. In the last analysis, we find that Judaism is the most tolerant religion known to man, having due regard for variations of opinion.

The Talmud relates that for three years the schools of Shammai and Hillel were divided in opposite camps, one declaring that the *halacha* was in conformity with its views, and the other claiming to express the authoritative halachic decisions. The Heavenly voice proclaimed, "Both decisions are the words of the living God, but the *halacha* of the School of Hillel prevails." The question was asked, if both decisions are the words of the living God, why grant priority to the School of Hillel? The answer was, because the Hillelites were conciliatory and humble, for they gave their own version and the version of the School of Shammai, and moreover, they gave precedence to the views of the School of Shammai over their own (Erubin 13b). Modern sectarians, as champions of democracy and liberalism, could profit from the teachings of Hillel, which they ought to emulate.

A similar understanding of the sacredness of diverse opinions is found in a statement of Rev. Frederick William Robertson. He said, "Whenever opposite views are held with warmth by religious minded men, we may take it for granted there is some higher truth which embraces both. All high truth is the union of two contradictions." How close this is to the talmudic expression, "Both are the words of the living God." But with regard to religious sects, which are characterized not by "the warmth of religious minded men," but rather by the friction of ambitious rivals, a noted English poet has this to say:

> And when religious sects ran mad
> He held, in spite of all their learning,
> That if a man's belief is bad
> It will not be improved by burning.

The fact that there is a legitimate as well as a negative side to raising questions may be found in the Passover Hagadah. The wise son and the wicked son raise practically the same question with reference to the Seder ritual. But there is a vast difference in the spirit of the questioner.

229

The wicked son does not ask for the purpose of gaining information; his intent is to ridicule. "He asks, What is this service to you? To you and not to himself. Excluding himself from the community, he has denied the essence of faith. Do thou, then, blunt his teeth and break his power." His wickedness consists in cutting himself off from the group to which he belonged. Sectarians do just that. They are not satisfied merely to raise questions. They look with disdain upon their brothers, and for that reason all their efforts lead to disintegration and destruction.

The *halacha* makes a distinction between *min b'mino*, two things that belong to the same species, and *min b'she'eno mino* and two things that belong to separate species. Diversity of sects may be termed *min b'she'eno mino*, in talmudic language. They do not belong to each other; the result is neutralization and nullification when one comes in contact with the other.

It is just a coincidence and not a play on words that the talmudic term for sect is also *min*. The *minim* in talmudic days were the heretics, the infidels and the sectarians, mostly applied to Jewish-Christians, against whom the rabbis directed their diatribes and anathemas. The sectarians of today are rendering the same kind of disservice to Israel as did the *minim* in ancient times. We are opposed to *minuth*, heresy and infidelity to Jewish traditional sanctities. But we favor *min b'mino;* that is, we want all Jews to feel that they belong to the same *min*, to the same species and class. Whatever differences may exist apply not to intrinsic characteristics, but only to variables of form and minor details.

It is in this spirit that we favor the scrapping of all sectarianism in Jewish religious life, and propose the promotion of a closer affiliation and a keener sense of kinship by sloughing off all pietistic pretense and imaginery superiority of wisdom and working together for a common destiny. We must learn to differ and to debate our differences without rancor or resentment. Any system of thought that cannot stand critical analysis will not live and endure.

Judaism, that has withstood the assaults of all the philosophies and the religions of the world, and has gone through the crucible of fire throughout the ages, will withstand open, friendly discussion and emerge stronger from such debate.

The unification of the diverse segments of Judaism is a complex question which has perplexed the wisest among us. It would be unwise for anyone to maintain that he has *the* answer. The solution will not come from a single person; it will come from an ensemble of ideas, from the collective wisdom of people of all walks of life, enjoying a diversity of experiences, so that no one biased point of view will be presented, but a composite of all ideas will come into being. We must not make light of any attempt to unify Judaism regardless of the source. It was a wise saying on the part of our elders who remarked, "Let not the blessing of a *hedyot*, commoner, be light in your eyes." More good is gained from the grass roots than from the tall cedars. The tall cedars vie with each other in a race for increased height, with the result that the sunshine is shut out and the darkness blights the grass roots which languish for a breath of air and the warmth of the light. While the great leaders of our religious sects are trying to outdo each other in the growth of their respective organizations, straining every nerve to meet the increasing budgetary requirements to keep their organizations alive, Judaism is dying at the base for want of proper care and spiritual nourishment. Perhaps, then, Jewish salvation will come eventually from an unknown source, from the bottom and not from the top.

The "Mature Mind," which Professor Overstreet at one time expounded, will some day develop, and people will begin to realize that they can no longer depend upon their leaders for deliverance. They will open their eyes to the fact that the rivalries among the leaders in every phase of life—economic, political and religious—is not in the interest of the masses, but exists for personal aggrandizement. The maturation of the human race as envisioned by Overstreet must take place soon, before it is too late. The feeling of the Oneness of the human race, epitomized in the Unity of God, is not just a rhetorical and theological doctrine, but a truth which must become an integral part of the consciousness of every individual. It must color every thought and act, and become the basis for every endeavor of man; no longer a fantasy and a utopia, but a motivation in all his business and social relations.

With the advent of the twentieth century, it was felt that we had overthrown the despotic *l'état c'est moi* enslavement and that the era of "We, The People" had dawned on the horizon. But the world has made little progress since Louis IV. His incarnation has appeared in the characters of Hitler and Stalin and other smaller dictators. And the immaturity of mankind is manifest in the humble submissiveness with which their votaries are willing to put their necks into the noose of slavery.

One of the cardinal doctrines of Judaism is indicated in the second commandment, "Thou shalt have no other gods before Me." Judaism cautions mankind against all forms of idolatry, not only the worship of inanimate objects, such as icons and statues, or animals, such as the crocodile or the bull, but even the hero worship of self-appointed leaders. Judaism bids man beware the false prophets, who aim to befog the mind with vain promises, with magic and miracle, and seductive designs. Judaism recognizes no king, priest or prophet as supreme authority. All are answerable to the one universal law, and all actions are tested and measured by the one standard, as proclaimed in the Holy Script, "There shall be one law for the home born and for the stranger among you" (Ex. 12:49). No law can be regarded as divine and universal which is restrictive, which sets one people against the other, or one class against another. Sectarianism, and cock-sureness, and a refusal to help build communicative linkages between the complex divisions of the human race constitute a basic sin, militating against the realization of man's fondest hope and dream—peace.

The spokes of a wheel go in different directions, but

they are united to one hub, and together they move the vehicle. Similarly, in the wheel of human relations, every individual may go his own way and differ from his neighbor in language, in religion, in likes and dislikes, in vocation and avocation, but he cannot sever his connections from the universal hub. Everything must stem from one source and go back to the same source. It is this principle which will guide us in an effort to indicate wherein the factions in Judaism may differ and separate if they choose, and wherein they must unite and become integrated into an unbreakable and indissoluble unit. If we closely examine the hub of Jewish life, and indicate where the spokes are loosely connected and where they need repair and strengthening, we will then enable the vehicle of Judaism to continue its course of historic progress to its destined goal.

THE BASIC PRINCIPLES

1. We regard the declaration: "Hear, O Israel, the Eternal our God, the Eternal is One," as the affirmation of the unity of God, the unity of the Jewish people, the unity of Judaism and the unity of Jewish Law, and that the Jews have been divinely ordained to champion the cause of one world.

2. We hold that the continuity of the Jewish people has been maintained uninterruptedly for two thousand years in the Diaspora by virtue of the comparative homogeneity of Jewish religious observances and the recognition of rabbinic authority as embodied in Jewish codes.

3. We hold that the future of Israel in the Holy Land and in the Diaspora is entirely dependent upon a continuation of the Jewish traditions, subject to change only by a universally recognized authoritative tribunal.

4. We believe that the Torah, divinely revealed to Moses and interpreted by the rabbis throughout the ages, is an immutable guide for the Jewish people and for all other peoples who choose to follow its teachings.

5. We believe that Judaism is a universal religion, capa-

233

ble of serving the spiritual interests of all classes in all parts of the world. Hence, there is no specific American Judaism as there is no Asiatic, European or African Judaism.

6. We regard the present segmentation of Judaism into diverse and conflicting denominations as a menace to the integrity of our people and a repudiation of the basic doctrine of unity, and hold that change of ritual and revaluation of Jewish concepts is not the answer to Jewish problems.

7. We hold that all present sects in Judaism should set aside their petty differences which cause confusion in the minds of the laity, resulting in alienation from the synagogue and religion.

8. We hold that all sects in Judaism should concentrate on the issues which are vital: i.e., maximum Jewish education, standardized for all age levels; training of youth for future Jewish leadership; intensification of religious observances in the home; revitalization of the Sabbath and holidays; restoration of the centrality of the synagogue in all communal activities; reclamation of the unsynagogued; strengthening the role of the rabbi as counsellor and guide in all matters pertaining to the individual and the community; achievement of Jewish world unity; dissemination of the Jewish ideals of justice, righteousness, brotherhood, equality and peace.

9. We believe that the Jewish way of life as embodied in the Torah is the most effective assurance of human happiness on this earth, and that it more closely approximates the ideal of world civilization.

10. We believe that man will some day learn the secret of eternal life and that there will be a reunion of all the spirits that have lived since the beginning of time.

11. We believe that God is the Creator of the universe and all that is therein, and that He is the Source of all wisdom and power. To believe in God and to be imbued with the divine spirit means to draw from His wisdom and power and become a partner in creative endeavor.

12. We believe that individual freedom to express opinions, suggest improvements and combat injustice, is an inalienable right which is the basis of progress. But the individual also has the duty to strengthen the solidarity of his group and avoid an act which will cause disruption and disintegration.

13. We believe that headquarters of Universal Judaism should be established in the Holy Land, and that a Tribunal or Sanhedrin be organized consisting of the representatives of duly ordained rabbis and scholars of every community in the world, to be recognized as the highest authority in the administration of Jewish religious law. Regional branches of the Sanhedrin should be established in every country to meet local needs.

14. We hold that the State of Israel, which guarantees freedom of religion to all faiths, should abide by the legal principles embodied in the Talmud and rabbinic codes, and continue further development of Jewish jurisprudence which was arrested by the Diaspora.

15. We hold that Israel shall be regarded, not only as the national home of the Jewish people, but above all, as the spiritual homeland to which all Jews in every country shall look for authoritative guidance. Regardless of the fate of the political state, Judaism shall not relinquish its claim upon the Holy Land, which shall continue to fulfill the same spiritual function as the Vatican does for Christendom.

Date Due